Royal Navy
Instructional Airframes

RAY STURTIVANT
ROD BURDEN

Mich

Best wishes

Ray

A JOINT BARG/AIR-BRITAIN PRODUCTION

Copyright 1997
Ray Sturtivant, Rod Burden, the British Aviation
Research Group and Air-Britain (Historians) Ltd.

First published in the United Kingdom in 1978 by the
British Aviation Research Group.

This second edition published jointly by
the British Aviation Research Group and
Air-Britain (Historians) Ltd,
1 East Street, Tonbridge, Kent.

Air-Britain Sales Dept, 5 Bradley Road, Upper Norwood
London, SE19 3NT

Correspondence to:

Rod Burden, 80 Beamish Road,
Canford Heath, Poole, Dorset BH17 7SH
and not to the Tonbridge address

ISBN 0 85130 263 7

Printed in the United Kingdom by
Bell & Bain Ltd
303 Burnfield Rd
Thornliebank
Glasgow G46 7UQ

Front cover photograph:
Wessex HU.5 XT762 still in its former Royal Aircraft
Establishment Bedford colour scheme, seen at SAH
Culdrose on 19 May 1988 after being allocated A2751. It
was later allocated A2662 [2]. (Geoff Wakeham)

Rear cover photographs (Top to bottom):

The FAA Museum's Swordfish II A2001/HS618 in 825
Sqdn marks as *"W5984/5H"* in which Lt Cdr Eugene
Esmonde was killed in the Channel Dash episode on
12.2.42, being awarded a posthumous Victoria Cross. It
is currently displayed as *"P4139"*. (FAA Museum)

Wasp HAS.1 A2722 [2]/XT778 '-/430' with AES
Lee-on-Solent on 22.7.89. It was later allocated A2642
[2]. (Bob Turner)

Hunter T.7 A2738/XX466 'DD/830' with SAH Culdrose
on 23.7.91. Still in RAF camouflage, the *"Double
Diamond"* marks can be seen on the tail - derived from
the initials for Dummy Deck training. It was later
allocated A2651 [2]. (Geoff Wakeham)

ORIGINAL FOREWORD (1978)

I am delighted to have been given the opportunity to write the foreword to this marvellously detailed monograph.

"Instructional Airframes" perhaps does not conjure up quite the impression of glamour conveyed by the names of some current operational aircraft. However, the reader, who opens the cover is immediately immersed in a fascinating study of old warriors who have returned from the Front Line to provide invaluable facilities for training the groundcrews of the future. I am full of admiration for the painstaking work of those who have followed the history of these old aircraft and compiled this most complete account of their use and locations.

The instructional airframe has been, and will continue to be a vital element in Fleet Air Arm training allowing young officers and ratings to gain knowledge and experience of real aircraft before they leave the closely supervised confines of the Schools and meet operational aircraft for the first time.

The summary of aircraft training establishments is a bonus which will I am sure awaken many fond memories of establishments which have served the Royal Navy well in former days.

Tony Monk

Rear Admiral A.J. Monk CBE MSc BSc(Eng) FIMechE MRAeS FIMarE
(Rear Admiral Engineering to the Flag Officer Naval Air Command)

ORIGINAL PREFACE

This is the third "Super-Monograph" produced by the Research Section of the Group, and to our knowledge the first book ever devoted entirely to Instructional Airframes. Like the first two "Super-Monographs" on the Douglas Skyraider AEW.1 and the Westland Wyvern, it is the culmination of extensive research and planning.

We have brought together information on the different classes of Naval Instructional Airframes, the various Airframe Training Establishments and the aircraft allocated to ground instructional roles since the Fleet Air Arm was transferred to the Admiralty in 1939. The aircraft have been listed by class and then by maintenance serial sequence within each class and a cross-reference has been included to assist readers who are interested in particular aircraft types.

For consistency, the format of this monograph has been modelled around our two previous publications. Deciding the photographic coverage has taken many hours of researching and deliberation, so we hope that you will agree that the selection is an interesting and unusual cross-section of the airframes in the text.

All the information in this monograph has been checked and cross-checked for errors and omissions but should you find any discrepancies or have any further information to add, please let us know. With 'A' numbers still being issued this publication will be suitable for revision in later years when any additions and amendments can be included.

If all goes according to plan, late 1979/early 1980 should see Gnats replacing Sea Hawks at the School of Aircraft Handling, and the arrival on the scene of Harriers at training establishments in preparation for the Sea Harrier era.

In the hope that this book will become a standard reference for researchers of Naval Aviation history in future years, we have continued our practice of presenting the first copy to the Fleet Air Arm Museum at RNAS Yeovilton.

PREFACE TO THIS EDITION

The compilation of this edition of "Royal Navy Instructional Airframes" was born out of necessity. It soon proved impossible to keep the first edition of the monograph up-to-date in its original format and with a word processor at my disposal, for the production of the Fleet Air Arm section of "British Aviation Review", this was an obvious platform on which to maintain a record of the disposition of instructional airframes.

As more additions and amendments became known so more of the original monograph was input to the word processor. A second edition was long overdue and during 1992/93, I added the remainder of the first edition to complete the record. Ray Sturtivant has continued his research of the available allocation records at Yeovilton and later HMS *Sultan*, and this edition brings the record of allocations up to date.

However, this research shows that both the airframe and engine number allocations have undergone two re-structuring exercises, the first in 1988 and then again in 1993. This is more fully described in the relevant sections but a consequence is the duplication of the allocations. This will undoubtedly result in a diminished interest in the subject for all but the serious researcher, especially as the relevant numbers are no longer painted on the aircraft concerned.

Rod Burden

ACKNOWLEDGEMENTS

The original monograph was researched and brought to fruition by a team of Research Section members:

Ray Sturtivant (Project Leader); Dave Allen; Mick Burrow; Pete Cooper; Geoff Cruikshank; Jim Davis; Jim Downing; John Dyer; Richard Foster; R M Keel; Tom MacFadyen; Eric Myall; Douglas Rough; David Smythe; John Tipp; Frank Tyler; Robin Walker.

The Group gratefully acknowledged the help of the following people in supplying research material and/or photographs for the original monograph:

Lt L.Allan RN; Peter Arnold; Gordon Bailey; Mike Bowyer; Lt Cdr M.M.S.Brown.RN; Phil Butler; Bill Chorley; P G Coker; Noel Collier; B Coussens (FAA Museum); Lt Cdr L.A.Cox RN Retired (Curator FAA Museum); "Flamingo"; P.Fletcher; R D Gee; HMS Ark Royal; HMS Sea Hawk; HMS Thunderer; Steve Hobden; John Huggon; J D Hunt; Imperial War Museum; Paul Jackson; Roger Lindsay; Brian Lowe; Fred Lynn; M.P.Marsh; Roy Montgomery; J.A.Morgan; L.G.Pain; S.Palmer; Brian Pickering (MAP - 'Military Aircraft Photographs'); J.Robertson; G.Scott; Captain M.F.Simpson RN; G.J.R.Skillen; Ian Stott; Lt Cdr K.G.Talbot RN Retired; Geoff Wakeham; West London Aviation Research Group; 'Wrecks and Relics' .... and "anyone else we have inadvertently omitted".

Thanks also went to the typists, Marie Finlay, Margaret Hogg and Jean Kendall, and Les Rockett of Gotelee Printers for his help and advice.

This edition would not have been possible without the help of the numerous correspondents who have contributed to the journals "British Aviation Review" and "Roundel" and our thanks are due to all of you. In particular we are grateful to:

Lt Cdr Theo Ballance, Glyn Coney, Terry Coombes, Colin Dawson, Pat Dobbs, Jim Gosling, Mike Hooks, Steve Mills, Eric Myall, Colin O'Neill, Graham Sheppard, Bob Turner (FAA Museum) and Geoff Wakeham.

We are also indebted to Ken Ellis and the team at Midland Publishing responsible for the publication "Wrecks and Relics", now in its 15th Edition after 35 years.

In this instance the "typist" was co-author Rod Burden.

CONTENTS

A view of the Dummy Deck, SAH Culdrose at work in October 1995. Leading the line up is Harrier T.4 XW271/X which was allocated A2692 [2]. (Crown copyright, via Geoff Wakeham)

INTRODUCTION

In January 1921, the Royal Air Force (RAF) introduced a special series of numbers for aircraft relegated to instructional use. A machine re-allocated for this purpose ceased to be identified by its operational serial, receiving instead a new serial number suffixed by the letter 'M'. This series, which probably started at 1M, has at the present time progressed beyond 9200M. At the time 'M' serials were initiated the Fleet Air Arm (FAA) had not come into existence, but did so on 1 April 1923 operating under the jurisdiction of the RAF. The normal sequence of RAF serials had by then reached the 'J' range, but naval aircraft had been allocated serials with 'N' prefixes in a special series which had commenced in 1916. The 'N' serials were exhausted by 1925, and were followed by a similar series of 'S' serials. Both series were intended for use by all aircraft which flew over the sea, and they therefore included flying boats and land-based torpedo bombers which formed no part of the FAA. Despite the fact that these special serial numbers were given to FAA aircraft in operational service, it was apparently deemed unnecessary to have a special series of instructional serial numbers at that time, and consequently aircraft downgraded for this purpose were given RAF 'M' serials.

Shortly before World War II, after campaigning for many years, the Navy was successful in gaining control of the Fleet Air Arm from the RAF. As a result of this transfer of responsibility, all aircraft on the strength of naval first and second line squadrons were transferred to Admiralty charge on 24 May 1939. Initially, instructional airframes at the new FAA shore bases at Donibristle, Ford, Gosport, Lee-on-Solent, Lympne, Southampton (Eastleigh) and Worthy Down continued to use 'M' serials; but early in 1942 a new series of instructional airframe numbers was begun, reserved entirely for FAA instructional aircraft. Details of the early allocations are scanty, and there is no evidence to suggest that existing airframes with 'M' serials were re-numbered in the new series, but this may well have been the case.

Airframe Classifications to June 1973

Until 1973 there were three classes of FAA instructional airframe, these being selected according to the amount of maintenance work required to be carried out on the maintenance work required to be carried out on the machine whilst in the particular class. Throughout the text, Roman numerals are used for each of these classes, but in practice either Roman or Arabic numerals could be used.

CLASS I

A machine in Class I was kept in full flying condition and serviced regularly. Modifications were kept up to date, the engines were run once a fortnight, and the aircraft was flown once a month. An aircraft in this Class did not receive an 'A' serial, but a large proportion of such machines were subsequently downgraded to Class II and consequently received 'A' serials at that stage. Occasionally a Class I aircraft was upgraded and returned to squadron service.

CLASS II

This was a lower Class from which machines could still be restored to flying condition though they rarely did so. Minimum standard anti-corrosion procedures were followed, but no modifications were made, nor were components changed. Many Class II aircraft were subsequently downgraded to Class III, but the majority were eventually written off charge (WOC). Machines in this category received 'A' serials, and for record purposes this then superseded the operational serial. However, there was no requirement to paint the 'A' serial on the aircraft or to overspray the operational serial, and consequently no record survives of the 'A' serials of many of the earlier instructional airframes.

CLASS III

Machines in Class III had been WOC for normal purposes, and were not restorable to flying condition. They could be sectioned or cut up if required. There are many instances of aircraft being downgraded to Class III on two or three occasions, but the reason for this is unknown. It is possible that they had been temporarily upgraded to Class II, but there is no evidence of this, and by their very nature it seems most unlikely. An alternative is that the later dates were simply book records confirming the category.

Airframe Classifications from June 1973

In June 1973 the classification system changed, and two new classes of Ground Reserve airframe were introduced. Class GRA was basically identical with the old Class I, but a few Class II airframes went into this category. Class GRB comprised the majority of airframes in the old Class II and all in the former Class III. It is interesting to note that Wessex' XP155 and XT457 were temporarily listed as Class DRB, but it is not recorded whether this was some other short-lived category, or simply a mistake for Class GRB. Under this new system, aircraft and/or aero engines allocated for instructional purposes were classified as either GRA or GRB, defined as follows:

CLASS GRA

Ground (Training) Reserve (A) airframes and Engine Change Units (ECU's) were to be maintained in a condition which allows them to be brought up to an authorised issue standard by work in a support unit. All aircraft/ECU's in this category remained on naval charge and had to be maintained in accordance with the relevant servicing schedules. The degree of servicing woould to some extent depend upon the instructional task and was determined by the Air Engineer Officer.

CLASS GRB

Ground (Training) Reserve (B) airframes and ECUs were functionally complete, and although they were dismantled or sectioned to meet training requirements, they retained their identity as aircraft, airframes or ECUs. GRB airframes/ECUs were transferred to maintenance/ instructional charge, and there was no requirement to maintain them in accordance with the relevant servicing schedules. If, however, ground running was intended, the Air Engineer Officer detailed the minimum standard of servicing necessary for the intended instructional use. Aircraft in this category could fly again, but would need a total rebuild.

CLASS GR(1) and GR(2)

By 1989 Class GRA and GRB appear to have been superseded by Class GR(1) and GR(2) respectively. The references in the half yearly returns are by no means consistent, but these classifications have been used in the sections of this book which cover the two re-organisations of the allocations in 1988 and 1993 (see 'A' Number Issues). These categories have now fallen into disuse.

Engine Classification

In addition to an 'A' serial, an instructional airframe could carry an 'E' number, and this relate to its engine, officially known as an Engine Change Unit (ECU). ECUs only acquire 'E' numbers when they are in Class GRB (or Class II), and this classification is quite independent of the classification held by the airframe, if any, in which it is installed. Thus a Class GRA engine installed in a Class GRB airframe would receive no 'E' number, but would do so if subsequently downgraded.

The current series of numbers appears to have commenced at either E3000 or E3001, and progressed slowly towards the E4800 series. It is possible that it was preceded by a wartime series commencing at E1, but this is pure conjecture. 'E' number allocations tended to proceed at more than double the rate of the 'A' serials, and this was due to several factors. Twin-engined aircraft are given two, usually consecutive 'E' numbers. Some instructional airframes are later given a new engine and this replacement is given a different 'E' number. There have been in addition many instructional engines which never fitted into airframes, being used solely for some form of engine instruction. No attempt was made to list these in the original monograph, but all known numbers of installed engines will be found amongst the details of their relevant airframes.

An example of an aircraft carrying both its airframe and engine ground instructional numbers, Sea Hawk FB.2 WF294, at Arbroath in 1967, has A2443 and E4370 on its nose. The code marking "FD/105" is spurious. (MAP)

In this edition we have included a section "Instructional Engines". This gives some details which have come to light since the original monograph but primarily concentrates on the re-allocation of 'E' numbers which occurred in 1988 and 1993 (see 'A' Number Issues below).

As with instructional airframes, instructional engines have operational numbers which are superseded by their 'E' numbers. Thus Wessex A2648 has a Gnome 10101 installed now numbered E4692, which had the previous identity of 619/664658; the first part represents the manufacturers' engine number, while the second part was the naval engine number. No attempt has been made to list these numbers in this publication.

Aircraft in Storage

Reference will occasionally be found in the later serial lists to aircraft in storage. There are two main categories of such aircraft, namely Short Term Storage (STS) and Long Term Storage (LTS), the latter being more relevant to the subject of this publication. An aircraft in STS has been flight tested and given certain preservative work on parts which are susceptible to rapid deterioration. It is then held in readiness for issue on 24 hours notice, for a maximum of six weeks. When the number of aircraft held in STS exceeds the number required to be held, the surplus machines are transferred to LTS1 or LTS2. Aircraft placed in LTS1 are brought out of storage after six months for renovation and incorporation of

modifications, whilst those in LTS2 are brought out once a year only. LTS3 applies to aircraft embalmed in a plastic cocoon to enable them to stand in the open without suffering deterioration. Aircraft stored in Category LTS2 which are not required to be worked on are designated LTS2(U), the 'U' suffix indicating 'Unworked'.

'A' Number Issues

The original series of 'A' numbers evidently commenced at A1, and issues were made in numerical sequence until 1948, when the series had reached around A752, or possibly slightly higher. In that year there was a re-organisation of the FAA in which the office of Rear Admiral Reserve Aircraft (RARA), which was responsible for the issue of 'A' serials, closed down at Arbroath. In its place a new authority known as the Flag Officer Reserve Aircraft (FORA) was established at Wykeham Hall, Lee-on-Solent, and as a consequence a new series of 'A' numbers was begun at either A2000 or A2001. All surviving machines in the old series were given numbers in the new series, which then proceeded with normal issues in sequence. This latter series is still in use, although the issuing authority is now the Flag Officer Naval Aviation (FONA) at Yeovilton.

However, there have been two major re-organisations of the issues in recent years. In 1988 it was decided to use only the block A2600 to A2799 (with E4600 to E4899 for engines) and vacant numbers were re-issued in an arbitrary fashion. In 1993 a similar exercise effectively scrapped all existing issues and the extant airframes were issued 'new' numbers commencing at A2600, with engines allocated in the range from E4700. The anomalies which have occurred as a result are more fully explained in the relevant sections.

Anomalies etc.

There are some points relating to the system which are worthy of special mention. Occasional reference is made to aircraft which are used for either fire fighting or exhibition purposes, but it is not normal practice to allocate 'A' serials to these, so they would therefore only carry them if previously used for other instructional purposes in Class II or GRB, although the possibility of such machines having crept into the system in the past is not a remote one. The issuing of 'A' numbers, although now well regulated, has not always been an exact science, probably indicative of its lesser importance than issuing normal operational serials.

The same is apparently true of naval 'M' numbers, since Skuas *"M1291"* and *"M1296"* were seemingly accurately recorded on a dump at Balado Bridge in March 1952, although the official records show that serials 1291M and 1296M were actually issued to Anson K8075 and Moth K1902 respectively.

At this point the original monograph made reference to a Defiant TT.III "5248M" (noted at Bridgnorth in 11.52) and to Spitfire VA P7964. This is now known to be in error since the Spitfire was correctly listed as 5262M and 5248M was in fact allocated to Liberator III FL932. The Defiant was actually recorded as "N5248" which, since it is not a genuine Defiant serial, was thought to be an error for M5248. Details of the real identity of the Defiant would be very welcome.

Several examples of such anomalies will be found amongst the 'A' serial lists. A2268 is officially listed as Seafire F.15 PR394, but it has been reported that this serial was actually painted on another aircraft of this type, SW867. Sea Hawk WF165 is shown in the records as A2405 but it was seemingly mis-painted as A2403 at some stage in its career. Another Sea Hawk, WF147, is recorded as A2376 except in one place where it was transposed as A2367, and possibly as a consequence of this it appears to have spent most of its life carrying the latter serial. Yet another Sea Hawk, XE368/A2534 was painted in error as A2555, a serial which correctly belongs to XE330, also a Culdrose-based Sea Hawk.

A further problem is that there is no permanent cross-recording of original serials and subsequent 'A' numbers, and occasionally a machine has received more than one 'A' number. The most outstanding example of this is probably Sea Vixen XN650, which initially had serial A2612, was briefly given A2620, then finally became A2639. Sea Hawk XE369 had two 'A' serials by virtue of its history as an instructional machine, being originally A2580, then transferring to the RAF as 8158M before returning to the FAA to receive the new number A2633. Occasionally an aircraft allocation will be cancelled after issue of an 'A' serial, and it is possible for this serial to be re-issued, as was the case with A2593 which was to be

a Sea Hawk, but instead became a Sea Vixen Flight Refuelling pod, the latter being yet another anomaly since it is not strictly an aircraft.

In theory a machine in Class I or GRA should never receive an 'A' serial, but in practice this has occasionally occurred in error, as instanced by Wessex HU.5's XT448 and XS509, which were inadvertently given serials A2596 and A2597 respectively. There have also been instances of machines being downgraded to Class II but receiving no 'A' serials. These include Scimitars WT854 and XD242, and Sea Venoms WM517 and XG694, where it would appear that the issue of 'A' serials was simply overlooked at the time of downgrading.

Application of 'A' Numbers

As previously stated, there is no official requirement that an 'A' serial be actually applied to the relevant airframe, although until recent years this was usually done, and consequently the mode of application, if any, has tended to vary. At Worthy Down the serial was often applied in small black symbols immediately below the operational serial. Bramcote tended to be rather inconsistent with some 'A' serials not being applied, whilst others were painted on the rear fuselage or the fin, with the operational serial sometimes deleted by a diagonal line. Arbroath evolved a system whereby both the Class and the 'A' serial were applied in black in a yellow circle carried on the nose of the aircraft. Culdrose and Lee-on-Solent used to apply the 'A' serial in most, but not all, cases. There are many instances where the operational serial was painted out before the 'A' serial was applied, adding to the difficulties in establishing previous identities. Conversely, since the late-1970's the practice of applying 'A' numbers seems to have disappeared completely.

Despite all the handicaps, it has proved possible to identify with accuracy all but three of the 'A' serials issued since the A2400 series was commenced in 1956, the three unconfirmed exceptions being A2403, A2442 and A2474. Earlier than this only representative coverage has proved possible, although more than half the A2300 series has been identified. The details given for each aircraft relate solely to its history whilst it was in the instructional role. Space considerations preclude giving the full service history of each machine mentioned in this publication. Previous units and markings are generally mentioned only where the aircraft came direct from that unit, or where it still carried its former marking. Where a Class I aircraft returned to service, no attempt is made to give its subsequent history. Even confined to that brief, and despite the prodigious amount of effort that went into preparing the original monograph and this subsequent edition, there still remain many gaps to be filled in the record of this somewhat fragmented subject, especially in relation to the 1942 - 1955 period. The readers help is sought in filling these gaps, and since this is a subject of a continuing nature, it is hoped that in future years it will prove possible to produce another updated and revised version of the publication from time to time, incorporating such additional information.

WRNS at Milmeece manoeuvring a Hurricane, probably 'Y1J' ex 759 Sqdn Yeovilton, in June 1943.

AIRFRAME TRAINING ESTABLISHMENTS

Instructional airframes are likely to be found at any United Kingdom naval air station, but as they are primarily intended for use in the training of apprentices, it follows that most of them are issued to schools. Such schools are usually situated on present or former aerodromes, but this is not always the case. Some of the wartime FAA training establishments were dispersed to the North of England and to Scotland, to be less vulnerable to enemy bombing. The primary units mentioned in this publication as holding instructional airframes at some time in their history are given below. In most cases they were given ship's names, as is the customary practice with naval shore bases.

ARBROATH (HMS CONDOR)

Arbroath was originally commissioned as HMS *Condor* on 19 June 1940. During World War II it accommodated the Naval Air Signals School and the FAA's No.2 Observer School. Flying continued on a limited basis after the War, but its main postwar use was as a ground instructional establishment. The Naval Air Apprentices School was set up in January 1946 on the closure of HMS *Daedalus II* at Newcastle-under-Lyme, and two months later the Artificer Training Establishment took up residence. Artificer training and mechanician training at Arbroath was supplemented late in 1958 by the Engine, Airframe and Ordnance Mechanics courses, transferring

from Bramcote when that station closed. By 1966 the Air Engineering School, as it was then known, was responsible for training all FAA maintenance ratings in the mechanical trades. On 4 September 1970 the School moved to Lee-on-Solent as part of the Royal Naval Air Engineering School (AES), and Arbroath paid off on 31 March 1971, to be taken over the following year by the Royal Marines for helicopter use.

BRAMCOTE (HMS GAMECOCK)

In 1947 the RAF vacated Bramcote, near Nuneaton, which they had used since 1940, mainly as a base for Operational Training Units (OTU). The station was then taken over by the FAA (HMS *Gamecock* was commissioned on 3 December 1946) who installed one of their newly formed Royal Naval Volunteer Reserve (RNVR) squadrons, No.1833, and also established an Initial Training School. After an initial period of three or four days at Lee-on-Solent, where they joined the service, all Naval Airmen and Naval Air Mechanics went to Bramcote for a six weeks New Entry Basic Training course, consisting of "square-bashing" and seamanship training. On completion of this course, they were then categorised into their various trades and drafted to the appropriate training camp. In the Naval Airmen Branch, the Aircraft Handlers went to the School of Aircraft Handling at Lee-on-Solent; the Safety Equipment ratings went to Seafield Park near Lee-on-Solent; the Photography ratings went to the Photography School at Ford; and the Meteorological ratings went to Kete. The Naval Air Mechanics remained at Bramcote for their technical training courses as Engine, Airframe or Ordnance Mechanics. A considerable number of instructional airframes were held on strength until October/November 1958 when those surviving were transferred to Arbroath and the station closed down (paid off 10 November 1958), being transferred to the War Department as the Gamecock barracks, to house the Junior Leaders School, Royal Artillery.

CULCHETH (HMS ARIEL)

In May 1942, the Radio Mechanic Branch of the Royal Navy was created to cope with the rapidly changing needs of the service for the maintenance and operation of its radio equipment. This newly formed branch was divided into two categories, General Service and Air. On 12 October 1942, HMS *Ariel* was commissioned at Culcheth, Risley, near Warrington, Lancashire for the training of FAA officers and ratings in air radio maintenance. By 1943 the establishment had expanded into three camps, and the third of these was provided with hangars and hardstandings to house a collection of fuselages and aircraft for practical training purposes to enable aircraft work to be as realistic as possible outside an actual airfield. Aircraft present at this time included an Albacore. Also used by HMS *Ariel* were a Barracuda II, a Swordfish with many radar/radio aerials, a Corsair coded '7J' and an Avenger coded '2Z'. Another camp was set up near Risley to give aerodrome defence training to naval airmen, this being known as HMS *Gosling*. On 1 January 1946 the Electrical Branch was formed, and in June 1952 the Air Electrical School, as HMS *Ariel* had become, was moved to Worthy Down, and the wartime base closed down.

CULDROSE (HMS SEAHAWK)

Culdrose commissioned as HMS *Seahawk* on 17 April 1947 and has since been used by a considerable number of first and second line FAA squadrons. In January 1959 the Royal Naval School of Aircraft Handling (SAH) was established at Culdrose, incorporating Aircraft Handling and Fire Fighting Schools formerly based at Lee-on-Solent and Gosport. The School is divided into four sub-sections, and instructional aircraft are used by two of them, the Aircraft Handling Section and the Fire Fighting School. In November 1995 the SAH was renamed the School of Flight Deck Operations to reflect the full scope of flight deck training. Details of the many aircraft operated by this unit will be found later in this publication.

CULHAM (HMS HORNBILL)

Culham commissioned on 1 November 1944 as HMS *Hornbill*. It was not primarily a training station, being mainly used by an Aircraft Receipt and Despatch Unit, a Ferry Pool and several RNVR squadrons, but it occasionally had an instructional airframe on strength. It closed down in July 1953 (paid off 30 September 1953), becoming an Admiralty stores and United Kingdom Atomic Energy Authority site.

GOSPORT (HMS SISKIN)

Gosport is one of the oldest names in British military aviation history, having been established as a Royal Flying Corps aerodrome in July 1914. It was used as one of the main FAA bases between the wars. In 1945 an Aircraft Handling, Safety Equipment and Fire Fighting School was established, using many instructional airframes. In July 1956 the aerodrome was closed down to become a housing estate, and in January 1959 the School moved to Culdrose as part of the Royal Naval SAH. Another unit at Gosport was the Naval Aircraft Maintenance Development Unit, which formed in 1951 and originated planned inspections and schedules.

GOSPORT (HMS SULTAN)

New facilities were completed here in 1995 to house the Royal Naval Air Engineering School (AES), formerly at Lee-on-Solent which closed on 31 March 1996. A pair of Wessex' had transferred here by May 1995 and the remaining airframes were due by the end of 1995. Most had transferred by June 1996 but several were not confirmed in residence until early 1997 by which time the facility was retitled the Air Engineering and Survival School.

GOSPORT (HMS VINCENT)

During the war a few instructional airframes were on strength for the initial training of FAA aircrew. In the postwar years, the Royal Naval New Entrant Training Establishment functioned and retained the occasional instructional airframe.

KIRKHAM (RAF STATION)

The RAF formed No.10 School of Technical Training (SoTT) at Kirkham, near Blackpool in 1940, and had a number of FAA instructional airframes on strength until at least 1946. These were used to give airframe training to FAA apprentices at this RAF station which gave different types of ground training to RAF recruits. The unit closed down in March 1958. Naval airframe training is known to have been carried out at other RAF SoTT's, including No.5 at Locking and No.6 at Hednesford, the latter unit, using amongst other aircraft a Barracuda and in 1945 a Seafire, continuing to give such training in the early post-war years.

LEE-ON-SOLENT (HMS DAEDALUS / HMS ARIEL)

Another old name in naval aviation history, Lee-on-Solent was opened on 30 July 1917 as a seaplane training station. It has been used as a naval aviation station throughout its existence, being transferred from the RAF on 24 May 1939 to become HMS *Daedalus*. On 1 November 1960 it was renamed HMS *Ariel*, but reverted to its former title on 5 October 1965. In the postwar years it has been the base for a number of FAA training units, several of which have used instructional airframes. It was used by the Aircraft Handling School, Gosport until that unit moved to Culdrose at the end of 1958. By 1958, the Accident Investigation Unit (AIU) was carrying out instruction in flight safety and accident prevention, and by 1960 the School of Safety Equipment was also in residence. On 1 November 1960 the Air Electrical Training Establishment moved in from Worthy Down. On 4 September 1970 the Air Engineering School at Arbroath combined with the old Air Electrical School (AES) at Lee-on-Solent to become the Royal Naval Air Engineering School (AES), the biggest unit at HMS *Daedalus*. All the FAA electrical and mechanical training was then concentrated at Lee-on-Solent, and consequently quite a number of instructional airframes are held. In recent years airframes have been used by *"760 Squadron"*; this is a dummy or shadow squadron set up to train engineers in the procedures used by the frontline units. 760 Squadron has used two Sea Kings and up to three Wasps drawn from the AES.

The Navy's facilities at Lee-on-Solent were withdrawn from the base from December 1995 with official closure on 31 March 1996. The AES moved to HMS *Sultan*, Gosport on completion of new facilities there in 1995, at which time the AIU moved to Yeovilton. The first two Wessex' had moved by May 1995 with the remaining airframes due to transfer by the end of the year.

LYMPNE / NEWCASTLE-UNDER-LYME (HMS DAEDALUS II)

Early in the war, a naval air mechanic school was opened at the former Royal Air Force aerodrome at Lympne in Kent, this base being attached to Lee-on-Solent (HMS *Daedalus*) for administrative purposes, and consequently known as HMS *Daedalus II*. After the fall of France, it became necessary to return Lympne to the RAF, and by 23 May 1940 the naval establishment had evacuated to Newcastle-under-Lyme, Staffordshire, where it stayed for the remainder of the war. It was known as the Royal Naval Aircraft Training Establishment, and undertook training of air apprentices, air fitters and air mechanics. In January 1942 technical training was given in the Westlands Girls School using a Swordfish, a Skua, a Fulmar, a Martlet and a Proctor. By the end of that year the establishment was using a large permanent hangar at nearby Clayton, and in addition to the aircraft held earlier in the year it had acquired a Shark, an Albacore, a Tiger Moth, a Spitfire, a Walrus and a Hurricane. On its closure in January 1946 the unit was replaced by the newly-formed Naval Air Apprentices School at Arbroath. The whole site is now occupied by an estate of bungalows.

MAHARAGAMA (HMS MONARA)

The Royal Naval Aircraft Training Establishment, Ceylon, commissioned on 1 December 1944 as HMS *Monara*. It was established to train Ceylonese recruits and used at least an Albacore, a Fulmar and a Seafox. The establishment was paid off after the war.

Sea Venom FAW.21 WW189/A2518, ex 'J/153' of 892 Sqdn and still in Suez stripes, at Lee-on-Solent on 15 June 1961. (MAP).

MILMEECE (HMS FLEDGLING)

HMS *Fledgling* was commissioned on 15 April 1943 at Milmeece, Eccleshall, Staffordshire for the training of Womens Royal Naval Service (WRNS) Air Mechanics. It was situated only a few miles away from HMS *Daedalus II* whose facilities it initially shared for the training of Ordnance Mechanics. The Air Branch of the Navy, which had previously had no WRNS Air Mechanics, initiated four categories, these being Airframe (A), Engine (E), Electrician (L) and Ordnance (or armament) (O). A variety of airframes were used for training purposes, including a Wildcat, a Fulmar, a Hurricane (coded 'Y1J', ex 759 Sqdn Yeovilton) and a Proctor. The school was closed down after the war.

ST.MERRYN (HMS VULTURE)

St.Merryn, in Cornwall, was commissioned on 10 August 1940 as HMS *Vulture*, and was used by numerous first and second line FAA squadrons. Recommissioned as HMS *Curlew* on 31 December 1952, becoming primarily a ground training base. Closed to flying on 14 December 1953. Shortly after World War II, selected experienced pilots were given intensive training at St Merryn, being attached to the School of Air Warfare and subsequently undergoing flying courses at either Eglinton or Culdrose to become qualified as Air Weapons Officers. This ground training was also carried out for a time by the School of Aircraft Maintenance and the Air Ordnance School, the latter unit having moved from Yeovilton. A number of instructional airframes were held for use by these units until the station finally closed down in 1955, when the airframes were dispersed, mainly to Arbroath and Bramcote. Paid off on 10 January 1956.

TOWNHILL (HMS WAXWING)

In 1942, a Naval Aircraft Depot was established at Townhill, Dunfermline and it was commissioned on 1 July 1942 as HMS *Waxwing*. The nucleus of a number of Corsair squadrons assembled here before sailing to the USA where they were officially commissioned. Initially the ratings were at Townhill, and the officers gathered at Donibristle. Squadrons whose crews assembled here included Nos. 1833, 1834, 1835, 1836 and 1846. 857 Avenger squadron also assembled here. Small numbers of instructional airframes were in use until the establishment closed at the end of the war. These included an Avenger fuselage which was the only airframe on strength in January 1944.

WORTHY DOWN (HMS ARIEL)

Worthy Down commissioned on 25 May 1939 as HMS *Kestrel*, being formerly an RAF bomber base. HMS *Kestrel* closed in late 1947, but in June 1952 the station was re-opened as HMS *Ariel II*, to house the Air Electrical School, formerly at Culcheth. On 1 November 1960 this unit moved again, this time to Lee-on-Solent, once more taking the title HMS *Ariel* with it, and on 1 December 1960 the station was handed over to the Royal Army Pay Corps.

YEOVILTON (HMS HERON)

Yeovilton commissioned on 18 June 1940 as HMS *Heron*, a name which it has held continuously ever since. From time to time it has had a number of instructional airframes, including some with the Air Ordnance School until at least 1951. Leading Airmen's courses for ratings were held at Yeovilton for Airframe and Engine Mechanics until 1958 when, on the closure of Bramcote, all mechanic training was concentrated at Arbroath. Some of the many aircraft held by the FAA Museum also have instructional numbers.

Other Royal Navy Units

From time to time other naval establishments, not primarily concerned with FAA training, hold an instructional airframe on strength. Reference to the following will be found in the main lists of this publication.

HMS Collingwood	RN Weapon and Electrical Engineering School, Fareham, Hampshire.
HMS Daedalus III	RN Camp, Bedhampton, Hampshire. New entry base for maintenance ratings, and a transit camp. Used until at least 1946.
HMS Excellent	RN Gunnery School, Whale Island, Portsmouth, Hampshire.
HMS Ganges	RN Junior Training Establishment, Shotley Gate, Ipswich, Suffolk. Closed for training early 1976 but retained on a care and maintenance basis. Completely closed by November 1976.
HMS Pembroke	RN Supply School, Chatham, Kent.
HMS Royal Arthur	RN Petty Officers School, Corsham, Wilts.
HMS Thunderer	RN Engineering College (RNEC), Manadon, Plymouth, Devon. Closed July 1995.
HMS Vernon	RN Torpedo, Anti-Submarine and Diving School, Gosport, Hampshire.

NAVAL 'M' SERIALS

Prior to the introduction of the 'A' series of airframe serial numbers in 1942, the instructional airframes of naval aircraft carried 'M' serial numbers in a common series with RAF aircraft. Records for the earliest examples of the 'M' series were destroyed some years ago, but most of the late pre-war and early wartime allocations have been traced. They include such nostalgic types as the Seal, Shark and Walrus. In addition to these, a number of RAF aircraft which had been transferred to the FAA for training or operational use returned to the RAF at the end of their flying lives to be used as ground instructional airframes at Radio Schools and Schools of Technical Training, in some cases for the training of naval apprentices attached to such schools. This explains the apparent overlap between the later 'M' serials

allocated to the former FAA aircraft, and the commencement of that service's own series of 'A' serials. In the 1970's a number of naval aircraft were issued to No.1 SoTT at Halton, and other RAF units, for instructional purposes and this continued through the 1980's with a variety of types, leading up to the early 1990's when the former FAA Buccaneers and Phantoms were withdrawn from RAF service.

Explanations of the many abbreviations used in the following listings are to be found in the Glossary of Terms. In the later allocations the name SERCO refers to the company which took over the recruitment display airframes from the RAF Exhibition Flight (RAFEF) by early 1994.

'M' No.	AIRCRAFT TYPE	SERIAL	DETAILS
622M	Nimrod I	K2833	SOC 25.6.34.
646M	Osprey I	K2774	SOC 6.6.35.
657M	Seal I	K3521	SOC 29.6.35 (ex Fairey Aviation).
666M	Tutor	K1230	SOC 6.35 (ex 'C' Flight Gosport).
695M	Hart I	K2464	SOC 9.35 (ex Gosport).
739M	Fairey IIIF	S1835	(ex MAEE Felixstowe).
873M	Osprey IIIL	K3915	SOC 17.7.36.
894M	Nimrod I	K2831	SOC 29.9.36 (ex HAD Henlow).
903M	Shark II	K5617	To Southampton 28.10.36, after a crash landing with 1 FTS at Donibristle 8.9.36.
922M	Osprey III	K3640	SOC 5.3.57 (ex Pool Gosport).
931M	Shark I	K4295	SOC 21.1.37 (ex MAEE Felixstowe).
962M	Osprey		To 5 SoTT Locking. Reduced to spares and produce 29.4.44.
965M	Osprey IIIL	K3914	SOC 25.3.37 (ex 'A' Flight Calshot).
971M	Osprey IIIL	K3918	SOC 1.7.37 (ex SoNC Lee-on-Solent).
985M	Swordfish I	K5986	SOC 25.8.37 (ex 'A' Flight, TTU Gosport).
990M	Shark I	K4357	SOC 30.9.37 (ex Stn Flt Gosport).
1000M	Osprey III	K3644	SOC 21.10.37 (ex Pool Gosport).
1028M	Fairey IIIF	S1317	SOC 17.8.38.
1046M	Nimrod I	K2826	SOC 22.3.38 (ex Pool Gosport).
1057M	Osprey I	K2777	SOC 3.5.38 (ex SoAC Old Sarum).
1069M	Seal	K4792	SOC 17.5.38 (ex Pool Gosport).
1070M	Seal	K4214	SOC 17.5.38 (ex Pool Lee-on-Solent).
1071M	Walrus	K8563	SOC 17.5.38 (ex Ford).
1090M	Seal	K4786	SOC 1.6.38 (ex 4 ASU Ternhill).
1091M	Seal	K4224	SOC 1.6.38 (ex 4 ASU Ternhill).
1096M	Seal	K4793	SOC 27.6.38 (ex DTD).
1098M	Seal	K3577	SOC 13.7.38 (ex MAEE Felixstowe).
1125M	Osprey III	K3655	SOC 16.9.38 (ex Pool Gosport).
1127M	Shark II	K8475	SOC 19.11.37 (ex 4 ASU Ternhill).
1146M	Nimrod I	K2823	SOC 18.10.38 (ex Kenley).
1172M	Osprey IV	K5760	SOC 10.11.38 (ex Pool Gosport).
1175M	Seal	K4202	SOC 10.11.38 (ex 2 AACU Lee-on-Solent).
1176M	Seal	K4204	SOC 10.11.38 (ex 2 AACU Lee-on-Solent).
1179M	Seal	K4218	To Lee-on-Solent 11.11.38 (ex 2 AACU Lee-on-Solent).
1183M	Nimrod II	K2910	Ex crash landing 1 FTS Netheravon 27.9.38.
1186M	Seal	K4203	SOC 5.12.38 (ex Pool Lee-on-Solent).
1188M	Walrus	L2203	SOC 26.11.38 (ex 8 ATS Evanton).

'M' No.	AIRCRAFT TYPE	SERIAL	DETAILS
1190M	Nimrod I	K2827	SOC 5.12.38 (ex Pool Gosport).
1200M	Skua	L2869	SOC 16.12.38 (ex 800 Sqdn Worthy Down).
1201M	Skua	L2870	SOC 11.1.39 (ex Worthy Down).
1228M	Osprey III	K3648	SOC 19.1.39 (ex Pool Gosport).
1229M	Osprey IV	K5755	SOC 19.1.39 (ex Pool Gosport).
1241M	Walrus	L2186	SOC 1.2.39 (ex 'A' Flight, SoNC Ford).
1247M	Avro 504N	K1813	SOC 3.39 (ex 'C' Flight Gosport).
1248M	Avro 504N	K1974	SOC 3.39 (ex Stn Flt Gosport), after ground collision with Swordfish L2729 27.10.38.
1249M	Avro 504N	K2349	SOC 3.39 (ex SoNC Lee-on-Solent).
1250M	Avro 504N	K2386	SOC 3.39 (ex SoNC Lee-on-Solent).
1251M	Avro 504N	K2402	SOC 3.39 (ex SoNC Lee-on-Solent).
"1291M"	Skua		Balado dump 3.52 [1291M was actually Anson K8705].
1294M	Skua	L2871	SOC 27.3.39 (ex A&AEE Martlesham Heath).
"1296M"	Skua		'X5W' Balado dump 3.52 [1296M was actually Moth K1902].
1311M	Swordfish	L7698	SOC 25.2.39 (ex Stn Flt Northolt).
1325M	Walrus	L2192	To 5 SoTT Locking 7.2.39 (ex Pool Lee-on-Solent).
1338M	Walrus	L2270	To 6 SoTT Hednesford 6.4.39 (ex Pool Lee-on-Solent).
1339M	Walrus	L2272	To 1 SoTT Halton 6.4.39 (ex Pool Lee-on-Solent).
1340M	Walrus	L2215	SOC 22.3.39 (ex 712 Sqdn Lee-on-Solent).
1356M	Swordfish	L2761	SOC 22.3.39 (ex 811 Sqdn Donibristle), after crash landing at Turnhouse 16.1.39.
1451M	Shark II	K8895	To 2 SoTT Cosford 24.4.39 (ex 2 AACU Lee-on-Solent).
1456M	Shark II	K8479	To 6 SoTT Hednesford 26.4.39 (ex 4 ASU Ternhill).
1457M	Shark II	K8450	To 6 SoTT Hednesford 26.4.39 (ex 24 MU Ternhill).
1458M	Shark II	K8451	To 6 SoTT Hednesford 26.4.39 (ex 4 ASU Ternhill). Cancelled.
1459M	Shark II	K8452	To 6 SoTT Hednesford 26.4.39 (ex 4 ASU Ternhill). Cancelled.
1460M	Shark II	K5641	To 2 SoTT Cosford 26.4.39 (ex 4 ASU Ternhill).
1461M	Shark II	K5633	To 2 SoTT Cosford 26.4.39 (ex 4 ASU Ternhill).
1462M	Shark II	K8500	To 2 SoTT Cosford 26.4.39 (ex 4 ASU Ternhill).
1463M	Seafox	K4304	To 5 SoTT Locking in 5.39 (ex MAEE Felixstowe).
1482M	Shark II	K5607	To 1 SoTT Halton in 5.39 (SOC 12.6.39, ex HMS Pegasus).
1507M	Fairey IIIF	S1851	To 2 SoTT Cosford in 6.39.
1568M	Seal	K4794	To Brize Norton 8.6.39.
1752M	Shark II	L2374	SOC 10.39 (ex 2 AACU Gosport).
1826M	Fairey IIIF	S1859	(ex SoNC Lee-on-Solent).
1827M	Fairey IIIF	S1826	
1867M	Shark II	K8906	SOC 8.1.40 at 3 SoTT Blackpool (ex 2 AACU Gosport/Roborough 5.12.39).
1929M	Fairey IIIF	S1800	SOC in 3.40.
1953M	Osprey III	K3631	At 10 SoTT Kirkham. To Yeovilton 8.7.43.
2757M	Hurricane I	V7111	To HMS Daedalus II Newcastle-under-Lyme 16.10.41.
2807M	Sea Hurricane IA	P5183	(ex Cat.B with MSFU Speke 3.11.41).
2876M	Hurricane I	N2669	To FAA, Yeovilton 15.1.42 (ex 23 MU).
3490M	Shark II	K8929	(ex 'C' Flight, 2 AACU Roborough).
3584M	Sea Hurricane IA	V7600	(ex Cat.B with MSFU Speke 26.6.42).
3585M	Hurricane I	P3119	(ex FAA).
3819M	Master I	N9005	(ex FAA).
3831M	Master I	N9004	(ex FAA).
4065M	Tiger Moth	T7910	To RN College, Keyham, Plymouth 20.8.43 (ex RIW at W.Mumford, Bibbacombe via 19 MU).
4350M	Sea Hurricane IA	V6990	(ex MSFU Speke).
4499M	Sea Hurricane IB	V7157	To 2 SoTT Cosford 28.1.44.
4501M	Sea Hurricane IB	L1663	To 2 SoTT Cosford 28.1.44 (ex Yeovilton).
4502M	Sea Hurricane IB	W9221	To 2 SoTT Cosford 28.1.44 (ex 759 Sqdn Yeovilton).
4503M	Sea Hurricane IB	P3111	To instructional 1.44 (ex 760 Sqdn Yeovilton).

'M' No.	AIRCRAFT TYPE	SERIAL	DETAILS
4504M	Sea Hurricane IB	R4089	To 2 SoTT Cosford 1.2.44 (ex 760 Sqdn Yeovilton).
4505M	Sea Hurricane IB	P3020	To 6 SoTT Hednesford 2.2.44 (ex 759 Sqdn Yeovilton).
4506M	Sea Hurricane IA	V7002	To 2 SoTT Cosford 28.1.44 (ex Yeovilton).
4507M	Sea Hurricane IB	Z7147	(ex 760 Sqdn Yeovilton).
4533M	Hurricane I	W9127	To 5 SoTT Locking 15.2.44 (ex 748 Sqdn St Merryn).
4534M	Hurricane I	L1568	To 5 SoTT Locking 15.2.44 (ex Yeovilton).
4535M	Sea Hurricane IB	Z4927	To instructional 15.2.44 (ex 760 Sqdn Yeovilton).
4536M	Sea Hurricane IB	V6933	To 5 SoTT Locking 15.2.44 (ex 759 Sqdn Yeovilton).
4537M	Sea Hurricane IB	Z7078	(ex 762 Sqdn Yeovilton).
4539M	Sea Hurricane IB	P3814	(ex Yeovilton).
4560M	Sea Hurricane IB	N2660	(ex 760 Sqdn Yeovilton).
4561M	Sea Hurricane IB	P3829	To 1 SoTT Halton 24.2.44 (ex 760 Sqdn Yeovilton).
4562M	Hurricane I	V7377	To 2 SoTT Cosford 26.2.44 (ex Yeovilton).
4574M	Hurricane I	V6850	To 6 SoTT Hednesford 25.2.44 (ex 759 Sqdn Yeovilton).
4576M	Sea Hurricane IB	P3701	(ex Yeovilton).
4577M	Sea Hurricane IB	N2435	(ex Yeovilton).
4578M	Sea Hurricane IB	V6579	To 7 SoTT Innsworth (ex Yeovilton).
4659M	Sea Hurricane IA	BW841	(ex 787Z Sqdn Wittering).
4660M	Sea Hurricane IB	Z7085	(ex 759 Sqdn Yeovilton).
4662M	Sea Hurricane IB	V6779	(ex 787 Sqdn Wittering).
4663M	Hurricane I	V7055	(ex 759 Sqdn Yeovilton).
4664M	Sea Hurricane IB	N2671	To 6 SoTT Hednesford 25.2.44 (ex 761 Sqdn Yeovilton).
4665M	Sea Hurricane IB	Z7091	
4684M	Sea Hurricane IA	Z4851	To instructional 20.3.44 (ex Yeovilton).
4685M	Sea Hurricane IB	P2859	To 2 SoTT Cosford 20.3.44 (ex 762 Sqdn Yeovilton).
4686M	Sea Hurricane IB	V7252	To 2 SoTT Cosford 20.3.44 (ex Lee-on-Solent).
4687M	Sea Hurricane IB	V6675	To 6 SoTT Hednesford 20.3.44 (ex 760 Sqdn Yeovilton).
4693M	Sea Hurricane IB	N2455	To 6 SoTT Hednesford 13.3.44 (ex 768 Sqdn Yeovilton). SOC 31.12.46.
4694M	Sea Hurricane IB	AF950	(ex Yeovilton).
4695M	Hurricane I	Z4790	To 6 SoTT Hednesford 22.3.44 (ex Yeovilton).
4696M	Sea Hurricane IB	AF981	
4697M	Spitfire VC	AR493	To 10 SoTT Kirkham 23.3.44 (ex 19 MU).
4725M	Sea Hurricane IB	N2591	To 1 RS Cranwell 24.3.44 (ex Yeovilton).
4726M	Sea Hurricane IB	V7421	To 4 RS Madley 24.3.44 (ex 759 Sqdn Yeovilton).
4727M	Spitfire IA	K9883	To RNAETE Milmeece 25.3.44 (ex 19 MU).
4746M	Sea Hurricane IB	Z7144	(ex 760 Sqdn Yeovilton).
4747M	Sea Hurricane IB	V6545	To 11 RS Hooton Park 27.3.44.
4748M	Sea Hurricane IB	W9318	(ex 880 Sqdn HMS Indomitable).
4749M	Sea Hurricane IB	W9134	Technical Training Comm Flight White Waltham (ex 762 Sqdn Yeovilton).
4750M	Spitfire IA	X4921	To St Merryn 28.3.44 (ex 19 MU).
4756M	Sea Hurricane IB	V7379	To 2 SoTT Cosford 2.4.44.
4757M	Sea Hurricane IB	V7623	To 4 RS Madley 2.4.44 (ex Yeovilton).
4758M	Sea Hurricane IB	AF945	(ex 748 Sqdn St Merryn).
4759M	Sea Hurricane IB	N2398	To 6 SoTT Hednesford 2.4.44.
5033M	Sea Hurricane IA	V6867	(ex MSFU Speke, later 59 OTU Milfield).
5034M	Hurricane I	V7166	(ex MSFU Speke, later 609 Sqdn Manston).
5035M	Sea Hurricane IB	V7246	(ex MSFU Speke).
5036M	Sea Hurricane I	V7653	(ex MSFU Speke, later 59 OTU Milfield).
5039M	Sea Hurricane IA	W9208	(ex MSFU Speke).
5042M	Sea Hurricane IA	Z7145	(ex MSFU Speke).
5044M	Sea Hurricane IA	P5397	(ex MSFU Speke, later 50 OTU Milfield). At Kegworth School, Notts 6.46.
5054M	Sea Hurricane IB	P2717	(ex MSFU Speke).
5207M	Sea Hurricane IB	W9182	(ex MSFU Speke).
5262M	Spitfire VA	P7964	To instructional 27.1.45 (ex FAA).
5367M	Hurricane FB.IIC	LF765	To 5 SoTT Locking 14.7.45 (ex FAA). At St Athan 1946.

'M' No.	AIRCRAFT TYPE	SERIAL	DETAILS
5371M	Hurricane FB.IIC	LF719	To 5 SoTT Locking 14.7.45 (ex 776 Sqdn Woodvale).
5372M	Hurricane FB.IIC	LF690	To 5 SoTT Locking 14.7.45 (ex 776 Sqdn Woodvale).
5373M	Sea Hurricane IIC	NF686	(ex 800 Sqdn at various bases).
5374M	Sea Hurricane IIC	NF737	
5396M	Spitfire VB	EP169	(ex Stretton).
5537M	Spitfire VB	W3127	(ex Yeovilton).
5572M	Spitfire LF.VB	W3229	To instructional 12.6.45 (ex Yeovilton). To Armée de l'Air 1946.
5684M	Wellington XI	MP519	To 8 RS Cranwell 10.45 (ex 762 Sqdn Yeovilton), coded 'P1X'.
5912M	Mosquito II	DD759	To Arbroath 29.3.46 (ex 44 MU Edzell), and still there 1.48 coded '53' (probably ex 51 OTU Cranfield).
5915M	Mosquito NF.30	NT560	To Yeovilton 1.4.46 (ex 9 MU Cosford) and still there 7.50 as A2026.
5982M	Tiger Moth II	N9211	To Yeovilton 6.7.46 (ex 20 MU).
5983M	Tiger Moth I	K2587	To Yeovilton 6.7.46 (ex 20 MU).
5987M	Tiger Moth II	T7682	To Yeovilton 6.7.46 (ex 11 EFTS Perth, probably via 20 MU). Became A2034.
6006M	Mosquito B.25	KB685	To Arbroath 27.6.46.
6049M	Tiger Moth II	R4752	To Yeovilton 6.7.46 (ex RAE Farnborough).
6116M	Mosquito NF.30	MT477	To Arbroath 10.9.46.
6120M	Mosquito PR.XVI	NS803	To Yeovilton 10.9.46.
6143M	Mosquito PR.XVI	MM389	To Yeovilton 30.9.46.
6153M	Mosquito PR.XVI	NS737	To Yeovilton 24.10.46.
6154M	Mosquito PR.XVI	MM327	To Yeovilton 24.10.46.
6155M	Mosquito PR.XVI	NS525	To Yeovilton 24.10.46.
6156M	Mosquito PR.XVI	NS640	To Yeovilton 24.10.46 (ex RAF). Later returned to FAA service.
6225M	Walrus II	X9580	To instructional 13.12.46 (ex MAEE Felixstowe). Allotted to RNethAF. Handed back at Lasham and SOC 5.1.48.
6956M	Sea Mosquito TR.37	VT726	To 12 SoTT Melksham, allotted 10.3.52 (ex CS(A) charge at RAE Farnborough).
7174M	Hawker P.1052	VX272	Allocated to 1 SoTT Halton 14.1.55. To 2 Recruit Centre, Cardington 20.6.61. To Colerne Museum 9.6.64. To St Athan Museum 8.9.75 and on to Cosford Museum 1.77. To Lee-on-Solent by road 3.5.90 for FAA Museum storage. To FAA Museum store Wroughton 15.2.95. Current.
7175M	Supermarine 517	VV106	[Former trials aircraft - as Supermarine 510 - for a Naval version of the Swift] Allocated to 1 SoTT Halton 17.1.55. To 2 Recruiting Centre, Cardington 20.6.61. To Colerne Museum 9.6.64. To St Athan Museum 29.9.75 and on to Cosford Museum 1.77. To Lee-on-Solent by road 2.90 for FAA Museum storage (dismantled). To FAA Museum store Wroughton 15.2.95. Current.
7703M	Dragonfly HR.3	WG725	To 8 SoTT Weeton 7.11.60 (ex RAE Farnborough). Later to Colerne, then Odiham, Middle Wallop and Southend [registered N9987Q circa 1982]. To Cornwall Aeronautical Park, Helston 21.9.86 (now named Flambards Village Theme Park) and restored as "WG754" "CU/912" in 1990. Current.
8051M	Buccaneer S.1	XN929	By sea to RAF Honington 11.69 (ex NASU Lossiemouth, departed 12.11.69 via Inverness and Belfast), marked '630½' (ex 'LM/630' 736 Sqdn Lossiemouth). Dumped circa 1973 and expired 1974, but cockpit section retained for use as a simulator at until at least 6.86. To Cranwell by 2.89 and current 1991. To G F Williamson's scrapyard, Elgin by 1.92 and current 1.96.

'M' No.	AIRCRAFT TYPE	SERIAL	DETAILS
8059M	Buccaneer S.1	XN956	To RAF Laarbruch 21.11.69 (ex NASU Lossiemouth). Used as a weapons loading trainer at Laarbruch until at least 1.77. Still current with 2 Sqdn for BDR training at Laarbruch in 6.90, spuriously marked as 15 Sqdn 'K'. Believed scrapped.
5368M	Hurricane FB.IIC	LF656	To 5 SoTT Locking 14.7.45, coded 'R7B' (ex 776 Sqdn Woodvale).
5369M	Hurricane FB.IIC	LF709	To 5 SoTT Locking 14.7.45 (ex 776 Sqdn Woodvale).
5370M	Hurricane FB.IIC	LF718	To 5 SoTT Locking 14.7.45 (ex 776 Sqdn Woodvale).
8087M	Buccaneer S.1	XN925	To FF&SS Catterick by 8.70 (ex A2602), coded 'LM/-'. Derelict by 3.88 and last noted 2.89.
8138M	Sea Vixen FAW.2	XN700	To 1 SoTT Halton 16.5.71 (ex Belfast). Coded '31' by mid-1974. To Farnborough by 7.76 and stored for the D.3 drone programme (current 9.82). Stripped for spares 12.83. North side scrap compound by 9.84.
8139M	Sea Vixen FAW.2	XJ582	To 1 SoTT Halton 7.71 (ex Belfast). Coded '32' by mid-1974. Scrap area 3-12.79. By road to Cottesmore 27.1.80 for the dump. To Hanningfield Metals, Stock, Essex by 11.91 and scrapped.
8140M	Sea Vixen FAW.2	XJ571	To 1 SoTT Halton 30.5.71 (ex Belfast), coded 'H/242' (ex 893 Sqdn). 1 SoTT code '33' added by mid-1974. To 2 SoTT Cosford circa 3.79, with local code 'R', and current 8.86 as 'H/242'. To Southampton Airport 11.9.87 for restoration project (with 8171M/XJ607). To Dunsfold 12.90 for continued restoration. For sale 2.92 but still at Dunsfold 6.94, coded 'R'. Prepared for display by BAe as 'H/242' 893 Sqdn and to Brooklands Museum 6.12.94. Current.
8141M	Sea Vixen FAW.2	XN688	To 1 SoTT Halton 4.7.71 (ex Belfast). Coded '34' by mid-1974. To RAE Farn-borough 18.4.77, stored for the D.3 drone programme (current 9.82). Stripped for spares 12.83. On western dump for FCR by 9.84. Noted 9.90-10.92 in poor state.
8142M	Sea Vixen FAW.2	XJ560	To 1 SoTT Halton 29.6.71 (ex Belfast). Coded '35' by mid-1974. To RAE Farnborough 2.4.77. To RAE Bedford 25.2.79, with code '35' in white on nose and '-/242' (ex 893 Sqdn code) visible underneath. Essentially a hulk. From RAE Bedford dump to Newark Air Museum, Winthorpe 10.8.86. Current as '-/242'.
8143M	Sea Vixen FAW.2	XN691	To 1 SoTT Halton 1971 (ex Belfast), coded 'H/247' (ex 893 Sqdn). 1 SoTT code '36' added by mid-1974. To 2 SoTT Cosford 9.3.79. WFU at 2 SoTT by 4.86. To Midland Air Museum, Baginton in 4.88. To North Weald 2.90 and current.
8144M	Sea Vixen FAW.2	XN707	To 1 SoTT Halton 5.6.71 (ex Belfast). Coded '37' by mid-1974. To RAE Farnborough 27.3.77. Dumped by 11.79 and noted minus booms 4.82.
8145M	Sea Vixen FAW.2	XJ526	To 1 SoTT Halton 7.71 (ex Belfast). Coded '38' by mid-1974, to at least 3.79. Scrap area by 3.79 to 6.81. To FF&SS Catterick by road 1-2.2.83 (via Finningley). Expired by 12.85.
8148M	Sea Vampire T.22	XA165	To 1414 ATC Sqdn Crowborough (ex 5 MU Kemble). Scrapped in 1977.
8151M	Sea Hawk FGA.6	WV795	To 1 SoTT Halton 20.1.71 (ex Belfast). By road to Belfast Harbour, where embarked in RFA Robert Dundas for Halton 12.3.71. Became A2661.
8152M	Sea Hawk FGA.6	WV794	To 1 SoTT Halton 20.1.71 (ex Belfast). By road to Belfast Harbour, where embarked in RFA Robert Dundas for Halton 12.3.71. Became A2634.

'M' No.	AIRCRAFT TYPE	SERIAL	DETAILS
8153M	Sea Hawk FGA.6	WV903	To 1 SoTT Halton 20.1.71 (ex Belfast). By road to Belfast Harbour, where embarked in RFA Robert Dundas for Halton 16.3.71. Became A2632.
8154M	Sea Hawk FGA.6	WV908	To 1 SoTT Halton 20.1.71 (ex Belfast). By road to Belfast Harbour, where embarked in RFA Robert Dundas for Halton 16.3.71. Became A2660.
8155M	Sea Hawk FGA.6	WV797	To 1 SoTT Halton 20.1.71 (ex Belfast). By road to Belfast Harbour, where embarked in RFA Robert Dundas for Halton 16.3.71. Became A2637.
8156M	Sea Hawk FGA.6	XE339	To 1 SoTT Halton 19.1.71 (ex Fleetlands). Became A2635.
8157M	Sea Hawk FGA.6	XE390	To 1 SoTT Halton 19.1.71 (ex Fleetlands). Became A2636.
8158M	Sea Hawk FGA.6	XE369	To 1 SoTT Halton 30.12.70 (ex A2580 at Arbroath). Became A2633.
8162M	Sea Hawk FB.5	WM913	'M' serial not taken up. To RAF Sealand still as A2510.
8163M	Sea Vixen FAW.2	XP919	To RAF Abingdon 2.8.71 by air coded 'VL/706' (ex 890 Sqdn Yeovilton). To 1 SoTT Halton 2.72. To Thorpe Park, Chertsey - date ? To City of Norwich Aviation Museum, Norwich Airport 13.9.81 as 'VL/706'. To Blyth Valley Aviation Collection, Walpole, Suffolk 12.95 and current.
8164M	Sea Hawk FB.5	WF299	[Formerly A2509] To FF&SS Catterick by 3.72 (ex SAH Culdrose), still 'SAH-8'. Remained to at least 9.74 and probably until 1977. Noted at Topcliffe 8.77. Re-allocated A2662.
8171M	Sea Vixen FAW.2	XJ607	To Cranwell Engineering Flight 3.8.71 by air (ex 'VL/701' 890 Sqdn Yeovilton). To 2 SoTT Cosford 11.80, marked 'VL/-'. WFU by 4.86. To Southampton Airport 15.10.87 for restoration project (with 8140M/XJ571). To Dunsfold 12.90 for continued restoration but for sale 2.92. Still in open store at Dunsfold 6.95 as 'VL/-' but scrapped 3.96. Cockpit section to Enstone, Oxon.
8172M	Sea Vixen FAW.2	XJ609	To Cranwell Engineering Flight 3.8.71 by air (ex 'VL/702' 890 Sqdn Yeovilton). To RAF Abingdon by 11.80 for BDR training and dumped by 9.81. Scrapped 23.6.85. Incorrectly marked as "8171M"
8173M	Sea Vixen FAW.2	XN685	To Cranwell Engineering Flight 3.8.71 by air (ex 'VL/703' 890 Sqdn Yeovilton). To 2 SoTT Cosford 11.80, marked 'VL/-', with 2 SoTT code 'P' added later. To BAe Hawarden on 10.8.87 for use there as a training aid by the apprentices. To Midland Air Museum, Baginton 14.9.92 and current.
8179M	Buccaneer S.1	XN928	To 4 SoTT St Athan by 9.71 (ex Belfast), coded 'LM/631' (ex 736 Sqdn Lossiemouth but with 12 Sqdn badge). To Honington via Ipswich docks 20.1.77. To South Wales APS, Rhoose 8.77. Repainted in desert colour scheme by 4.95. To Bruntingthorpe, Leics 24.2.96 and reduced to the nose section only. Current.
8180M	Buccaneer S.1	XN930	To 4 SoTT St Athan by 9.72 (ex NASU Lossiemouth), coded 'LM/632' (ex 736 Sqdn Lossiemouth). To RAF Honington via Ipswich docks 20.1.77. Derelict at Honington by 11.85 and in use for BDR training until 1991. To Hanningfield Metals, Stock, Essex and cockpit noted there 12.91 but had gone by 2.93.
8181M	Buccaneer S.1	XN972	To 4 SoTT St Athan by 9.72 (ex NASU Lossiemouth). To P&EE Foulness 4.80 and last noted 3.84.
8182M	Buccaneer S.1	XN953	Left Inverness by sea 15.9.71 (ex NASU Lossiemouth) for 4 SoTT St Athan, coded 'LM/637' (ex 736 Sqdn Lossiemouth). Current 7.75. Became A2655.

'M' No.	AIRCRAFT TYPE	SERIAL	DETAILS
8183M	Buccaneer S.1	XN962	To 71 MU Bicester 9.71 (ex NASU Lossiemouth), coded 'LM/635' (ex 736 Sqdn Lossiemouth). Cockpit section only by 8.74 retained with 71 MU/RAFEF for displays. To Abingdon with RAFEF by 4.76. Marked "XN972" (see 8181M) by 2.89 and current 6.92. To EP&TU St Athan by 6.93 and current 1.94. To Cosford Museum by 7.95 and current.
8222M	Sea Vixen FAW.2	XJ604	To 1 SoTT Halton 6.72, via Abingdon (ex 'VL/755' ADS Yeovilton). To Cranfield Institute of Technology 23.10.86 for tyre assessment trials, but found to be unsuitable. Allocated to the Otterburn ranges 4.11.87 and moved by road 15.4.88. Still present early 1996.
8223M	Sea Vixen FAW.2	XN658	To 1 SoTT Halton 11.71, via Abingdon (ex 'VL/750' ADS Yeovilton). To RAE Farnborough by 10.76 and stored for the D.3 drone programme (current 9.82). Stripped for spares 12.83. North side scrap compound by 9.84.
8224M	Sea Vixen FAW.2	XN699	To 1 SoTT Halton 4.72, via Abingdon (ex 'VL/752' ADS Yeovilton). To North Luffenham 31.10.86 and derelict there 3.90. Scrapped by 10.92.
8225M	Sea Vixen FAW.2	XN705	To 1 SoTT Halton 6.72, via Abingdon (ex 'VL/751' ADS Yeovilton). Gone by 6.77, presumably scrapped.
8226M	Sea Vixen FAW.2	XP921	To 1 SoTT Halton 2.72, via Abingdon (ex 'VL/753' ADS Yeovilton). To RAF Hereford for gate guard duties 20.11.86. To North Luffenham by 4.88. Reportedly preserved there by 2.89 (?) but scrapped by 10.92.
8356M	Whirlwind HAS.7	XL835	At NASU Culdrose 1974. 8356M allocated but not taken up. Fuselage to Predannack by 10.74, coded ''-/509' (ex 771 Sqdn Culdrose). Remains only by 8.76 and gone by 1978.
8382M	Sea Fury FB.11	VR930	SOC 5.11.62 (ex AHU Lossiemouth). Stored Colerne. To Yeovilton (date?) as spares for RNHF. To Wroughton 20.5.76. Delivered by road to storage at Lee-on-Solent 1.5.86. To Boscombe Down by 1989. Arrived Yeovilton by road 1.2.90 as spares source for RNHF. To BAe Brough 27-28.6.94 (for restoration with T.20S VZ345) and at Dunsfold by 9.95.
8387M	Tiger Moth T.2	T6296	To RAF Museum store Henlow 15.3.72 (ex RNAY Fleetlands). To the RAF Museum, Hendon 9.5.72 and current.
8397M	Sea Vixen FAW.2	XS583	Not taken up. Believed scrapped at Sydenham.
8403M	Buccaneer S.1	XK531	To RAF Honington 2.10.69 (ex NASU Lossiemouth). Gate guard by 5.73, and by 8.74 coded 'LM/-' (700S Sqdn marks). Removed from gate 16.2.83 (replaced by XK526/8648M) and placed on field. To Boscombe Down circa 4.84. Airlifted by Chinook HC.1 to NBC Defence School, Winterbourne Gunner 5.12.84. Current to at least 1991 but presumed scrapped.
8430M	Sioux HT.2	XV312	See A2631.
8432M	Whirlwind HAS.7	XK937	To RAF Bicester 4.4.75 (ex RNAY Wroughton) as a recruiting exhibit. Reported dumped at Bicester by 10.75 and 8432M not taken up.
8457M	Wessex HAS.1	XS871	To RAF Odiham 1976, coded 'H/265' (ex HMS Hermes SAR Flt). Repainted in RAF camouflage and spuriously coded "AI". Last noted 1989. Fate ?
8550M	Phantom FG.1	XT595	To RAF Coningsby for GI by 3.77 (ex HSA Brough). Officially transferred to St Athan 3.4.81. Broken up 9.81 and dumped at St Athan. Cockpit section to RAFEF Abingdon and current 1986 (fate ?). Hulk retained at St Athan for BDR and re-allocated 8851M.

'M' No.	AIRCRAFT TYPE	SERIAL	DETAILS
8564M	Whirlwind HAR.9	XN387	To RAF Odiham for BDR training 19.10.77 (ex RNAY Wroughton). Derelict by 5.87. To Spadeadam ranges 1988 and current 6.93.
8601M	Gannet AEW.3	XL450	To 431 MU RAF Bruggen 5.12.78 (ex 849 Sqdn Lossiemouth). To Air Classik, Monchengladbach by 1.85 and current 5.86.
8610M	Gannet AEW.3	XL502	To RAF Leuchars 27.11.78 (ex AHU Lossiemouth) for BDR training, coded 'LM/-' (ex 849 Sqdn Lossiemouth). Restored to flying condition and flown to Carlisle Airport 19.5.87 as G-BMYP. CoA expired 29.9.89 and stored. Flown to Sandtoft, Lincs 25.2.95. Current.
8611M	Sea Prince T.1	WF128	To RAF Honington by road 5.2.79 (ex 5 MU Kemble). Repainted olive drab overall. To Flixton 25.9.81 for Norfolk & Suffolk Aviation Museum and current.
8627M	Jet Provost T.4	XP558	[Formerly A2628] To 4 SoTT St Athan 19.3.79 (ex SAH Culdrose), coded '20' on nose-wheel door (ex CAW, "Macaws" aerobatic team colour scheme). Current 4.92, but dumped by 7.92. Current 12.93.
8634M	Sea Prince T.1	WP314	Flown to 1 SoTT Halton 6.79 (ex 5 MU Kemble), coded 'CU/573' (ex 750 Sqdn Culdrose). To Syerston by 1.82 with RAF Police Training School. 8634M not applied. Offered for sale in 1.89, but in poor condition. Transported to Aviation Marine Specialist Spares, Hedon Road, Hull 5.3.89 and current there 4.89 dismantled. Moved to a new yard at Preston, Humbs 3/4.2.92 and to Carlisle Airport 2.94. Current.
8636M	Gnat T.1	XR540	To SAH Culdrose 11.12.81 (ex Cranwell and "Red Arrows"). Became A2708.
8637M	Gnat T.1	XR991	To SAH Culdrose 28.1.82 (ex Cranwell and "Red Arrows"). Became A2709.
8648M	Buccaneer S.2	XK526	To RAF Honington 9.3.80 for BDR training (ex RAE Bedford). To gate guard at Honington 16.2.83 (resprayed in RAF camouflage) and current.
8653M	Wessex HAS.1	XS120	To RAF Abingdon by 7.80 for BDR training (ex RNAY Wroughton), coded 'CU/520' (ex 771 Sqdn Culdrose). Noted in BDR compound 9.81 to 9.84 but not found 6.85. [Note: this aircraft did not return to Wroughton by 1.87 for the dump; it is possible that it passed through en route to one of the ranges]
8654M	Whirlwind HAR.9	XL898	To RAF Abingdon by road 20.5.80 (ex RNAY Wroughton), coded 'ED/30' (ex 829 Sqdn Endurance Flt). By road to Boscombe Down on 28.10.81 for rescue training and parked out on airfield at Boscombe Down 21.9.85. Still present 6.90. Sold as scrap 12.90. To a private collector at New Byth, Grampian in 1991 but scrapped late 1992.
8658M	Buccaneer S.2C	XV358	To 431 MU Bruggen for BDR training by 5.81 (ex BAe Bitteswell). Cockpit retained to at least 1.90. Fuselage noted at RAF Wildenrath 4.85.
8659M	Buccaneer S.2B	XV340	To instructional at RAF Honington and fuselage dumped 1.81 (ex 208 Sqdn Honington). To P&EE Foulness 22.9.83. To P&EE Pendine Ranges, Dyfed 21.2.84 and current 3.94.
8705M	Buccaneer S.2B	XT281	To RAF Lossiemouth 10.80 by road/sea (unloaded from Landing Craft *Ardennes* at Inverness on 17.1.80) for weapons loading training (ex 12 Sqdn Honington). Coded "ET" (spurious) by 6.86, last noted 10.91. To G F Williamson's scrapyard, Elgin by early 1992 and current 3.96.

'M' No.	AIRCRAFT TYPE	SERIAL	DETAILS
8716M	Buccaneer S.2B	XV155	Fuselage to BAe Brough as static test airframe in 1981 (ex St Athan) and current 6.86 with apprentices. Hulk to Lovaux, Macclesfield by 2.89. Due to leave 1992 for scrapping.
8719M	Wessex HAS.3	XT257	To 1 SoTT Halton 1981 (ex A&AEE Boscombe Down). Transferred to 1 SoTT Cosford (renumbered from 2 SoTT on closure of Halton) late-1994 and had arrived by 3.95. Current.
8742M	Canberra TT.18	WH856	Flown to RAF Abingdon 2.3.82 for BDR training, coded '849' (ex FRADU Yeovilton and still coded '56' from RAF/7 Sqdn service). Current 3.86 but sectioned by 12.86. To Staravia, Ascot by 4.87.
8747M	Canberra TT.18	WJ629	Flown to RAF Chivenor 24.3.82 for BDR training, coded '845' (ex FRADU Yeovilton and still coded '29' from RAF/7 Sqdn service). Derelict 4.92 and removed by road 9.3.94, destination unknown.
8751M	Wessex HAS.3	XT255	At 14 MU Carlisle for FCR training by 6.83 (ex ETPS Boscombe Down). Current.
8754M	Gannet T.5	XG882	Rescued from the dump at RAF Lossiemouth and refurbished with parts of XA463/XG889. Displayed at the main gate as 'LM/771' (849 Sqdn HQ Flt marks) by 6.82. Tendered for sale 7.89 but still on the gate early-1991. To former airfield site at Errol, Tayside on 30.5.91 and current.
8773M	Buccaneer S.2A	XV156	At RAF St Athan for FCR training by 8.83 (ex-store) to at least 2.89. Fuselage on dump by 9.89 and scrapped 10.91.
8774M	Buccaneer S.2A	XV338	Cockpit to GI at RAF Honington by 8.83 (ex St Athan). [Rest to P&EE Pendine Ranges, Dyfed]. Reported to RAFEF Abingdon by 1988 but still listed as current for FCR at Honington early 1992. Fate unknown.
8775M	Buccaneer S.2A	XV354	To CTE Manston by 8.83 (ex St Athan). Last noted 1.84.
8776M	Buccaneer S.2A	XV152	To CSDE Swanton Morley for GI training by 8.83 (ex St Athan). Scrapped by 6.88.
8796M	Whirlwind HAS.7	XK943	[Formerly A2653] To BDR training at RAF Abingdon by 9.83, still code '57'. Dumped by 9.1.87 and current 2.92 for FCR training, but removed from dump 3.92.
8802M	Sea Vixen FAW.2	XJ608	To RAF North Luffenham by road 17.3.84 (ex Flight Refuelling Ltd, Hurn). Current 4.92 but scrapped by 10.92.
8803M	Sea Vixen FAW.2	XJ572	To FF&SS Catterick by road 26-27.3.84 (ex RAE Farnborough), marked *"Thunderbird 1"*. Last noted in a burnt state 3.88.
8804M	Sea Vixen FAW.2(TT)	XJ524	To FF&SS Catterick by road 13-14.3.84 (ex Flight Refuelling Ltd, Hurn). Expired by 11.84.
8805M	Wessex HU.5	XT772	To SARTU at RAF Valley by road 24.2.84 for BDR training (ex RNAY Wroughton), uncoded (ex 781 Sqdn Lee-on-Solent). Mounted in hangar for winch training by 11.85. Rear fuselage at RAF Finningley by 4.87, possibly for repair/refurbishment. Current at Valley 8.94.
8806M	Wessex HAS.3	XP140	To RAF Chilmark by road 4.4.84 for FCR training (ex RNAY Wroughton), coded 'PO/654' (ex 737 Sqdn Portland). Current 2.93 (for sale) and disposed of by 3.94.
8814M	Wessex HAS.3	XM927	To RAF Shawbury by road 24-25.4.84 (ex RNAY Wroughton) for FCR training, coded 'PO/660' (ex 737 Sqdn Portland). On dump by 11.5.84 for FCR and current.
8817M	Sea Vixen D.3	XN652	Allocated to FF&SS Catterick by 6.84 but still derelict at Hurn 3.85 (ex Flight Refuelling Ltd). To FF&SS Catterick by 4.86. Current 3.88 but gone by 4.92, presumably expired.

'M' No.	AIRCRAFT TYPE	SERIAL	DETAILS
8818M	Buccaneer S.2D	XK527	Allocated to RAF Lossiemouth for BDR training by 6.84 (ex BAe Scampton) but 8818M not taken up. To BAe Brough and rear fuselage in use for static tests 10.84. To a scrapyard in Blackburn 8.8.85. Cockpit section left Brough 12.87 for Lutterworth, Leics. To New Milton, Hants in 1990 for restoration and current.
8819M	Wessex HU.5	XS479	To JATE Brize Norton by road 20.6.84 (ex RNAY Wroughton), coded '-/XF' (ex 847 Sqdn Yeovilton). Current 3.95.
8826M	Wasp HAS.1	XV638	To Air Movements School, Brize Norton late-1984 (ex Portland as *"A430"* - see *"Unidentified Class II Airframes"*), coded '-/430' (ex 829 Sqdn HMS Achilles Flt). Current 1.88. To RAF High Wycombe by 10.90 and dumped. Scrapped 1991.
8828M	Sea Vixen FAW(TT).2	XS587	Allocated to 2 SoTT Cosford by 10.84 (ex Flight Refuelling Ltd) but not taken up. Awaiting collection at Hurn by Manchester Air & Space Museum 3.85 but sold to Brencham Historic Aircraft Collection, Hurn and registered G-VIXN 11.85. In outside storage at Hurn as G-VIXN 6.88. To Peter Vallance Collection, Charlwood, Surrey in 1990 and current.
8845M	Wasp HAS.1	XS572	To 16 MU Stafford by road 15.10.84 (ex RNAY Wroughton), coded '-/414' (ex 829 Sqdn HMS Hecate Flt). Dumped by 4.90 and current 9.92.
8846M	Hunter GA.11	XE673	To RAF Wattisham for BDR training 20.2.85 (ex Shawbury), coded 'VL/680' (ex 764 Sqdn Lossiemouth) and marked *"XE689"* (fitted with rear fuselage of XE689) and *"No 13(BD)Sqn"*. To RAF Bawdsey for BDR training by 10.85. Still at Bawdsey 12.89, marked 'VL/-'. To Hanningfield Metals, Stock, Essex by 11.91. Noted 6.93 but scrapped by 2.94.
8851M	Phantom FG.1	XT595	[Formerly 8550M] Noseless hulk allocated to BDR St Athan by 6.85 (formerly on the dump). To RAF Wattisham 12.85 for BDR training and last noted 11.91.
8852M	Buccaneer S.2C	XV337	To RAF Abingdon for BDR training by 6.85 (ex-A&AEE Boscombe Down) until at least 2.92. To BDR training at St Athan 8.92 and current 4.94.
8853M	Buccaneer S.2A	XT277	To 2 SoTT Cosford by 7.86 (ex Shawbury), coded 'F' (ex 237 OCU Honington). Coded 'M' with 2 SoTT by 7.86. In open store 4-6.93 and scrapped, the nose going to Bruntingthorpe, Leics by 10.93 and on to Welshpool, Powys 11.93. Current.
8854M	Buccaneer S.2A	XV154	Allocated for BDR at RAF Wattisham by 6.85 (ex St Athan), but not wfu until 7.2.86. Instead to Lossiemouth for BDR training by 6.86, uncoded (ex 12 Sqdn), and current to at least 10.90. Broken up 1992 and to G F Williamson's scrapyard, Elgin by 10.92. Current 1.96.
8855M	Buccaneer S.2A	XT284	To RAF Abingdon for BDR training by 11.85 (ex St Athan), coded 'H' (ex 237 OCU Honington). Current 2.92 but to St Athan 8.92 for BDR training. Current 11.93 but disposed of by 3.94.
8856M	Buccaneer S.2A	XT274	To RAF Abingdon for BDR training 5.1.86 (ex St Athan), coded 'E' (ex 237 OCU Honington) and last noted 9.89. To P&EE Pendine Ranges, Dyfed 23.1.90 and current 3.94.
8867M	Buccaneer S.1	XK532	[Formerly A2581] To RAF Lossiemouth in 1982 (ex Manadon), coded 'LM/632' (ex 736 Sqdn Lossiemouth), for preservation and placed on the gate 15.8.84, still coded 'LM/632'. Tendered for sale 3.92 and removed from the gate 30.6.92. To Inverness/Dalcross 23.9.92 for preservation and stored. Current.

'M' No.	AIRCRAFT TYPE	SERIAL	DETAILS
8877M	Wessex HAS.1	XP159	To RAF Odiham for BDR training by 3.86 (ex 2407 Sqdn ATC, Fleet), coded 'R/047' (ex HMS Ark Royal SAR Flight). To Brands Hatch by 4.88 and current 3.89, but not found 1993 - fate ?
8878M	Gnat T.1	XR993	Not taken up. See A2677.
8893M	Hunter T.8C	WT745	Forward fuselage to 4 SoTT St Athan by late-1986 (ex Shawbury), coded '-/745' (ex FRADU Yeovilton), for paint training. Reported sold to Ed Stead in the USA in late 1987. To ASF Coltishall 1987 (fitted with a rear fuselage from XL565). To Park Aviation Supply, Faygate 13.8.90 but moved on to Jet Heritage, Hurn 26.10.90. Nose to Ed Stead in the USA, the rest was scrapped in 1993. [The rear fuselage of WT745 was reported with Staravia, Ascot 3.82].
8913M	Phantom FG.1	XT857	To instructional with ASF Leuchars by 9.85 (damaged 7.85), coded 'C' (ex 111 Sqdn Leuchars). WFU in shelter area by 9.87 and marked *"MP"* by 9.88. Last noted 9.91 with ASF. Reported scrapped mid-1995.
8919M	Wessex HU.5	XT486	To JATE Brize Norton by road 3.2.87 (ex RNAY Wroughton), coded '-/XR' (ex 847 Sqdn Yeovilton). On display outside JATE HQ by 10.90, uncoded. Current 3.95.
8920M	Wessex HU.5	XT469	To 16 MU RAF Stafford by road 10.12.86 (ex RNAY Wroughton), coded '-/XN' (ex 847 Sqdn Yeovilton), for GI with Tactical Supply Wing. Current 1.94.
8921M	Wessex HU.5	XT466	To 2 SoTT Cosford by road 3.2.87 (ex RNAY Wroughton), coded '-/XV' (ex 847 Sqdn Yeovilton). Current 8.90 but reportedly disposed of by 2.92. To Duke of Wellington's Regt at Weeton Barracks, Preston for de-emplaning exercises. Became A2617 [4] (q.v.) by 7.97 at AESS.
8922M	Wessex HU.5	XT467	To RAF Gutersloh for BDR training 1.87 (ex RNAY Wroughton by road 8.1.87). Marked *"XR504/BF"* (18 Sqdn) in RAF camouflage by 6.87. Allocated to 431 MU RAF Bruggen for BDR training by 7.90 and current 6.93. To Laarbruch for BDR use by 18 Sqdn as *"BF"* by 7.93. To Odiham dump by 4.96.
8941M	Wessex HU.5	XT456	To RAF Aldergrove for BDR training (ex RNAY Wroughton by road 9.11.87, arrived 11.11.87), coded '-/XZ' (ex 847 Sqdn Yeovilton). Current.
8998M	Phantom FG.1	XT864	Allocated by 8.89 for gate guard duties at RAF Leuchars and there by 9.89, coded 'BJ' (ex 111 Sqdn Leuchars). Current.
8999M	Phantom FG.1	XT859	To BDR training at RAF Leuchars by 8.89, coded 'BK' (ex 111 Sqdn Leuchars) and current 11.91. To Adams scrapyard in Glasgow by 4.92 and gone by 6.92.
9037M	Whirlwind HAS.7	XN302	[Formerly A2654] To RAF Finningley for FCR by 5.90 (ex HMS Royal Arthur, Corsham). Current on the dump 1.94, remains noted 9.94.
9050M	Whirlwind HAR.3	XG577	[Formerly A2571] To RAF Leconfield for FCR duties 10.90 (ex Duxford), coded 'PO/752'. Current.
9052M	Canberra TT.18	WJ717	To St Athan in 1990 for FCR training (ex St Athan store), coded '841' (ex FRADU Yeovilton). Stored at St Athan 9.92 but with CTTS by 9.93. Current 11.95.
9053M	Wessex HU.5	XT755	To 1 SoTT Halton by road 22.1.91 for ET (ex RNAY Wroughton), coded '(Y)V' (ex 845 Sqdn Yeovilton). Current 7.92. To Phoenix Aviation, Bruntingthorpe, Leics by 10.93. Scrapped 1.96.
9054M	Wessex HU.5	XT766	To 1 SoTT Halton by road 23.1.91 for ET (ex RNAY Wroughton), coded 'CU/822' (ex 771 Sqdn Culdrose). Left Halton by road 25.11.92, reportedly for Bruntingthorpe, Leics, but officially listed as BDR at St Athan late 1993. To AESS at HMS Sultan, Gosport by 10.4.97, as A2620 [3].

'M' No.	AIRCRAFT TYPE	SERIAL	DETAILS
9055M	Wessex HU.5	XT770	To 1 SoTT Halton by road 23.1.91 for ET (ex RNAY Wroughton), coded '(Y)P' (ex 845 Sqdn Yeovilton). Current 4.93 but gone by 3.94. Reported as going to Bruntingthorpe, Leics but on to Shawell, Leics by 10.93 for use in a civilian assault course. Current 9.94.
9056M	Wessex HU.5	XS488	To 1 SoTT Halton by road 22.1.91 for ET (ex RNAY Wroughton), coded '-/XK' (ex 847 Sqdn Yeovilton). Current 7.92 but gone by 3.94. To AAC Air Mobile Training Centre, Wattisham by 4.96.
9063M	Phantom FG.1	XV569	To RAF Bruggen for FCR by 2.91 (ex WLT at Wildenrath), coded 'BQ' (ex 111 Sqdn Leuchars) and current 4.95 on the dump.
9064M	Phantom FG.1	XT867	To BDR training at RAF Leuchars by 2.91 (ex Leuchars store), coded 'BH' (ex 111 Sqdn Leuchars). Current.
9065M	Phantom FG.1	XV577	To BDR training at RAF Leuchars by 2.91 (ex Leuchars store), coded 'AM' (ex 43 Sqdn Leuchars). Current.
9066M	Phantom FG.1	XV582	To Operational Turn Round training at RAF Leuchars by 2.91, coded 'M' (black colour scheme, ex 111 Sqdn Leuchars), but preserved on base 9.93. Current.
9067M	Phantom FG.1	XV586	To 43 Sqdn RAF Leuchars for BDR training by 2.91 (ex Leuchars store), coded 'AJ' (ex 43 Sqdn Leuchars), but preserved in 43 Sqdn HAS area 9.93. Current.
9068M	Phantom FG.1	XT874	To BDR training at RAF Wattisham by 2.91 (ex Wattisham store), coded 'BE' (ex 111 Sqdn Leuchars). Current 10.92. Left by road 11.5.93 to Phoenix Aviation, Bruntingthorpe, Leics but disposed of by 2.94 to Hanningfield Metals, Stock, Essex. Gone by 5.95.
9069M	Phantom FG.1	XV570	To BDR training at RAF Wattisham by 2.91 (ex Wattisham store), coded 'BN' (ex 111 Sqdn Leuchars). Dumped 4.92 and scrapped 9.92 by Mayer & Perry, Snailwell, Cambs.
9070M	Phantom FG.1	XV581	To Operational Turn Round training at RAF Wattisham by 2.91 (ex Wattisham store), coded 'AE' (ex 43 Sqdn Leuchars). Current 10.91. To RAF Buchan, Grampian 24.4.92 for gate guard duties and current.
9088M	Phantom FG.1	XV587	Dumped at RAF Wattisham for FCR training by 3.91 (ex store), coded 'BR' (ex 111 Sqdn Leuchars). Current 10.92 but to Hanningfield Metals, Stock, Essex by 4.93 as scrap.
9096M	Hunter T.8C	WV322	To SIF Cranwell by 7.91 (ex 237 OCU Lossiemouth) and coded 'Y'. Current.
9102M	Wessex HU.5	XS241	To RAF Benson by road 25.1.91 for spares use (ex RNAY Wroughton and RAE Farnborough; r/w/b scheme). Dumped by 7.92 and scrapped by 12.92, although still listed for FCR duties 3.94.
9108M	Wessex HU.5	XT475	Front fuselage to CTE Manston by road 16.7.91 (ex RNAY Wroughton), coded '-/624' (ex 772 Sqdn Portland). Current 9.95 lying on its side.
9115M	Buccaneer S.2B	XV863	Wfu 4.91 at RAF Lossiemouth (ex 'S'/Gulf Det) for display but replaced by XW533. Role changed and re-allocated 9139M.
9117M	Buccaneer S.2B	XV161	Wfu 4.91. To BDR training at RAF Lossiemouth by 4.92 and current 11.92. To Lossiemouth ASF by 11.93 (grey/green camouflage, no marks), marked for scrapping (the dreaded blue cross!) and current as such 3.94. Nose section to East Fortune for temporary store soon after and then to a yard in Birtley, Tyne & Wear by 8.95. Current.
9123M	Wessex HU.5	XT773	Left RNAY Wroughton by road 2.10.91 (uncoded in SAR scheme) for BDR at RAF Abingdon, although reportedly did not arrive until 8.10.91. Current 2.92. To BDR training at RAF St Athan by 6.92 and current 1.94.

'M' No.	AIRCRAFT TYPE	SERIAL	DETAILS
9134M	Buccaneer S.2B	XT288	Wfu 4.91 (ex 12 Sqdn Lossiemouth) and allocated for Weapon Load Training at RAF Lossiemouth by 4.92. Current 4.94 but marked with the blue cross (for scrapping). Acquired by the Museum of Flight, East Fortune by 7.94 and current in store.
9139M	Buccaneer S.2B	XV863	[Formerly 9115M] For BDR at RAF Abingdon but cancelled. Re-allocated 9145M.
9144M	Buccaneer S.2B	XV353	For BDR training at RAF St Athan (ex 12 Sqdn Lossiemouth) but allocation cancelled and a/c still in use 2.93.
9145M	Buccaneer S.2B	XV863	[Formerly 9115M/9139M] Re-allocated for display at RAF Lossiemouth (replacing XW533 once again). Placed on the gate by 2.92, in *"desert"* scheme coded 'S' (retaining the *"Sea Witch/Debbie"* nose art applied during the Gulf conflict). Current.
9182M	Hunter T.8C	XF967	For GI at SIF Cranwell but cancelled. Re-allocated 9186M.
9186M	Hunter T.8C	XF967	[Formerly 9182M] To SIF Cranwell by 4.93, coded 'T' (ex 237 OCU Lossiemouth, black colour scheme) and current.
9226M	Buccaneer S.2B	XV865	To RAF Coningsby 26.1.94 for FCR training (ex 208 Sqdn Lossiemouth). Current, but allocated for transfer to Culdrose where it will be repainted and put on display at the public viewing enclosure.
9232M	Buccaneer S.2B	XV332	To RAF Marham by air 5.4.94 for FCR training (ex 208 Sqdn Lossiemouth; grey scheme). Current.
9234M	Buccaneer S.2B	XV864	To CTE Manston by air 5.4.94 for FCR training (ex 208 Sqdn Lossiemouth; grey/green scheme). Current.
9237M	Hunter T.8B	XF995	To SIF Cranwell by air 11.4.94, coded 'W' (ex 208 Sqdn Lossiemouth; grey/green scheme). Recoded 'K' by 6.94 and current.

Buccaneer S.1 XN930', ex 'LM/632' of 736 Sqdn, marked 8180M in 1979 at Honington. (MAP)

Allocated to Class I instructional duties at Lee-on-Solent in 1958, Skyraider AEW.1 WT965 is seen here the previous year coded 'J/417' with 849 Sqdn 'A' Flt. (MAP)

CLASS I and GRA AIRFRAMES

AIRCRAFT TYPE	SERIAL	DETAILS

Gannet T.2

XA510 — To Class II at Arbroath 26.9.61 (ex-Abbotsinch ADW) coded 'GN/544' (ex 719 Sqdn). Upgraded to Class I 29.10.62. Downgraded to Class II 8.7.65, but no 'A' serial allotted. To NARIU, Lee-on-Solent 14.7.66 and from there to Brawdy end 7.67, to be declared ADW and WOC to be reduced to spares and produce.

XA518 — To Class I at Arbroath 7.11.62 (ex-Abbotsinch ADW). To Westland Aircraft 19.5.67 for modernisation and conversion to T.5 standard. Re-allocated 15.1.68 to be reduced to spares and produce 1.5.68. To Fleetlands 7.2.68 and for sale as scrap at Fleetlands 25.4.69.

Gannet ECM.6

XA460 — To Class I at Lee-on-Solent 2.6.66 (ex 831 Sqdn Watton). To NASU Brawdy 5.4.67 and reverted to operational status.

XG797 — To Class I at Arbroath 2.6.66 (ex 831 Sqdn Watton). Returned to operational service and to NASU Brawdy 15.5.57. To 849 Sqdn HQ TAE 10.7.67 at Brawdy, to NASU Brawdy STS 2.2.68. Reverted to Class I at Arbroath 7.8.68. To MARTSU Lee-on-Solent 23.3.71 to ADW. To IWM Duxford 7.12.73, coded 'BY/766'. (Was offered to Canada). Current.

Hunter F.4

WV404 — Allocated to Class I at Arbroath 10.62 (ex 19 MU St Athan) but cancelled and became 7768M instead, at 4 SoTT. Sold to HSA and became G-9-384 (to Switzerland as F.58A J-4137).

XE707 — To Class I at Arbroath 1.61 (ex 5 MU Kemble). To Hawker Aircraft 4.6.62 for conversion to GA.11 standard. Offered to Class I as an alternative to WV404 for Arbroath (ex 19 MU St Athan) but similarly cancelled 10.62 and became 7772M. (Sold to HSA and became G-9-387 and to Switzerland as F.58A J-4136).

Seafire F.47

PS954 — To Class I at Yeovilton 24.6.51 (ex Yeovilton).

Sea Fury F.10

TF904 — To Class I at Yeovilton 24.6.51. Returned to service [with 767 Sqdn Henstridge by 6.52; used for DLCO training].

TF912 — To Class I at Yeovilton 14.6.51, coded 'VL/-' (ex 767 Sqdn Yeovilton), to at least 7.51.

AIRCRAFT TYPE	SERIAL	DETAILS
Sea Fury F.10 (contd)	TF918	To Class I at Yeovilton 30.8.51 (ex 767 Sqdn Yeovilton, crashed 29.8.51).
	TF943	To Class I at Yeovilton 14.6.51 (ex Yeovilton).
Sea Fury FB.11	TF973	To Class I at Yeovilton 14.6.51, coded 'VL/119' (ex 799 Sqdn Yeovilton), to at least 7.51.
	VR927	To Class I at Yeovilton 14.6.51 (ex Yeovilton). At Bramcote by 8.58.
Sea Hawk FB.3	WF289	To Class I at SAH Culdrose 18.3.60 (ex Abbotsinch AHU). Allocated 'SAH-2' and coded '2' on nose by 15.7.60. Taxyable. Returned to Abbotsinch AHU for LTS2(U) 18.7.62 and sold as scrap 19.12.62. SOC 13.2.63. Remains on Staravia dump at Ascot, Berks 9.65.
	WM908	To Class I at SAH Culdrose 18.2.60 (ex Abbotsinch AHU). Allocated 'SAH-5' and coded '5' by 15.7.60. Taxyable. Returned to Abbotsinch LTS2(U) 15.2.62. On Abbotsinch dump 4.62, coded '5'. Sold as scrap 19.12.62 and remains reported on the Lasham scrap heap circa 1963.
	WM988	To Class I at SAH Culdrose 18.2.60 (ex Abbotsinch AHU 17.2.60). Allocated 'SAH-6' and coded '6' by 15.7.60 with a red Ace of Spades motif below the cockpit. Taxyable. Returned to Abbotsinch LTS2(U) 8.12.61 via Lee-on-Solent. At Lee-on-Solent by 1.62 (sic). On AHU Abbotsinch dump 4.62-7.62, coded '6' with red Ace of Spades badge.
	WN114	To Class I at SAH Culdrose 31.3.60 (ex Abbotsinch AHU 30.3.60). Allocated 'SAH-7' and coded '7' by 15.7.60, with a red Ace of Spades motif below the cockpit. Taxyable. Returned to Abbotsinch LTS2(U) 24.3.62. On AHU Abbotsinch dump 4.62-7.62, coded '7' (red Ace of Spades badge).
Sea Hawk FB.5	WN115	To Class I at RNEC Manadon 7.59. To Lee-on-Solent 24.9.59. To Abbotsinch LTS2(U) 24.3.62. On Abbotsinch AHU dump 4.62. Sold to Staravia, Ascot, Berks 4.9.63. Fuselage at Lasham by 8.70.
	WN116	To Class I at RNEC Manadon 4.2.59 (ex Abbotsinch), coded 'R/134' (ex 820 Sqdn). To Abbotsinch LTS2(U) 22.1.62. Sold to Staravia, Ascot, Berks 4.9.63. Fuselage at Lasham by 8.70.
Sea Hawk FGA.6	WF284	To Class I at Fleetlands 15.3.63 (ex Abbotsinch). Scrapped 1964. To Nelson Stanley, scrap metal merchants, Poole, Dorset 22.11.65.
Sea King AEW.2A	XV704	To "Class IR" [i.e. to Initial Reserve"] at AES Lee-on-Solent 13.1.88 on loan, uncoded (ex 849 Sqdn FIR). Engines also "Class IR". To AMG Culdrose by road 27.7.89 and returned to service.
Sea Mosquito TR.33	LR387	At Worthy Down 16.5.47. To Class I 23.4.48 (ex CS(A) at De Havillands). Possibly later Class II. At Yeovilton 7.50, with prototype markings, to at least 9.51.
Sea Vampire F.20	VV137	To Class I at Yeovilton 14.6.51 (ex Yeovilton). May have returned to service as reported with 702 Sqdn Culdrose in 1.52.
Sea Vixen FAW.1	XN704	To Class I with 890 Sqdn Yeovilton 23.10.67 (ex NASU Brawdy), becoming 'VL/750'. To Class II at Yeovilton 28.7.69 (or 4.9.69), but possibly not taken up as no 'A' number allotted. To Yeovilton LTS2(U) 1969, then to Class III scrap.
Sea Vixen FAW.2	XN694	To Class I at Belfast 15.1.69 - date unconfirmed (ex Belfast LTS).
Skyraider AEW.1	WT965	To Class I at Lee-on-Solent 12.6.58 (ex AHU Culdrose). SOC 23.10.61 and reduced to spares.
Wasp HAS.1	XS539	To Class I (later GRA) at Yeovilton 10.4.72. No engine. Lent to the Royal Tournament 30.7.73 to 23.8.73 alias "XS566" for display purposes, then to MARTSU Lee-on-Solent on temporary charge. To RNAY Wroughton 3.10.73 (uncoded) and returned to service. [Later to Class GRB allocated A2718 (2)].

AIRCRAFT TYPE	SERIAL	DETAILS
Wasp HAS.1 (contd)	XT429	To Class I (later GRA) at AES Lee-on-Solent 7.9.70. To RNAY Wroughton 23.6.75 (uncoded). Returned to service. To Lee-on-Solent and held for Air Weapons Group. [Later to Class GRB allocated A2720 (2)].
	XT441	To Class I at Lee-on-Solent by 7.69 (ex Fleetlands). To Fleetlands 12.70 and returned to service. [Later to Class GRB allocated A2703].
	XT778	To Class I (later GRA) at Yeovilton 12.2.73 (by road ex RNAY Wroughton LTS, uncoded). Returned to RNAY Wroughton 5.7.73 and returned to service. [Later to Class GRB allocated A2722 (2)].
	XT779	To Class I at Arbroath 16.1.69 (ex Fleetlands). To Fleetlands 14.5.70 and returned to service.
	XT789	To Class I at Arbroath 27.3.68 (ex Fleetlands). Withdrawn 16.1.69 and returned to service.
	XT795	To Class I (later GRA) at 829 Sqdn Portland 3.73. Returned to operational use with 829 Sqdn 8.75 (being coded '-/617').
	XV626	To Class GRA at AES Lee-on-Solent 20.10.75 for vibration trials at Southampton University. To NATIU Lee-on-Solent 20.4.78 and flying again by 4.78, marked 'HMS Hero' and "-/471" for TV series "Warship". To Fleetlands by 8.78 and returned to service.
Wessex HAS.1	XM832	To Class I (later GRA) at AES Lee-on-Solent 12.10.72 (by road, ex RNAY Wroughton LTS), coded 'CU/576' (ex 706 Sqdn). Returned to RNAY Wroughton by road 14.11.75 and returned to service.
	XM843	To Class I at Arbroath 30.5.69 (ex Fleetlands), to replace XM329 which became A2609. Reported at Fleetlands between 3.68 and 12.71, coded 'CU/572' (ex 706 Sqdn Culdrose). Flown to RNAY Wroughton 10.10.72 and returned to service. [Later to Class GRB allocated A2693].
	XS871	To Class GRA at Lee-on-Solent. To 8457M.
	XS872	To Class I (later GRA) at AES Lee-on-Solent 17.10.72 (by road, ex RNAY Wroughton LTS), coded 'CU/572' (ex 706 Sqdn). Returned to RNAY Wroughton 12.11.75. [Later Class GRB allocated A2666].
Wessex HU.5	XS510	To Class I at Yeovilton 13.3.72. No engine. To Lee-on-Solent as Class GRA 19.6.73 (ex Ground Training School, Yeovilton). Returned to service 7.11.77. [Later to Class GRB allocated A2765].
	XS520	To Class I (later GRA) at Yeovilton 13.3.72 (ex Fleetlands and Cat.3 repair). Returned to service.
Whirlwind HAR.9	XN309	To Class GRA at RNEC Manadon 25.7.75, coded 'CU/590' (ex Culdrose SAR Flt). To RNAY Wroughton 10.2.76 by road for disposal. [Later Class GRB allocated A2663].
	XN359	Ditched in Antarctic 9.1.67. To Fleetlands for rebuild, then to Class I at Arbroath 30.5.69. Returned to Fleetlands 20.4.70. Held at Fleetlands until issued to HMS Endurance Ship's Flight 13.9.72 and returned to service. Retired to RNAY Wroughton 7.9.76. [Later Class GRB allocated A2712 and A2759].
Whirlwind HAR.21	WV193	To Class I at RNEC Manadon 20.8.58. Intended for Class II at Manadon but to Fleetlands as LTS2(U) 11.7.61 pending disposal. To St Athan 17.4.63 on temporary loan for the Royal Tournament. Returned to Fleetlands and prepared for sale as scrap on 7.6.63. WOC on 29.11.65 and sold to Marine Salvage Ltd, Portsmouth 30.11.65. Also reported Class I at Manadon 15.9.68 (sic).
	WV194	To Class I at Lee-on-Solent 12.12.58 (ex Donibristle). To Fleetlands LTS2(U) 11.7.61. Reduced to scrap at Fleetlands 29.8.63. SOC 30.9.63 and sold to Westland's who are believed to have converted the fuselage into a helicopter simulator. However, the conversion is also reported as being undertaken at Teversham circa 28.8.63! The final fate of the aircraft is unknown.
	WV195	To Class I at Arbroath 9.58. To Fleetlands LTS2(U) 21.7.61. Transferred to RAF Cardington 7.6.63 (to replace WV193 ?), moving on to RNAS Culdrose 20.7.63 for a fire sequence in an instructional film. Allocated for ground instructional use 26.8.63. SOC 30.9.63, presumably having been burnt.

Brewster Buffalo AS426 was handed over by the RAF in March 1942 to became A39. (MAP)

CLASS II AIRFRAMES 1942-1948

The original series of 'A' numbers was introduced in 1942 and used throughout the remainder of the war, continuing into the early post-war period. Few details have survived of this series, which included a wide variety of aircraft types ranging from the nostalgic Buffalo, Swordfish and Fulmar to the Barracuda, Firebrand and later marks of Seafire. Use of this series was discontinued in 1948 when RARA disbanded.

'A' No.	AIRCRAFT TYPE	SERIAL	DETAILS
A37	Buffalo I	AS417	SOC by RAF 27.3.42.
A38	Buffalo I	AS427	SOC by RAF 27.3.42.
A39	Buffalo I	AS426	SOC by RAF 27.3.42.
A78	Albacore	L7074	To 6 SoTT Hednesford 22.10.42 (ex Rolls-Royce, Hucknall).
A105	Hurricane		At Yeovilton.
A132	Wildcat IV	FN174	To 10 SoTT Kirkham 28.3.44 (ex Abbotsinch).
A167	Hurricane		SOC 21.2.44.
A201	Hurricane		SOC 21.2.44.
A202	Hurricane	W....	At RNEC Manadon 8.54.
A203	Hurricane		SOC 21.2.44.
A305	Firefly I		At Yeovilton 7.50.
A325	Barracuda III		At 10 SoTT Kirkham 1.46, coded 'E1L' (ex 767 Sqdn Easthaven).
A337	Barracuda II	MD612	At St Merryn 7.53.
A350	Seafire 1B	MB364	At RNEC Manadon 8.54. Burnt at Manadon 1957.
A367	Avenger I		At 10 SoTT Kirkham 1.46.
A372	Hellcat F.II		At 10 SoTT Kirkham 1.46.
A373	Hellcat F.II		At 10 SoTT Kirkham 1.46.
A388	Beaufort		To Class II on 20.11.45 at RNARY Coimbatore.

'A' No.	AIRCRAFT TYPE	SERIAL	DETAILS
A417	Barracuda		At St Athan in 1946.
A438	Seafire III	PX913	At St Athan in 1946.
A454	Seafire F.III		
A455	Barracuda II	LS955	At St Athan in 1946 (ex 710 Sqdn Crail).
A456	Seafire III		At St Athan in 1946.
A463	Barracuda		At St Athan in 1946.
A464	Barracuda		At St Athan in 1946.
A466	Barracuda		At St Athan in 1946.
A467	Barracuda		At St Athan in 1946.
A471	Barracuda		At St Athan in 1946.
A472	Barracuda		At St Athan in 1946.
A480	Firefly NF.II		
A483	Seafire		At St Athan in 1946.
A486	Seafire		At St Athan 1946. From dump at Gosport to Lee-on-Solent by road 6.49.
A494	Firebrand TF.III		
A495	Firefly I		At St Athan in 1946.
A498	Seafire		At St Athan in 1946.
A502	Seafire L.III	RX217	From dump at Gosport to Lee-on-Solent by road 4.49, coded 'S7A' (ex 748 Sqdn St Merryn).
A505	Seafire III	NN570	From dump at Gosport to Lee-on-Solent by road 4.49, coded 'K' (probably ex 748 Sqdn St Merryn).
A506	Seafire L.III	NN336	At Stretton 4.50, coded 'S7P' (ex School of Naval Air Warfare, St Merryn).
A509	Seafire LF.III	NF531	At Yeovilton 5.47.
A511	Seafire III	NN585	Coded 'G4F' (ex 761 Sqdn Henstridge). Seen at Ratcliffe around 1949.
A513	Seafire III		
A517	Seafire XVII	SX336	Became A2055.
A518	Seafire III		On Balado dump 3.52.
A530	Seafire F.XV		
A543	Firefly I		At St Athan in 1946.
A551	Barracuda		At St Athan in 1946.
A559	Firebrand TF.III		
A564	Seafire III		On Balado dump 3.52.
A575	Seafire III		At Yeovilton 7.50.
A577	Seafire III		At Yeovilton 7.50.
A633	Seafire III		At Yeovilton 7.50.
A634	Seafire prototype		On Balado dump 3.52 with 'P' prototype markings.
A646	Seafire F.17	SX300	Engine No E3056. At Yeovilton 7.51. At Bramcote 7.54 as A2054. (But see A696).
A656	Seafire F.III		At Bramcote 6.49.
A661	Seafire F.III		At Bramcote 6.49.
A680	Tiger Moth T.2	DE373	Became A2127.
A687	Tiger Moth T.2		At Bramcote 6.49.
A696	Seafire F.III	SX300	At Bramcote 6.53-7.54. At Stretton 6.55. (But see A646).
A703	Firebrand		From dump at Gosport to Lee-on-Solent by road 4.49, coded 'L'.
A707	Seafire F.III		At Bramcote 6.49.
A714	Firefly F.1	DT932	At Bramcote 6.49.
A717	Firebrand TF.4		
A718	Seafire F.17		
A719	Seafire III		
A727	Seafire F.17	SX341	
A728	Tiger Moth T.2	BB731	[Originally G-ADCG] To Class II at Bramcote 27.2.48. Became A2126.
A750	Tiger Moth T.2	NL750	SOC 12.6.48. Became A2123.
A752	Tiger Moth T.2		At Yeovilton 5.47.

CLASS II and GRB AIRFRAMES 1949 to 1988

A2000 to A2099

The new series of 'A' numbers commenced in 1948 when RARA was replaced by FORA. It is not known whether it commenced at A2000 or A2001. The range A2000 to A2099 was probably taken up entirely by renumbered airframes from the superseded A1 to A752 range, and comprised types then in service or currently becoming obsolescent. Like the wartime series, few details have survived, but the range is known to have included numerous Fireflies, Firebrands, Tiger Moths and various marks of Seafire.

'A' No.	AIRCRAFT TYPE	SERIAL	DETAILS
A2001	Swordfish II	HS618	At RNEC Manadon in 1960. Engine No E3001. Downgraded to Class III 3.7.63. To FAA Museum Yeovilton by 1974, and displayed as *"W5984"* coded '5H' to represent the aircraft of 825 Sqdn in which Lt Cdr E Esmonds, VC was killed on 12.2.42. Repainted as *"P4139"* (uncoded) by 20.8.87 and current as such.
A2007	Firefly FR.4	TW694	To instructional at RNEC Manadon 3.12.47 (ex A&AEE Boscombe Down), to at least 8.54.
A2010	Firefly F.1	MB388	At Yeovilton 7.50 to at least 1951.
A2012	Firefly F.1	Z2117	At Bramcote 4.55 (scrap).
A2014	Firefly F.1	Z2013	At Yeovilton 7.50, coded 'K2K' (ex 766 Sqdn Inskip).
A2015	Firefly FR.5		At Yeovilton 7.50.
A2023	Firefly FR.1	MB572	At Yeovilton 7.51. To Bramcote by 1953 to at least 7.54.
A2024	Firefly FR.1	DK512	At Yeovilton 7.50. To Bramcote by 1953 to at least 7.54.
A2026	Mosquito NF.30	NT560	At Yeovilton 7.50 (ex 5917M). Dumped by 12.53.
A2030	Firefly FR.1		At Yeovilton 7.50.
A2033	Tiger Moth T.2	DE661	To GI at Donibristle 6.7.46 (ex RAF Leuchars). At Yeovilton by 7.51.
A2034	Tiger Moth T.2	T7682	[ex 5987M] At Yeovilton 7.50.
A2036	Sea Fury F.10	TF899	At Yeovilton 7.50.
A2051	Sea Hornet NF.21	PX239?	See A2059.
A2053	Seafire F.17		At Stretton 5.56.
A2054	Seafire F.17		At Stretton 5.56.
"A2054"	Seafire F.17	SX300	[ex A646] At Bramcote 7.54 with 'A2054' on fin and 'A646' on fuselage. Engine No E3056. Derelict at Stretton 25.4.55 for fire-fighting practice ('A' numbers not visible). Parts with Neville Franklin at Newark in 1978 for rebuild of SX336/A2055. Fuselage under restoration in the Warwick area by 1982. To Twyford, Bucks by 6.95 as spares for SX336/A2055. Current.
A2055	Seafire F.17	SX336	[ex A517] At Yeovilton 7.50. At Bramcote 6.53. At Stretton 25.4.55 to at least 7.55, in use for fire-fighting practice. At Baylis's scrapyard, Warrington until going to Neville Franklin at Newark 1973 for rebuild (with parts of SX300/A2054) to at least 1979. On rebuild by Peter Woods at Twyford, Bucks by 1987 and current. Registered G-BRMG.
A2059	Sea Hornet NF.21	PX239	To instructional at Yeovilton 7.1.49 (ex CS(A) charge at A&AEE Boscombe Down) to at least 7.50. No engines. [Also reported as A2051]
A2064	Firefly NF.2	Z2048	(ex 798 Sqdn Lee-on-Solent).
A2071	Firefly FR.1	MB553	To instructional 15.3.49. At Yeovilton 7.50, coded 'MV/219' (ex 766 Sqdn). At Bramcote 4.55 (scrap).
A2077	Seafire L.111	PR181	At Bramcote 6.49-6.53. Scrap by 4.55.
A2080	Seafire F.17	SX360?	At Stretton 6.53. [Previous identity unconfirmed]
A2086	Tiger Moth T.2	T7695	At Bramcote 4.55 (scrap).
A2087	Tiger Moth T.2	DE627	At Bramcote 6.53 to at least 11.58. Engine No E3094.
A2088	Tiger Moth T.2		At Bramcote by 6.53 to at least 10.56. Engine No E3095, later E3185.
A2090	Seafire F.15		At Bramcote 6.51-6.53.
A2093	Seafire F.15	PR377	SOC 7.2.49. At Bramcote 6.49-6.53.
A2097	Firebrand TF.4	EK608	Coded 'H'. At Bramcote 4.55 (scrap).
A2099	Firefly		

A2100 to A2199

The early part of this range was largely devoted to further renumbering from the A1 - A752 range, but the remainder were newly downgraded aircraft of the period. For the most part they were the mixture as before, but near the end of the series A2193 was issued to Sea Vampire VF315, which in all probability became the first jet-powered aircraft to grace the naval instructional ranks.

'A' No.	AIRCRAFT TYPE	SERIAL	DETAILS
A2104	Firefly 1		At St Merryn 7.53, coded 'AROK' (probably ex 730 Sqdn Ayr).
A2106	Seafire L.III	NF630	On Balado dump 3.52, coded 'D5H' (ex 807 Sqdn HMS Hunter).
A2106	Firefly		[Apparent duplication with a Seafire L.III]
A2113	Seafire F.15		At St Merryn 7.53.
A2115	Seafire F.15		At Arbroath 1950, coded 'J'. At Farnborough 9.51, semi-derelict with 13 short vertical blades on top of fuselage. Still there 9.53.
A2123	Tiger Moth T.2	NL750	[ex A750] At Arbroath 4.59 to at least 6.60. Engine No E3122. Downgraded to Class III 4.9.62. To BRNC Flight at Roborough 10.62, presumably for spares. At Yeovilton 9.67-1968. Fuselage still in store 1978 and last noted 6.82. Next noted as G-AHUF at Lower Upham, Hants in 1986 and still present 12.91. To Thruxton (restoration?) by 6.94 and current.
A2124	Tiger Moth T.2		
A2126	Tiger Moth T.2	BB731	[ex A728] At Arbroath 7.55-6.60. Engine No E4214. Downgraded to Class III 4.9.62. To BRNC Flight at Roborough 10.62, presumably for spares. At Yeovilton 9.67-1968. Fuselage still in store 1978. Last noted 6.82.
A2127	Tiger Moth T.2	DE373	[ex A680] At Arbroath 7.55-6.60. Engine No E3125. Downgraded to Class III 4.9.62. To BRNC Flight at Roborough 10.62, presumably for spares. Fuselage at Yeovilton 1968. Believed still in store 1978 but not reported since.
A2162	Seafire F.15	PR634	To instructional at Bramcote 21.2.49 (ex Lossiemouth). Still at Bramcote 6.53, coded 'LM/134' (ex 767 Sqdn Lossiemouth).
A2169	Firefly FR.1	DK504	To instructional 25.3.49. At Bramcote by 10.50, coded JB/254' (ex 796 Sqdn St Merryn). Scrap by 4.55.
A2173	Firefly FR.1	MB415	To Class II at Yeovilton 4.3.49 (ex Yeovilton) to at least 7.51. At Bramcote 7.54, coded 'VL/203' (ex 767 Sqdn Yeovilton).
A2178	Seafire F.15	PR463	To instructional at Bramcote 28.4.49 (ex Vickers-Armstrong (Aircraft)). At Bramcote to at least 6.55.
A2179	Seafire F.15	SW866	To instructional 28.4.49 at Bramcote (ex Vickers-Armstrong). Scrap by 4.55.
A2182	Firefly FR.1	DK538	On Gosport dump 7.55. A2186 Seafire F.47 PS945 To instructional at Arbroath 24.6.49 (ex Vickers-Armstrong, Chilbolton). At Ford by 9.52.
A2187	Seafire F.15	PR406	To instructional at Bramcote 21.2.49 (ex Lossiemouth). Still at Bramcote 6.53, coded 'LM/141' (ex 767 Sqdn Lossiemouth).
A2189	Seafire F.15	SR453	To instructional 14.2.49 at Bramcote (ex Yeovilton). Scrap by 4.55.
A2190	Seafire F.15	PR433	SOC 29.6.49. At Yeovilton 7.50. At Bramcote 6.53-7.54. Engine No E3181. Still at Bramcote 4.55 (scrap).
A2193	Sea Vampire F.20	VF315	To instructional at Arbroath 25.8.49 (ex 703 Sqdn Lee-on-Solent) until at least 5.53.
A2195	Tiger Moth T.2	W7951	[Originally G-AFSP] To Class II at Arbroath 29.9.49 (ex Gosport). Engine No E3094. At Bramcote 6.51-6.53. Returned to Arbroath by 4.59, presumably on the closure of Bramcote. Downgraded to Class III 1.2.60 and sold as scrap in autumn 1960.
A2199	Seafire F.15	SW820	To instructional 15.10.49 at Bramcote, coded 'BR/168' (ex 1833 Sqdn Bramcote). Scrap by 4.55.

A2201 to A2300

This block highlighted the changing pattern of naval aircraft with the further appearance in the instructional ranks of jet-powered aircraft in the form of a Vampire and a Meteor. Later marks of Firebrand and Firefly were in evidence, as were the first instructional Wyverns. At this stage the FAA was still comparatively large, with many front-line, second-line and RNVR squadrons in existence. The need for instructional airframes was correspondingly great, and the block was rapidly exhausted, ending up in July 1951 about 18 months after it had begun.

'A' No.	AIRCRAFT TYPE	SERIAL	DETAILS
A2203	Seafire F.17	SW916	To Class II 17.11.49 (ex CS(A) charge at Vickers Armstrong, Eastleigh). At Bramcote by 6.51 to at least 6.53.
A2209	Sea Fury FB.11	VW651	To instructional 27.10.49. At RNEC Manadon 8.54, coded 'T/124' (ex 807 Sqdn HMS Theseus).
A2210	Firebrand TF.5	EK788	To Class II 21.12.49. Engine No E3197. At Bramcote 6.51-6.53.
A2211	Firebrand TF.4	EK827	To instructional 21.12.49 (ex Anthorn). At Bramcote 4.55 (scrap).
A2213	Firefly AS.5		At Worthy Down 6.56, coded *"VM/200"* (spurious).
A2217	Firefly		On Gosport dump 7.55, coded *"912"* (spurious - believed to be SAH Gosport local number).
A2218	Firebrand TF.5	EK840	To Class II 13.3.50. At Bramcote 6.53-7.54, coded 'C/913' (ex HMS Implacable Ships Flight).
A2227	Wyvern TF.1	VR135	To Class II at Yeovilton 5.5.50 (ex CS(A) charge) to at least 7.50. At Bramcote 7.54-2.59.
A2231	Firebrand TF.4	EK733	To instructional 6.4.50. At Bramcote 4.55 (scrap) to at least 1956.
A2232	Firebrand TF.4	EK735	To instructional 6.4.50. At Bramcote 4.55 (scrap) to at least 1956.
A2235	Firefly F.1	Z1889	From Gosport dump to Lee-on-Solent by road 5.52, coded *"908"* (spurious - believed to be SAH Gosport local number).
A2240	Firefly F.1	MB618	To Class II at Abbotsinch 26.9.50. At Lee-on-Solent 9.51, coded '216' (possibly ex 781 Sqdn Lee-on-Solent).
A2241	Firefly F.1	MB592	To Class II at Abbotsinch 26.9.50. At SAH Gosport, coded '213'.
A2245	Firefly 5	VT434	To Class II at Abbotsinch 26.9.50. At Lee-on-Solent 31.8.57, coded 'O/208'.
A2246	Firefly AS.5		
A2249	Vampire F.1	VF269	To Class II at Worthy Down 8.9.50 (ex Culham). At Yeovilton by 7.51 to at least 7.56.
A2255	Firefly FR.1	PP642	To Class II at Culham 8.9.50. At Stretton 7.51-6.55, coded 'P/282' (ex 827 Sqdn HMS Triumph). SOC 27.1.55.
A2256	Seafire F.15	SW800	To Class II 14.9.50, coded 'JA/109' (ex 1831 Sqdn Stretton). Remains at Worthy Down 6.55, coded *"VM/109"* (spurious). In Brownhills scrapyard 1978.
A2257	Firefly FR.1	PP596	To Class II at Culham 8.9.50. On Worthy Down dump 6.56, coded '273' (ex 827 Sqdn).
A2258	Firefly FR.5	VT417	To Class II at Abbotsinch 28.9.50. At Worthy Down 6.56, coded *"VM/202"* (spurious).
A2259	Seafire		Noted in a scrapyard near Stretton 2.3.57.
"A2259"	Meteor F.3	EE387	More likely A2295.
A2268	Seafire F.15	PR394	To Class II at Stretton 7.7.50 (ex RNARY Fleetlands). Engine No E3264. To Bramcote 26.8.52. WOC 26.9.56.
"A2268"	Seafire F.15	SW867	[Presumed mis-painted but correct 'A' serial unknown] To instructional 28.11.50. At Bramcote 6.53-10.56.
A2269	Firefly 5	VT373	To instructional 11.11.55 (ex RNAY Fleetlands). At Lee-on-Solent 8.58 and dumped, coded *"911"* (spurious - believed to be SAH Gosport local number).
A2270	Sea Fury F.10	TF900	To Class II 26.9.50 (ex Anthorn). At RNEC Manadon by 6.51 to at least 8.54. On Culdrose dump by 5.58.
A2291	Firefly FR.5	VT421	To Class II 23.1.50. At Worthy Down 6.56, coded 'K/223' (ex 816 Sqdn HMAS Sydney). [NB Downgrading date is inconsistent with 'A' number].

'A' No.	AIRCRAFT TYPE	SERIAL	DETAILS
A2294	Sea Hornet F.20	TT192	To Class II at Yeovilton 14.6.51. Downgraded to Class II at Worthy Down 5.6.53 (ex Yeovilton). Still at Worthy Down 6.56, with wings of NF.20 VW960.
A2295	Meteor F.3	EE387	[Meteor F.3 navalised. See A2259]. Derelict at Arbroath 7.55.
A2298	Wyvern TF.2	VW874	To Class II at Yeovilton 5.7.51 (arrived 11.7.51, ex Westland Aircraft). Engine No E3286. Dismantled 28.10.52. To St Merryn for *"Operation Solitaire"* 28.10.53. To Bramcote 18.3.55. WOC 24.11.58 at Bramcote and remains still there 2.59.
A2299	Firefly FR.4	TW687	To Class II 10.7.51 (ex 782 Sqdn Donibristle). At Bramcote 6.53, coded 'DO/201' (ex 782 Sqdn). Scrap at Gosport 7-8.55, still as '201'.

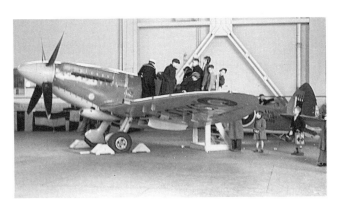

At Bramcote 3.7.54, Seafire F.17 SX300 has former allocation A646 on the fuselage and A2054 on the fin. (MAP/M P Marsh)

Seafire F.15 A2115 semi-derelict at Farnborough 9.51 with 13 short vertical blades on top of the fuselage.

Seafire F.15 A2190/PR433 jacked up at Bramcote on 3.7.54. (MAP/M.P.Marsh)

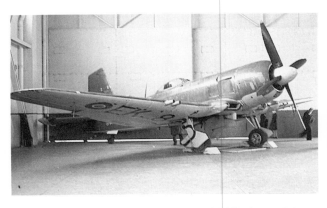

Firebrand TF.5 A2218/EK840 (code 'C/913' obscured) is pictured at Bramcote 3.7.54. (MAP/M P Marsh)

Wyvern TF.1 A2227/VR135 at Bramcote in 1956. (J.Colver/MAP)

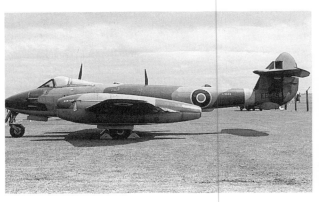

Meteor F.4 A2332/EE545 has number E3108 on the port engine at Bramcote 3.7.54 (M.P.Marsh/MAP)

A2301 to A2399

Indicative of the shrinkage in the size and scope of British naval aviation in the early 1950's is the period of over four years to reach the end of the A2300 range, which occurred towards the end of 1955. Wyverns and later marks of Firefly were still in evidence, but these were now joined by several Sea Furies, the last of the FAA's piston-engined fighters, and a host of second-generation jet fighters including the Attacker and Sea Hawk. As a foretaste of yet another revolution in naval air warfare, an S.51 and a production Dragonfly found their way into the list.

'A' No.	AIRCRAFT TYPE	SERIAL	DETAILS
A2301	Firefly FR.4	TW719	To Class II 10.7.51. Scrap at Gosport 8.55.
A2308	Wyvern TF.2	VW877	To Class II at Arbroath 24.2.52 (arrived 2.3.52, ex Westland Aircraft). Engine No E3288. WOC at Arbroath 19.1.59 and removed to scrap pen.
A2309	Wyvern TF.2	VW878	To Class II at Gosport 20.6.51 (or 5.12.51) (ex Gosport). To RNEC Manadon by 8.54. Believed broken up at Coypool Army Depot, Plymouth.
A2310	Wyvern TF.2	VW879	To Class II at Gosport 30.5.52 (ex HMS Eagle). At Worthy Down 6.56, coded *"LM/203"* (spurious).
A2311	Wyvern TF.2	VW880	To Class II at Arbroath 1952 (ex Westland Aircraft, force-landed 23.2.52). At Arbroath to at least 6.55 (front fuselage). Centre fuselage used for underwater ejection experiments at Arbroath and dumped at Abbotsinch by 6.57 to 1959.
A2312			A2312 or A2314 may be Attacker F.1 WA483 (see "Unidentified Class II Airframes" later).
A2313	Attacker	TS409	Type 392. To Class II at Arbroath 10.2.53 (ex CS(A) charge at Vickers-Armstrong, Chilbolton). Still at Arbroath 7.55 and scrapped there during 1956.
A2314			See A2312.
A2315	Oxford I	NM661	To instructional at Arbroath 4.3.53 (ex storage at Arbroath). Engine Nos E3290/3291. WOC 26.6.58.
A2318	Firefly AS.7	WJ216	To instructional 24.3.53. At Worthy Down 6.56, coded *"300"* (spurious).
A2320	Vampire F.1	VF317	To Class I at Worthy Down 29.5.53 (ex CS(A) charge). Downgraded to Class II. Still at Worthy Down 6.56, coded *"101"* (spurious). Dumped at Yeovilton by 3.59.
A2326	Avenger 3	KE442	To instructional 17.7.53 (ex Belfast), coded 'FD/064' (ex 703 Sqdn Ford). At Abbotsinch 2.56-3.61. Remains removed mid-1961 to J N Connell scrapyard at Coatbridge.
A2327	Venom FB.1 prototype	VV613	To instructional at Arbroath 14.8.53 (ex CS(A) charge at de Havilland, Hatfield). Still at Arbroath 7.55.
A2328	Firefly FR.5	VX394	To Class II at Yeovilton 12.9.53. Engine No E3103. To St Merryn 22.10.53 for *"Operation Solitaire"*. Returned to Yeovilton 28.4.55 and reduced to scrap on site 26.11.56.
A2332	Meteor F.4	EE545	To instructional at Bramcote 23.10.53 (ex CS(A) charge at Gloster Aircraft). Engine No E3108. WOC and reduced to scrap on site 13.10.55. Remains still at Bramcote 10.56.
A2336	Sea Hawk F.1	WF151	To Class II 15.2.54. At Arbroath 7.55-6.59. Downgraded to Class III 6.11.61. Fuselage still at Arbroath 7.68.
A2339	Sikorsky S.51	VW209	To instructional at RNEC Manadon 12.1.54 (ex CS(A) charge). To Staravia and stored at Blackbushe 12.58. Remains at Hall Farm, Yateley autumn 1961 but removed by 4.63.
A2343	Sea Fury FB.11	VX665	To instructional 30.3.54 at RNAY Fleetlands (ex Gosport). Downgraded to Class III components 2.3.60. Rear fuselage still at Fleetlands for apprentice instruction in 1974.
A2346	Vampire FB.5	VV215	To instructional at Bramcote 1.7.54 (ex CS(A) charge at A&AEE Boscombe Down). Engine No E3320 removed 30.5.56 and E4320 installed 2.6.56 at Bramcote. SOC 24.11.58 but still at Bramcote 2.59.

'A' No.	AIRCRAFT TYPE	SERIAL	DETAILS
A2347	Sea Hawk F.1	WM903	To instructional 25.10.54. At Yeovilton by 7.56, coded '161 (ex 806 Sqdn HMS Eagle). At Arbroath between 3.60 and 6.60 still coded '161'.
A2348	Sea Fury F.10	TF947	To Class II at Arbroath 19.10.54 (ex Anthorn 12.10.54). Engine No' E3302. WOC at Arbroath 8.10.59. Downgraded to Class III 4.9.62. Still at Arbroath 7.63. Scrapped at Lasham 1963 and still there 9.66.
A2349	Sea Fury F.10	TF908	To instructional at Arbroath 22.10.54 (ex Anthorn). Engine No E3303. WOC 19.1.59.
A2350	Sea Fury F.10	TF946	To instructional at Arbroath 27.10.54 (ex Anthorn). Engine No E3304. WOC 19.1.59.
A2351	Sea Fury F.10	TF922	To instructional at Arbroath 29.10.54 (ex Anthorn). Engine No E3305. Still at Arbroath 7.55.
A2352	Sea Fury F.10	TF955	To instructional at Arbroath 8.11.54 (ex Anthorn). Engine No E3306.
A2354	Vampire F.3	VV190	To instructional at Bramcote 30.9.54 (ex CS(A) charge at A&AEE Boscombe Down). WOC 22.6.57 but still at Bramcote 8.58.
A2355	Sea Fury FB.11	TF963	To instructional at Bramcote 14.10.54, coded '162' (ex 1833 Sqdn Bramcote). Engine No E3309. WOC 24.11.58 at Bramcote but still there 2.59.
A2356	Sea Fury FB.11	WE733	To instructional at Bramcote 14.10.54, coded 'BR/154' (ex 1833 Sqdn Bramcote). Engine No E3310. WOC 24.11.58 at Bramcote but still there 2.59.
A2357	Sea Fury FB.11	WN487	To instructional at Bramcote 15.10.54 (ex 1833 Sqdn Bramcote). Engine No E3311. WOC 14.10.58 at Bramcote but still there 2.59.
A2358	Sea Fury F.10	TF950	To instructional at Bramcote 19.11.54 (ex Anthorn). Engine No E3312. WOC 24.11.58 at Bramcote but still there 2.59.
A2359	Sea Fury FB.11	WE722	To instructional at Bramcote 28.10.54. Engine No E3313. WOC 24.11.58 at Bramcote but still there 2.59.
A2360	Attacker F.1	WA512	To Class II at Bramcote 5.11.54 (ex Abbotsinch). Engine No E3314. WOC 14.10.58 at Bramcote but still there 2.59.
A2361	Attacker FB.1	WA533	To Class II at Bramcote 27.10.54 (ex AHU Lossiemouth). Engine No E3315. Still at Bramcote 1.59, coded 'LM/115' (ex 736 Sqdn Lossiemouth).
A2362	Attacker F.1	WA481	To Class II at Bramcote 19.11.54 (ex Abbotsinch). Engine No E3316. WOC 14.10.58 at Bramcote but still there 2.59.
A2363	Attacker FB.1	WA530	To Class II at Bramcote 26.11.54 (ex LTS2 at Abbotsinch). Engine No E3317. Still at Bramcote 8.57, coded 'LM/150' (ex 738 Sqdn Lossiemouth). WOC 17.9.57 at Bramcote but still there 2.59.
A2364	Attacker F.1	WA505	To Class II at Bramcote 19.11.54 (ex LTS2 at Abbotsinch). Engine No E3318. WOC 17.9.57 at Bramcote.
A2365	Attacker FB.1	WA528	['A' serial unconfirmed] To Class II at Bramcote 3.12.54 (ex Abbotsinch). WOC 26.9.56.
A2366	Attacker FB.1	WA532	To Class II at Bramcote 3.12.54 (ex LTS2 at Abbotsinch). Engine No E3320. WOC 17.9.57 at Bramcote but still there 2.59. Used for fire practice at Brawdy 1960.
A2367	Sea Hawk F.1	WF147	To Class II at Yeovilton 18.3.55 (ex CS(A) charge at Hawker Aircraft, Dunsfold 14.3.55). Engine No E3330. To HMS Centaur 1.9.58. Transferred to Arbroath 23.10.58 and received 2.11.58. WOC and downgraded to Class III 12.2.59. [NB Both A2367 and A2376 are quoted officially for WF147. See also A2371]
A2368	Sea Hawk F.1	WF143	To Class II at St Merryn 1.2.55 (ex St Merryn, but previously with Armstrong-Whitworth Aircraft, Baginton until 19.10.54). Engine No E3322. Transferred to Arbroath by SNATSU 29.2.55. Engine replaced by E3112 1.5.56. Downgraded to Class III 10.7.58. WOC 19.1.59. Again downgraded to Class III 30.5.60. (Sometimes reported incorrectly as A2336 - possibly mis-painted).
A2369	Vampire T.11/T.22	WW458	To Class II at Lee-on-Solent 28.1.55 (ex Lee-on-Solent). Engine No E3323. At Yeovilton 5.56-4.57, coded 'LS/-'. At Donibristle 1958, still coded 'LS/-'.

'A' No.	AIRCRAFT TYPE	SERIAL	DETAILS
A2370	Vampire T.11/T.22	WW461	To Class II at Lee-on-Solent 28.1.55 (ex Lee-on-Solent). Engine No E3324. At Yeovilton 7.56. At Culdrose 7.57. Outside a public house at Goudhurst, Kent in early 1960's.
A2371	Sea Hawk F.1	WF155	To Class II at St Merryn 1.2.55 (ex St Merryn). Downgraded to Class III 18.3.55. WOC 24.3.55. At Bramcote by 11.58 to at least 2.59. ['A' serial unconfirmed. Could also be A2367].
A2372	Sea Fury T.20	WE825	To Class II at Bramcote 3.3.55 (ex SAD Benson 11.1.55). Engine No E3326, later E4309 (at Bramcote). To Arbroath 9.9.56. WOC and downgraded to Class III at Arbroath 12.2.59. At Staravia, Crookham 1961 to late 1960's. Derelict at Lasham 8.70, coded '270' (ex SAD Benson).
A2373	Attacker F.1	WA496	To Bramcote 22.1.55 (ex Abbotsinch). Engine No E3327. SOC 24.11.58 at Bramcote but still there 2.59.
A2374	Firefly FR.5	WB250	To Class II at Gosport 12.2.55 (ex Gosport). Engine No E3328.
A2375	Firefly FR.5	VT476	To Class II at Gosport 12.2.55 (ex Gosport). Engine No E3329. At Lee-on-Solent 5.57-8.57, coded '205'. At Gosport 1958, still coded '205'.
A2376	Sea Hawk F.1	WF147	To instructional at Arbroath 21.3.55 (ex CS(A) charge). Engine No E3330. Downgraded to Class III 1.2.60. [There is some confusion over the correct 'A' number of this aircraft, as both A2367 and A2376 have been officially quoted for WF147. A2376 seems almost certainly correct, but it is most likely that a mis-painting occurred as A2367 was reported as WF147 at Yeovilton between 7.56 and 8.58].
A2377	Sea Fury FB.11	WE801	To Class II at Yeovilton 10.3.55 (ex 738 Sqdn Lossiemouth). Engine No E3331. Reduced to produce at Yeovilton 4.5.56.
A2378	Firefly AS.6	WD848	To Class II at Yeovilton 8.3.55 (ex CS(A) charge at A&AEE Boscombe Down). Engine No E3332. Reduced to scrap on site 26.11.56. Remains noted in a scrapyard at Brownhills in 4.57.
A2379	Sea Fury FB.11	VX664	To Class II at Yeovilton 25.3.55 (ex 1834 Sqdn Yeovilton). Engine No E3334. Reduced to scrap 4.5.56.
A2380	Sea Fury FB.11	WE734	To Class II at Yeovilton 29.3.55 (ex 1834 Sqdn Yeovilton). Engine No E3334. Reduced to scrap 4.5.56.
A2381	Sea Fury FB.11	VR937	To Class II at Yeovilton 24.3.55, coded '155' (ex 1834 Sqdn Yeovilton). Engine No E3335. To Arbroath 5.5.56. WOC 19.1.59 at Arbroath.
A2382	Firefly AS.6	VT429	To Class II at Yeovilton 4.4.55, coded 'FD/207' (ex 1840 Sqdn Ford 28.3.55). Reduced to scrap on site 26.11.56.
A2383	Firefly AS.6	WD850	At Yeovilton 7.56, coded 'FD/214' (ex CAD Ford).
A2384	Dragonfly HR.3	WN495	To instructional at Arbroath 1.4.55 (ex SAY Donibristle 28.3.55). Remains at Arbroath 6.55, coded 'GJ/707' (ex 705 Sqdn Gosport). WOC 26.6.58 at Arbroath.
A2385	Firefly AS.6	WH630	To Class II at Yeovilton 30.4.55 (ex permanent CS(A) charge at Fairey Aviation, Ringway). Reduced to scrap on site 26.11.56.
A2386	Firefly AS.6	WD909	To Class II at Yeovilton 2.5.55 (ex SAD Abbotsinch 26.4.55), coded 'AC/222' (ex 1840 Sqdn Abbotsinch). To HMS Collingwood 24.11.56. WOC 3.12.59 at RNAY Fleetlands. [Note: A2387 - A2391 and A2393 were probably Fireflies MB641, WB254, WB349 and WB379, plus Sea Fury TF910 and one other aircraft (see "Unidentified Class II Airframes").]
A2392	Firefly 5	WB313	To SAH Gosport 6.8.55 (ex Sembawang, via HMS Vengeance). WOC for instructional purposes 16.11.55. Noted at Lee-on-Solent 31.8.57, coded 'K/255'.
A2394	Firefly 5	VX420	To SAH Gosport 6.8.55 (ex Sembawang, via HMS Vengeance). WOC for instructional purposes 16.11.55. Wreck at Lee-on-Solent 7.57, coded 'K/237' (ex 816 Sqdn HMAS Sydney). At Ford 8.57.
A2395	Firefly T.3	MB408	To instructional 13.6.55. On Culdrose scrap dump 5.58, coded 'CU/211' (ex 766 Sqdn Culdrose).
A2396	Attacker F.1	WA469	To instructional at Arbroath 29.9.55 (ex Ford). Engine No E3347. WOC 19.1.59 at Arbroath.

'A' No.	AIRCRAFT TYPE	SERIAL	DETAILS
A2397	Wyvern S.4	VW873	To Class II at Arbroath 24.10.55 (arrived 21.10.55, ex Merryfield, ex CS(A) charge at Westland Aircraft, Yeovil). WOC and downgraded to Class III 26.6.58. Used as fire fighting hack until scrapped in late 1963.
A2398	Sea Venom FAW.20	WM505	To Class II at RNEC Manadon 3.11.55 (ex Lee-on-Solent). Engine No E3349. Downgraded to Class III 20.11.61.
A2399	Venom FB.1	WE279	['A' number unconfirmed] To instructional at Gosport 15.11.55 (ex CS(A) charge at Folland Aircraft, Chilbolton). WOC 2.12.55. Burnt on Chivenor dump in 1959. Wreck to Yeovilton 1961 and on Yeovilton dump 6.61-6.62.

Rotorless Westland S.51 A2339/VW209 at Blackbushe in 1958. (MAP)

Sea Fury F.10 A2348/TF947 has its A-number painted below the original serial, at Arbroath in 1959. (MAP)

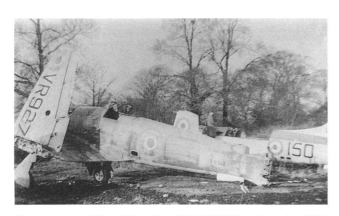

The remnants of Class I Sea Fury FB.11 VR927 and Attacker FB.1 A2363/WA530 ex 'LM/150' at Bramcote in 1959. (Brandon White).

Sea Hawk F.1 A2405/WF165, ex 'LM/123' of Lossiemouth-based No.738 Sqdn at Arbroath in 1959. (MAP)

Apprentices removing the engine of Attacker F.1 A2407/WA482 at Arbroath.

Sea Hawk F.1 A2409/WF200, ex 'LM/640' of No.736 Sqdn Lossiemouth, at Lee-on-Solent in 1961. (MAP)

A2400 to A2499

Issues of instructional serials during the latter part of the 1950's continued to slow down, and this block lasted until October 1960. A few Fireflies still adorned the naval scene, but the emphasis was now largely on Sea Hawks, Sea Venoms and Gannets. Dragonflies and Whirlwinds were now becoming quite common, and at the end of this series the first Scimitar appeared on the scene. A number of aircraft in this range are still in existence, some of them being used for exhibition purposes.

'A' No.	AIRCRAFT TYPE	SERIAL	DETAILS
A2400	Attacker FB.2	WZ279	To Class II at Arbroath 9.1.56 (ex Arbroath). Engine No E3351. WOC 26.6.58 at Arbroath. Remains still at Arbroath 7.60, coded 'J/103' (ex 800 Sqdn).
A2401	Attacker FB.2	WZ289	To Class II at Arbroath 14.1.56, coded '175' (ex Stretton by road 10.12.55, ex 1831 Sqdn Stretton). Engine No E3352. WOC 19.1.59 at Arbroath.
A2402	Attacker F.1	WA520	To Class II at Arbroath 27.1.56 (ex Abbotsinch by road). Engine No E3353. WOC 19.1.59 at Arbroath.
A2403	Blackburn YB.1	WB797	['A' serial unconfirmed] To Gosport 5.12.55 (ex CS(A) charge at Armstrong-Siddeley Motors, Bitteswell.
A2404	Sea Hawk F.1	WF211	To instructional 24.1.56 (ex Ford). Reduced to components at RNEC Manadon 2.12.59. Remains at Manadon 1970.
A2405	Sea Hawk F.1	WF165	To Class II at Yeovilton 24.2.56, coded 'LM/123' (ex 738 Sqdn Lossiemouth 21.1.56). Engine No E3356. Transferred to Arbroath 17.3.58 and received there 24.3.58. WOC and downgraded to Class III 12.2.59. Again downgraded to Class III 1.2.60. Remains still at Arbroath 4.60, mis-painted as "A2403".
A2406	Sea Hawk F.1	WF201	To Class II at Yeovilton 24.2.56, coded 'FD/162' (ex 764 Sqdn Ford). Engine No E3301. To Arbroath 20.2.58, coded "103" (spurious). Downgraded to Class III 20.7.64.
A2407	Attacker F.1	WA482	To Class II at Arbroath 7.3.56 (ex Abbotsinch 16.2.56). Engine No E3358; replaced by E4372 20.1.58, removed 4.58. WOC 19.1.59 at Arbroath.
A2408	Attacker F.1	WA506	To Class II at Arbroath 7.3.56 (ex Stretton 27.2.56). Engine No E3358 (see A2407 above). WOC 19.1.59 at Arbroath.
A2409	Sea Hawk F.1	WF200	To instructional 24.1.56 at Worthy Down (ex Lossiemouth). Engine No E4321. At Worthy Down 6.56, coded 'LM/640' (ex 738 Sqdn Lossiemouth). At Lee-on-Solent by 7.60. Downgraded to Class III at Lee-on-Solent 5.7.66.
A2410	Sea Hawk F.1	WF146	To instructional at Arbroath 22.5.56 (ex CS(A) charge at NTPS 11.5.56). Engine No E4323. WOC and downgraded to Class III at Arbroath 4.7.58.
A2411	Sea Venom FAW.20	WM564	To Class II 28.4.56 (ex CS(A) loan to De Havilland Aircraft. Engine No E4324. Delivered to HMS Excellent by road 8.5.56, ex Christchurch. Downgraded to Class III at HMS Excellent 1962 or 1963.
A2412	Gannet AS.1	WN354	To St Merryn by air for Class I 1.6.54 (ex AHU Anthorn). To Arbroath by road 1.3.55. Downgraded to Class II 20.7.56. Engine No E4391. WOC as Class III 26.2.59, and also on 12.2.59 and 6.11.61.
A2413	Firefly AS.6	WD910	To instructional at Bramcote 21.6.56, coded 'BR/891' (ex 1844 Sqdn Bramcote). Engine No E4326. WOC 24.11.58 at Bramcote.
A2414	Gannet AS.1	WN341	To instructional at Arbroath 20.7.56 (ex CS(A) charge at RAE Bedford 7.5.56). WOC 26.6.58 at Arbroath.
A2415	Firefly T.2	DK531	To Class II at HMS Ganges 5.7.56, coded 'GN/919' (ex Eglinton Stn Flt). Engine No E4328. Reduced to scrap 2.2.60.
A2416	Gannet AS.1	WN462	To instructional at Arbroath 21.9.56 (ex 744 Sqdn St Mawgan via Yeovilton 14.9.56). Engine No E4331. Downgraded to Class III 12.2.59, and on 1.2.60.
A2417	Sea Venom FAW.21	WM569	To instructional at Arbroath 5.6.56 (ex CS(A) charge at De Havilland Aircraft, Christchurch). No engine. Downgraded to Class III 25.9.61.

'A' No.	AIRCRAFT TYPE	SERIAL	DETAILS
A2418	Attacker FB.2	WK320	To instructional at Arbroath 16.10.56, coded '833' (ex 1833 Sqdn Honiley). Engine No E4333. WOC 19.1.59 at Arbroath.
A2419	Gannet AS.1	WN421	To Class II at Yeovilton 20.10.56, coded 'CU/657' (ex 744 Sqdn St Mawgan). Engine No E4338. To Arbroath 24.9.58, where coded *"64"* (spurious) in 6.59. SOC and downgraded to Class III at Arbroath 12.2.59, and also 1.2.60 and 4.3.63.
A2420	Sea Hawk F.1	WF159	To instructional at Stretton 11.5.56 (ex Stretton). Engine No E4340. To SAD Benson 15.10.56. WOC 29.10.56. At Culdrose by 25.7.59, coded '-/125' (ex 767 Sqdn Stretton). Taxyable. Reduced to scrap/fire drill at Culdrose 15.12.59. Allocated 'SAH-1' and coded '1' on nose by 15.7.60. Current 1964 but to Predannack late 1964 for fire-fighting practice.
A2421	Gannet AS.1	WN393	To Class II at Arbroath 24.11.56 (ex Fairey Aviation, Stockport 29.10.56). Engine No E4383, installed 31.3.58. WOC and downgraded to Class III at Arbroath 12.2.59, and again 24.4.63. Coded 'GN/-' at Arbroath 1959 and still there 1965.
A2422	Gannet AS.1	WN373	To instructional at Arbroath 21.11.56, coded 'O/298' (ex 815 Sqdn Eglinton 17.11.56). Engine No E4342. Downgraded to Class III and WOC 12.2.59. Also downgraded to Class III at Arbroath 6.11.61. Still at Arbroath 1965.
A2423	Attacker F.1	WA491	To instructional at Arbroath 16.1.57 (ex CS(A) charge at Airwork Services, Gatwick). Engine No E4345. WOC 19.1.59 at Arbroath.
A2424	Sea Hawk F.1	WF182	To Class II at SAH Culdrose 9.1.57 (ex Fleetlands). Engine No E4346. Reduced to scrap/fire drill at Culdrose 15.12.59.
A2425	Sea Hawk FB.5	WF243	To Class II at Lee-on-Solent 6.12.56 (ex CS(A) charge at Armstrong-Whitworth Aircraft, Baginton). Engine No E4347. To SAH Culdrose and reduced to scrap/fire drill there 15.12.59.
A2426	Sea Hawk F.1	WF183	To instructional at Lee-on-Solent 19.3.57 (ex SAD Benson 13.2.57). Engine No E4348. To SAH Culdrose and reduced to scrap/fire drill there 15.12.59.
A2427	Sea Hawk F.1	WF172	To instructional at Lee-on-Solent 13.3.57. Engine No E4349. To Fleetlands. Downgraded to Class III at Fleetlands 4.3.63.
A2428	Sea Hawk F.1	WF163	To instructional at Ford 12.1.57. Engine No E4351. To SAH Culdrose and reduced to scrap/fire drill there 15.12.59.
A2429	Venom NF.2	WL806	To Bramcote 2.5.57 (ex CS(A) charge at Armstrong-Whitworth Aircraft, Baginton. WOC at Bramcote 14.10.58. Broken up at Bramcote 2.59.
A2430	Meteor F.8	WF752	To instructional at Bramcote 7.5.57 (ex CS(A) charge at Armstrong-Whitworth Aircraft, Baginton 30.4.57 - ex Firestreak trials). Engine Nos E4354/4355. To Arbroath 29.10.58 on transfer of instructional task from Bramcote. WOC at Arbroath 8.10.59. Downgraded to Class III at Arbroath 1.2.60.
A2431	Sea Hawk F.1	WM901	To instructional at SAH Lee-on-Solent 31.1.57 (ex CS(A) charge). Engine No E4356. Transferred to Culdrose by early 1959 on move of SAH. Reduced to scrap/fire drill there 15.12.59. At Predannack by 1964 for fire fighting purposes.
A2432	Sea Hawk FB.3	WN118	To Class II at Lee-on-Solent 7.5.57 (ex 802 Sqdn Lossiemouth). Engine No E4357. Downgraded to Class III and scrapped on site at Lee-on-Solent 2.3.60. Scrap at Lasham 10.63.
A2433	Sea Hawk FB.3	WM924	To Class II at Lee-on-Solent 7.5.57 (ex 802 Sqdn Lossiemouth). Engine No E4358. Downgraded to Class III and scrapped on site at Lee-on-Solent 2.3.60.
A2434	Wyvern S.4	WL881	To Class II at Arbroath 21.5.57 (ex CS(A) charge at Merryfield, via Lee-on-Solent 16.5.57). WOC at Arbroath 26.6.58 and broken up.
A2435	Gannet AS.1	WN376	To Class I at Yeovilton 31.7.56 (ex 700 Sqdn). Downgraded 7.8.57 and converted to Class II use 16.9.57. Coded 'FD/521' (ex 700 Sqdn Ford). Engine No E4407. Transferred to Arbroath 27.7.58 and received there 31.7.58. WOC 4.12.59. Downgraded to Class III 4.3.63. Remains still at Arbroath 7.63, coded 'FD/521', but uncoded on the dump by 4.67.

'A' No.	AIRCRAFT TYPE	SERIAL	DETAILS
A2436	Gannet AS.1	WN453	To Class I at Yeovilton 7.8.56 (ex Lee-on-Solent). Downgraded to Class II 7.8.57. To Arbroath 6.3.58, where received 11.3.58. Engine No E4363. Coded 'FD/522' (ex 700 Sqdn Ford) in 1960, later coded *"FD/111"* (spurious) and *"FD/682"* (spurious) to at least 7.68. Downgraded to Class III at Arbroath 30.6.67.
A2437	Gannet AS.1	WN344	Converted to Class II at Bramcote 10.9.57 (ex CS(A) charge at Fairey Aviation, White Waltham 24.7.57). Engine No E4379 was allocated to this airframe, but it was never installed. WOC at Bramcote 19.1.59. At Arbroath by 4.60 until at least 7.60.
A2438	Wyvern S.4	VW870	To Class II at Bramcote 2.9.57 (ex Lee-on-Solent 9.8.57, ex HMS Albion Navy Days 6.8.57). WOC and being broken up at Bramcote 14.10.58 but still there 2.59.
A2439	Sea Hawk F.1	WF219	To Class II at Bramcote 14.8.57 (ex Lee-on-Solent) and converted to Class II use 9.9.57. To Arbroath 4.11.58, where received 9.11.58. Engine No E4365. Coded '824' at Arbroath (ex 1832 Sqdn Benson). Downgraded to Class III at Arbroath 25.9.61, to at least 1965. Rear fuselage, wings and tail stored by FAA Museum by 12.69 and last reported 1974. Rear fuselage/tail loaned to Cornwall Aero Park (later Flambards etc), Helston by 6.76. To FAA Museum store Wroughton 22-23.10.95 and current.
A2440	Sea Hawk F.1	WF213	To Bramcote 8.8.57 for Class II (ex HMS Ocean) and received 15.8.57. Engine No E4366. Converted to Class II use 9.9.57. To Arbroath 24.10.57, where received 29.10.57. Coded 'FD/702' (ex 764 Sqdn Ford) at Arbroath 6.59. WOC 22.10.59. Downgraded to Class III 25.9.61. Small parts on Arbroath dump 4.67.
A2441	Sea Hawk F.1	WF158	To Class II at Bramcote 30.8.57 (ex Brawdy). Engine No E4367. To Arbroath 9.11.58, coded 'FD/697' (ex 764 Sqdn Ford). WOC 22.10.59. Downgraded to Class III at Arbroath 25.9.61. On Staravia dump, Ascot 4.66.
A2442	Whirlwind HAS.7	XK908	['A' serial unconfirmed] Allocated to instructional at Arbroath 17.10.57, coded '-/505' (ex 700 Sqdn 'H' Flight Lee-on-Solent; damaged 10.9.57 in collision with Hunter F.5 WP144). It is likely that conversion proved impossible and therefore it was authorised to be reduced to spares and produce 21.10.57. WOC 26.6.58.
A2443	Sea Hawk FB.3	WF294	To Class II at Yeovilton 20.9.57 (ex Yeovilton). Engine No E4370. Coded 'FD/514' (ex 700 Sqdn Ford). To HMS Centaur 1.9.58. Transferred to Arbroath 23.10.58, where received 2.11.58. Still at Arbroath 7.63-1965, coded *"FD/105"* (spurious). WOC at Arbroath 22.10.59. Downgraded to Class III at Arbroath 14.12.66 and still on Arbroath dump 3.67.
A2444	Wyvern S.4	VZ777	To instructional at Bramcote 14.9.57 (ex Lee-on-Solent 19.8.57, arrived 11.9.57). Engine No E4371. WOC 24.11.58. Broken up at Bramcote 3.59.
A2445	Attacker FB.2	WZ299	To instructional at Arbroath 14.2.57 (ex Lossiemouth). Engine No E4372; replaced by E3358 20.1.58, in turn removed 6.11.58. WOC at Arbroath 19.1.59.
A2446	Attacker FB.2	WP286	To instructional at Arbroath 11.10.57 (ex Lossiemouth AHU 2.10.57). Engine No E4373. WOC at Arbroath 19.1.59.
A2447	Sea Venom FAW.20	WM503	To instructional at Arbroath 10.10.57 (ex CS(A) charge at RAE Farnborough). Engine No E4373. WOC 26.6.58 and remains still at Arbroath 7.58.
A2448	Sea Venom FAW.21	WW148	To Class II at Arbroath 14.10.57 and converted there to Class II use 24.10.57. Engine No E4375. WOC 28.10.58. Downgraded to Class III 4.3.63. On Portland dump by 1.64.
A2449	Sea Venom FAW.21	WW219	To Class II 11.11.57 (ex Yeovilton). At Lee-on-Solent by 7.60, coded 'O/096' (ex 893 Sqdn Merryfield). Engine No E4377. Downgraded to Class III at Lee-on-Solent 5.7.66. To Predannack by 8.67 for fire fighting purposes, still coded 'O/096'.

'A' No.	AIRCRAFT TYPE	SERIAL	DETAILS
A2450	Gannet AS.1	WN343	To Class II at Bramcote 27.11.57 (ex CS(A) charge at Fairey Aviation, White Waltham). Engine No E4412. To Arbroath 12.10.58 on cessation of training at Bramcote, becoming coded *"106"* (spurious). WOC 12.10.59. Downgraded to Class III at Arbroath 24.4.63, and still there 1965.
A2451	Sea Hawk F.1	WF196	To Class II at SAH Lee-on-Solent 3.2.58 (ex CS(A) charge at A&AEE Boscombe Down), coded '27' (ex ETPS). Engine No E4380. To Class III at Lee-on-Solent 9.4.62. Engine No E4379 was fitted at Lee-on-Solent by 3.64. At Lee-on-Solent 6.66, mis-painted as *"A2541"*/E4379.
A2452	Sea Hawk F.1	WF144	To Class II at Lee-on-Solent 19.2.58 (ex Airwork FRU, Hurn by road 10.2.58). Engine No E4381. Downgraded to Class III and scrapped on site 2.3.60. WOC at Lee-on-Solent 1.7.60.
A2453	Sea Venom FAW.21	WW223	To Class II at Arbroath 5.4.58 (ex Yeovilton 27.3.58). Engine No E4384. WOC 28.10.59. Still at Arbroath 7.60 coded 'O/098' (ex 893 Sqdn Merryfield). Downgraded to Class III at Arbroath 4.3.63. Badly burnt remains on Yeovilton dump 1.65.
A2454	Sea Hawk F.2	WF277	To Class II 15.11.57 (ex Lossiemouth). At RNEC Manadon. Engine No E4385. To Roborough by 6.59, coded '608' (ex 736 Sqdn Lossiemouth). Returned to Manadon by 1961/62, still coded '608'. Downgraded to Class III at Manadon 29.9.63.
A2455	Sea Venom FAW.20	WM514	To Class II 15.11.57 (ex Stretton). Engine No E4386. To RNEC Manadon by 6.59 to at least 7.61, coded '201' (ex 890 Sqdn). To HMS St Vincent 5.9.62. To Chatham as Class III 13.8.65. Scrap at Chatham 1967.
A2456	Sea Venom FAW.21	WW261	To Class II at Arbroath 6.5.58 (ex Yeovilton 30.4.58). Engine No E4389. At Arbroath 6.59, coded 'O/094' (ex 893 Sqdn Merryfield). At Arbroath 7.59-7.63, coded *"O/122"* (spurious). WOC 21.11.59. Downgraded to Class III at Arbroath 4.9.62. Derelict at Lasham in 1963.
A2457	Sea Venom FAW.21	WW269	To Class II at Arbroath 6.5.58 (ex Yeovilton 2.5.58). Engine No E4390 (and/or E4399). At Arbroath 6.59, coded 'O/093' (ex 893 Sqdn Merryfield). WOC 21.11.59. Downgraded to Class III at Arbroath 4.9.62. Derelict at Lasham 8.63.
A2458	Sea Venom FAW.21	WM570	To Class II at Arbroath 6.5.58 (ex Stretton 28.4.58). Engine No E4392. Downgraded to Class III at Arbroath 4.3.63. Derelict at Predannack in 1965 for fire fighting purposes.
A2459	Gannet T.2	XA523	To Class II at Arbroath 9.5.58, coded 'CU/769' (ex 796 Sqdn Culdrose 25.4.58). Engine No E4393; later E4442, then E4456, then E4501. WOC 4.12.59. Downgraded to Class III at Arbroath 3.1.68.
A2460	Sea Hawk FB.3	WM981	To Class II at Arbroath 19.5.58 (ex Lossiemouth by road 15.5.58 after flying accident 28.4.58 with 764 Sqdn), coded 'LM/702'. Engine No E4394. WOC 22.10.59. Downgraded to Class III at Arbroath 6.11.61.
A2461	Sea Venom FAW.21	WW146	To Class II at Arbroath 27.5.58 (ex Yeovilton 15.5.58). Engine No E4395. At Arbroath 6.59, coded 'O/099' (ex 893 Sqdn Merryfield). WOC 21.11.59. Downgraded to Class III at Arbroath 25.9.61.
A2462	Sea Hawk F.2	WF257	To Class II at HMS Ganges 19.5.58 (ex Lossiemouth, via NATSU Lee-on-Solent). Engine No E4396. Coded 'LM/613' at HMS Ganges (ex 736 Sqdn Lossiemouth). Downgraded to Class III at HMS Ganges 22.8.62. Remains at Staravia, Ascot 9.65.
A2463	Dragonfly HR.5	WH990	To Class II at Arbroath 20.5.58 (ex 705 Sqdn Lee-on-Solent 14.5.58). No engine. WOC and downgraded to Class III 12.2.59 and again 25.9.61. Still at Arbroath 7.63.
A2464	Sea Venom FAW.21	WW285	To Class II at Arbroath 29.5.58 (ex Yeovilton 21.5.58). Engine No E4390 ! (see A2457 above). At Arbroath 6.59, coded 'O/091' (ex 893 Sqdn Merryfield) and carrying Suez markings. WOC 21.11.59. Downgraded to Class III at Arbroath 25.9.61.

'A' No.	AIRCRAFT TYPE	SERIAL	DETAILS
A2465	Dragonfly HR.5	VX596	To Class II Arbroath 11.6.58 (ex Ford 9.6.58). No engine. WOC 22.10.59. Coded '923' (ex Ford Stn Flt) at Arbroath 7.60. Downgraded to Class III at Arbroath 4.9.62, to at least 1963. Remains at Lasham 1964 and on Staravia dump, Ascot 1969.
A2466	Gannet AS.1	WN364	To Class II at Arbroath 17.6.58, coded 'GN/544' (ex 719 Sqdn Eglinton). Engine No E4400. Downgraded to Class III at Arbroath 25.9.61.
A2467	Gannet AS.1	WN454	To Class II at Arbroath 17.6.58 (ex 737 Sqdn Eglinton). Engine No E4401. WOC 1.12.59. Coded 'GN/-' (ex 737 Sqdn) at Arbroath 7.60. Still at Arbroath 7.63-7.68, coded "FD/103" (spurious). Downgraded to Class III 30.6.67.
A2468	Whirlwind HAR.1	XA871	To Class I at Arbroath 16.1.58 (ex Arbroath). Downgraded to Class II 14.6.58 and converted to Class II use 17.6.58. Engine No E4402. WOC 23.10.59. Downgraded to Class III 20.7.64. Derelict at Arbroath 7.68.
A2469	Whirlwind HAR.3	XG581	To Class II 24.5.58 (ex Lee-on-Solent after flying accident 21.1.58 with 701 Sqdn). To RNAY Donibristle (arrived 20.3.58) but repairs were abandoned and moved to Arbroath 18.6.58. WOC 4.7.58 and believed scrapped at Arbroath in the late 1960's.
A2470	Gannet AS.1	WN391	To Class II at Lee-on-Solent 23.6.58 (ex Lee-on-Solent), coded 'O/334' (ex 824 Sqdn HMS Ark Royal). Engine No E4403. Downgraded to Class III at Lee-on-Solent 5.7.66. At Culdrose by 10.66, and derelict there by 8.67. At Predannack by 7.68.
A2471	Gannet AS.1	XA342	To Class II 23.6.58. No engine. At Lee-on-Solent by 6.61, coded 'O/292' (ex 815 Sqdn Culdrose). Engine No E4468 fitted by 1.64. Downgraded to Class III at Lee-on-Solent 5.7.66. At Culdrose 10.66-7.71. At Predannack by 3.73.
A2472	Gannet T.2	XA508	To Class II at RNEC Manadon 23.6.58, coded 'GN/627' (ex 737 Sqdn Eglinton). Engine No E4404 (later removed for Royal Australian Navy). To FAA Museum, Yeovilton by road 8.9.75 (received 11.9.75), and displayed as 'GN/627'. Transferred to south side storage hangar (9.2.81 ?). To the Midland Air Museum, Baginton by road 25-26.9.82 on loan and current, still 'GN/627'.
A2473	Sea Hawk F.1	WF220	To Class II 27.1.58 (ex Fleetlands). No engine. At Abbotsinch 6.59. Downgraded to Class III as components at Fleetlands 2.3.60. Scrap at Lasham 10.63.
A2474	Gannet T.2	XG871	['A' serial unconfirmed] To Class II 5.3.58 at RNAY Donibristle (ex 719 Sqdn Eglinton after landing accident 6.12.57).
A2475	Sea Venom FAW.20	WM557	To Class II at Arbroath 10.11.58 (ex Abbotsinch 29.10.58), coded 'BY/017' (ex Airwork FRU St Davids). Engine No E4414. WOC 22.10.59. Downgraded to Class III at Arbroath 26.5.61. Parts noted at Lasham in 1966.
A2476	Sea Venom FAW.20	WM520	To Class II at Arbroath 12.11.58 (ex RNAY Belfast 5.11.58). Engine No E4415. WOC 22.10.59. Downgraded to Class III at Arbroath 4.3.63.
A2477	Sea Venom FAW.20	WM513	To Class II at Arbroath 26.1.59 (ex Abbotsinch 23.1.59), coded 'BY/010' (ex Airwork FRU St Davids). Engine No E4416. WOC 28.10.59. Downgraded to Class III at Arbroath 4.3.63. Derelict at Culdrose 7.63, coded "107" (spurious). To Predannack for fire fighting purposes by 1965.
A2478	Sea Venom FAW.20	WM512	To Class II at Arbroath 2.2.59 (ex Abbotsinch 4.11.58), coded 'BY/012' (ex Airwork FRU St Davids). Engine No E4419. WOC 28.10.59. Downgraded to Class III at Arbroath 25.9.61. To Predannack for fire fighting purposes by 1965.
A2479	Sea Venom FAW.20	WM509	To Class II at Arbroath 16.2.59 (ex Abbotsinch, allocated 4.11.58 and received 13.2.59). Engine No E4420. WOC 28.10.59. Downgraded to Class III at Arbroath 30.5.60.

'A' No.	AIRCRAFT TYPE	SERIAL	DETAILS
A2480	Sea Venom FAW.20	WM553	To Class II at Arbroath 13.3.59 (ex Stretton, allocated 4.11.58 and received 4.3.59). Engine No E4421. WOC 28.10.59. Downgraded to Class III at Arbroath 30.5.60.
A2481	DH.110 prototype	WG240	To Class II at Arbroath 13.2.59 (ex CS(A) charge). Engine Nos E4422/4423. To RNEC Manadon 7.62. Scrapped 5.7.65.
A2482	Sea Hawk FB.5	WM939	To Class II at Arbroath 26.3.59 (ex 802 Sqdn Lossiemouth, received 2.3.59, after mid-air collision with WM926 on 13.1.59). Engine No E4431. Reported at Abbotsinch 6.59, coded 'E/-'. WOC 4.12.59. Downgraded to Class III at Arbroath 4.9.62. Tail still marked 'E/-' at Lasham 8.63-11.63 but disappeared soon afterwards. Fuselage at Arbroath to at least 9.67.
A2483	Sea Hawk F.2	WF259	To instructional at Lossiemouth 22.6.59 (ex Lossiemouth). Engine No E4432. On Lossiemouth fire dump 1967. Gate guardian at Lossiemouth by 7.68. To Museum of Flight at East Fortune by road in 1972, coded *"A/171"* (spurious 804 Sqdn code). Current.
A2484	Sea Hawk FB.5	WM907	To Class II 20.4.59 (ex Fleetlands). At Dartmouth without engine and wings. Downgraded to Class III at Dartmouth 7.8.63.
A2485	Whirlwind HAR.3	XJ397	To instructional 9.7.59 (ex Donibristle after flying accident 29.4.59 with 815 Sqdn). At Arbroath. Engine No E4434. Downgraded to Class III at Arbroath 6.11.61 and presumably scrapped there.
A2486	Sea Venom FAW.20	WM543	To Class II 3.7.59 (ex Lee-on-Solent). Engine No E4435. At HMS Collingwood. Downgraded to Class III at HMS Collingwood 2.9.60.
A2487	Whirlwind HAR.3	XG584	To Class II at Arbroath (ex Portland after being ditched 20.7.59 and salvaged). Engine No E4438. WOC 2.10.59. Downgraded to Class III at Arbroath 30.5.60.
A2488	Sea Venom FAW.21	WW194	At Lossiemouth. Engine No E4440. Downgraded to Class III at Lossiemouth 22.3.60. Bits in Quarrywood scrapyard 3.67.
A2489	Sea Hawk FB.3	WM918	To Class II at SAH Culdrose 29.2.60 (ex Abbotsinch AHU 21.1.60). Engine No E4444, later E4486. Allocated code 'SAH-4' and coded '4' on nose by 15.7.60. Taxyable. To RNAY Belfast 29.10.65. Downgraded to Class III at Belfast 11.7.68.
A2490	Sea Hawk FB.3	WM920	To Class II at SAH Culdrose 22.1.60 (ex Abbotsinch AHU 21.1.60). Engine No E4445. Allocated code 'SAH-3' and coded '3' on nose by 15.7.60. Painted black overall and marked 'SAH-3' by 7.66. Taxyable. Downgraded to Class III at Culdrose 26.10.66. Remains to Predannack for fire-fighting practice by 6.7.68, coded 'SAH-3' (wings to XE330).
A2491	Sea Venom FAW.21	WW275	To Class I at Lee-on-Solent 25.9.59. Downgraded to Class II 21.3.60. Engine No E4447. Coded 'VL/735' (ex 766 Sqdn Yeovilton) at Lee-on-Solent 7.60-8.63. To SAH Culdrose 4.4.67. Nothing further known.
A2492	Sea Venom FAW.21	XG616	To Class I at Lee-on-Solent 30.7.59. Downgraded to Class II 21.3.60. Engine No E4449 to at least 3.64, later E4464. Coded 'VL/736' (ex 766 Sqdn Yeovilton) at Lee-on-Solent 7.60-10.66. At SAH Culdrose by 30.8.67. Downgraded to Class III and fire fighting 5.3.70. Derelict in Culdrose fire pits 9.71-1972 and later burnt.
A2493	Gannet AS.1	WN346	To Class I at Lee-on-Solent 24.9.59. Downgraded to Class II 22.3.60. Engine No E4448. At Lee-on-Solent 6.61-1967, uncoded (ex 815 Sqdn). To SAH Culdrose by 21.10.68. Used by the Air Command Driving School but WFU by 5.71. Downgraded to Class III 4.10.71. To fire pits by 6.72 and at Predannack for fire-fighting practice by 10.3.73.
A2494	Sea Hawk FB.5	WM937	To Class II at Arbroath 29.6.60 (ex Abbotsinch), coded 'E/137' (ex 802 Sqdn Lossiemouth). Engine No E4454. At Arbroath 1965 coded *"114"* (spurious). Downgraded to Class III 20.7.64.
A2495	Sea Hawk FB.5	WM965	To Class II at Arbroath 21.7.60 (ex Abbotsinch), coded 'E/135' (ex 802 Sqdn Lossiemouth). Engine No E4455. At Arbroath 7.63, coded *"104"* (spurious). Downgraded to Class III at Arbroath 20.7.64.
A2496	Whirlwind HAS.7	XK933	To Class II at Arbroath 26.9.60 (ex Lee-on-Solent, after ditching 17.5.60), coded '-/770' (ex 737 Sqdn Portland). Engine No E4463. Downgraded to Class III 8.1.64. Still at Arbroath 7.68, coded '-/770'.

'A' No.	AIRCRAFT TYPE	SERIAL	DETAILS
A2497	Sea Hawk FGA.4	WV904	To Class II at Arbroath 14.10.60 (ex Abbotsinch). No engine. Upgraded to Class I 27.10.61. To LTS2(U) 4.12.62. Sold to Star Metal Co, Ascot 20.6.63. Fuselage at Lasham 8.70, coded '516' (ex 700 Sqdn Yeovilton).
A2498	Sea Venom FAW.21	XG621	To Class II at Arbroath 19.10.60 (ex Abbotsinch). No engine. Downgraded to Class III at Arbroath 4.9.62. Parts at Lasham 11.63.
A2499	VAS.544	WT859	[Scimitar prototype] To instructional Lee-on-Solent 21.8.60 (ex CS(A) charge at RAE Bedford). To Class II at SAH Culdrose 29.10.60 on HMS Victorious (ex RNAY Fleetlands). WOC 29.11.60. Engine Nos E4466/4467. In use by Air Command Driving School at Culdrose by 7.72, but to P&EE Foulness soon afterwards. Noted derelict at P&EE Foulness 3.88. Fuselage and rear end to Mayer & Perry scrapyard, Snailwell, Cambs 4.91 and scrapped. Nose section to The Vampire Collection, Ruislip 25.4.91. To Brooklands Museum 18.7.92 on loan.

Sea Hawk FB.3 A2443/WF295, ex 'FD/514' of No.700 Sqdn Ford, at Arbroath, also bearing engine number E4370. (MAP)

Wyvern S.4 A2444/VZ777 in the process of being scrapped at Bramcote in March 1959. (Brandon White)

Sea Venom FAW.21 A2449/WW219, ex 'O/096' of No.893 Sqdn, at Lee-on-Solent in 1961. (MAP)

The semi-derelict fuselage of Sea Hawk F.2 A2451/WF196 (engine number E4379) mis-painted as A2541 at Lee-on-Solent. (MAP)

Sea Venom FAW.21 A2458/WM570 at Arbroath in 1959. (MAP)

Gannet T.2 A2459/XA523, ex 'CU/769' of No.796 Sqdn Culdrose at Arbroath 6.59. (J.Chalmers via C.H.Thomas)

A2500 - A2599

Almost a decade was to elapse before the end of this block was reached in July 1969, and consequently it encompassed a wide range of types. Fixed-wing aircraft included further Sea Hawks and Sea Venoms, a miscellany of Scimitars, Gannets and Buccaneers, together with a gaggle of ex RAF Hunters, most of which were later to be refurbished and modified by HSA for sale to the Swiss Air Force. Indicative of the changes taking place in the equipment for the FAA during the decade were the numerous Wasp, Whirlwind and Wessex helicopters becoming available for ground instructional use. An oddment in this block was the second allocation for A2593 which related to the only non-airframe known to have been allocated an instructional airframe number. This was apparently easier to fit into the instructional numbering system as an airframe than an engine.

Reference is also made in this section to the re-allocations of numbers from A2600 in both 1988 and 1993 (see later).

'A' No.	AIRCRAFT TYPE	SERIAL	DETAILS
A2500	DH110 Mk.20X	XF828	To Class II at SAH Culdrose 28.11.60 (ex RAE Bedford). Marked *"de Havilland All-Weather Fighter"* on the nose. Engine Nos E4471/4472. WFU by 8.67 and placed in open store. Downgraded to Class III 16.1.68. Derelict at Culdrose fire pits by 7.70 and burnt hulk still present 6.78.
A2501	Whirlwind HAS.7	XN307	To Class II at Lee-on-Solent 14.2.61 (after being written off in a crash 28.10.60 while with 814 Sqdn coded '286'). Engine No E4477. To HMS Ganges 5.7.66, where downgraded to Class III 30.12.68.
A2502	Sea Hawk FB.5	WM936	To Class II at Arbroath 9.3.61 (ex Abbotsinch), coded '035' (ex Airwork FRU Brawdy. Coded *"113"* (spurious) in 1963. Engine No E4478. Downgraded to Class III at Arbroath 14.2.66. On Arbroath dump 3.67. At Quarrywood 9.69, still coded *"113"*.
A2503	Sea Hawk FB.5	WM994	To Class II at Arbroath 17.3.61 (ex Abbotsinch). Engine No 4479. Coded *"101"* (spurious). To Cranfield College of Technology on loan 25.6.63, still coded *"101"*. Downgraded to Class III 30.6.67. Believed intended to become Sea Hawk Executive G-APYG, but registration re-allocated. Departed Cranfield 26.4.74 and purchased by MAPS. At Swansea by 1978 undergoing restoration by Mr H Webborn. To Southend 9-10.4.82 to continue restoration. Registered G-SEAH 5.4.83 to Roger Boot and another. To Hunter One Collection, Hurn 10.83 for restoration. To Southampton Docks 11.11.94 en route to Amjet Aircraft Corporation, Minnesota, USA. Registered N994WM.
A2504	Sea Venom FAW.21	XG622	To Class II at Arbroath 17.3.61 (ex Abbotsinch). Engine No E4480. Downgraded to Class III 21.4.61.
A2505	Sea Hawk FB.5	WM943	To Class II at Arbroath 19.3.61 (ex Abbotsinch). Engine No E4482. Coded *"102"* (spurious) in 7.63. Downgraded to Class III 20.7.64. Scrap at Lossiemouth 7.68.
A2506	Sea Venom FAW.21	XG655	To Class II at Arbroath 8.7.61 (ex Abbotsinch). Engine No E4485. Downgraded to Class III 4.3.63. Still at Arbroath 7.63, coded *"123"* (spurious). On Arbroath dump 4.67.
A2507	Sea Vixen FAW.1	XJ583	To Class II at Lee-on-Solent 27.4.61 (ex MARTSU Lee-on-Solent). No engine. To Arbroath 7.7.61. Downgraded to Class III 14.12.66. On Arbroath dump 1968.
A2508	Sea Venom FAW.21	WW218	To Class II at HMS Ganges 13.3.61 (ex Brawdy via Lee-on-Solent), coded 'BY/104' (ex Airwork FRU, Brawdy). Engine No E4488. Downgraded to Class III at HMS Ganges 30.12.68. To Crawley Technical College by 9.75. Gone by 1980.
A2509	Sea Hawk FB.5	WF299	To Class II at SAH Culdrose 1.9.61 (ex Abbotsinch AHU by road 16-21.7.61), coded 'E/133' (ex 802 Sqdn Lossiemouth). Engine No E4489. Allocated 'SAH-8'. Painted black overall and recoded 'SAH-8' by 7.66. Taxyable. Still at Culdrose 3.68 marked 'SAH-8' with fin code 'E' visible under paint. To Lee-on-Solent store by 7.71, still as 'SAH-8'. At Catterick Fire School by 3.72, allocated 8164M. [Later allocated A2662].

'A' No.	AIRCRAFT TYPE	SERIAL	DETAILS
A2510	Sea Hawk FB.5	WM913	To Class II at SAH Culdrose 24.6.61 (ex Abbotsinch AHU), coded 'LM/616' (ex 736 Sqdn Lossiemouth). Engine No E4490. Allocated 'SAH-7' and coded '7' by 15.7.61. Painted black overall and recoded 'SAH-1' by 7.66. Taxyable. Still at Culdrose 3.68, marked 'SAH-1' with code 'LM/616' still visible under paint. WFU by 5.71. Preserved on the gate at RAF Sealand by 9.71 and with 30 MU Training School, Sealand 1974. Allocated 8162M but not taken up. Left Sealand 19.3.76 to Fleetwood Sea Cadets. To Newark Air Museum, Winthorpe 1984, coded '-/616' and current 6.91. Restored as 'J/456' and current.
A2511	Sea Hawk FB.5	WM983	To Class II at Culdrose 22.7.61 (ex Abbotsinch AHU 21.7.61). Engine No E4491. Allocated 'SAH-9' and coded '9' by 7.64. Painted black overall and recoded 'SAH-9' by 7.66. Recoded 'SAH-6' by 3.73. Fitted with wings of WV909/A2549 and repainted in original dark grey/sky colour scheme but uncoded. To Cornwall Aeronautical Park Ltd, Helston 29.5.75. To Brencham Historic Aircraft Collection, Hurn 8.85. Fuselage mated to tail section and wings of FGA.6 XE489/G-JETH for restoration to flying condition, which did not happen. Sold to P.G. Vallance and on display at Charlwood, Surrey by 6.88 in all over red scheme minus all marks. Current. Wings and tail of WM983 and fuselage of XE489 restored for Chilton Cantello House School, Somerset and displayed there as *"WM983"* by 3.87. To Soesterberg, Netherlands 8.8.89 for RNAF Museum.
A2512	Sea Venom FAW.21	XG637	To Class II at Arbroath 11.9.61 (ex Abbotsinch 23.8.61). Engine No E4492. Downgraded to Class III 4.3.63. At Lasham 1963.
A2513	Sea Venom FAW.21	WW267	To Class II at Arbroath 31.8.61 (ex Abbotsinch). Engine No E4493. Coded 'BY/012' (ex Airwork FRU Brawdy) in 1963. Downgraded to Class III at Arbroath 4.3.63.
A2514	Wessex prototype	XL722	To Class II at Arbroath 25.7.61 (ex CS(A) charge at Westland Aircraft, via Lee-on-Solent). No engine. Downgraded to Class III 4.9.62. Still at Arbroath 7.63. On Staravia dump at Ascot 1967.
A2515	Sea Hawk FGA.6	XE366	To Class II at Arbroath 10.12.61 (ex Abbotsinch). No engine. Downgraded to Class III at Abbotsinch 4.9.62.
A2516	Wessex HAS.1	XM835	To Class II at Arbroath 10.12.61 (ex AIU Lee-on-Solent , after crashing in Falmouth Harbour 3.5.61). No engine. Downgraded to Class III 14.12.66. Still at Arbroath 7.68.
A2517	Sea Hawk FB.5	WM961	To Class II at SAH Culdrose 13.10.61 (ex Abbotsinch AHU). Engine No E4497. Allocated 'SAH-6' and coded '6' by 7.64. Painted black overall and recoded 'SAH-6' by 7.66. Taxyable. WFU by 5.71 and to Torbay Aircraft Museum by 6.71. Repainted by 6.74 with yellow and black Suez stripes and coded 'J/-'. To Caernarfon Air Museum, Caernarfon Airport, Gwynedd in 1988 and current.
A2518	Sea Venom FAW.21	WW189	To Class I at Lee-on-Solent 10.1.57 (ex 892 Sqdn HMS Eagle). At Lee-on-Solent 6.61, coded 'J/451' (ex 892 Sqdn) in Suez markings to at least 3.64. Downgraded to Class II 18.1.62. Engine No E4502. Still coded 'J/451' at Lee-on-Solent 6.66, and downgraded to Class III there 5.7.66. Bits of this aircraft were reported on the dump at Culdrose 8.67 and the remainder went to Predannack by 8.67.
A2519	SARO P.531-O/N	XN333	To Class II at Arbroath 28.4.62 (ex AIU Lee-on-Solent, via MARTSU). Engine No E4505. Downgraded to Class III at Lee-on-Solent 8.1.64.
A2520	Sea Venom FAW.21	WW270	To Class II at RNEC Manadon 14.2.62 (ex Abbotsinch). Engine No E4506. Downgraded to Class III at Manadon 14.12.66.
A2521	Sea Hawk FGA.6	WV841	To Class II at RNEC Manadon 15.1.62 (ex AHU Abbotsinch). Engine No E4507. Painted as *"A2520/E4506"* in error. Downgraded to Class III at Manadon 14.12.66.

'A' No.	AIRCRAFT TYPE	SERIAL	DETAILS
A2522	Sea Hawk FB.5	WM993	To Class II at Culdrose 23.2.62 (ex Airwork FRU Hurn 22.2.62), coded '034'. Engine No E4508. Allocated 'SAH-7' and coded '7' by 7.66, still with '034' on the nose. Taxayable. Downgraded to Class III at Culdrose 15.3.67. To HMS Royal Arthur by 1972 minus wings, still coded '034' and '7' on the nose (the wings were stored at SAH Culdrose 1.76 until burnt in the fire pits in 6.78). From HMS Royal Arthur to a private owner at Peasedown St John, Avon by 27.7.85 (spares for A2661/WV795). For sale 1987 - fate?
A2523	Sea Hawk FB.5	WM915	To Class II at Lee-on-Solent 24.1.62 (ex Lee-on-Solent for MARTSU). Engine No E4509. Still at Lee-on-Solent 1967 but to SAH Culdrose by 11.67, and downgraded to Class III 26.6.68. In use with the Air Command Driving School 9.68 minus wings. Wings to XE368/A2534. At Predannack by 10.3.73.
A2524	Sea Hawk FB.3	WM998	To Class II at SAH Culdrose 14.2.62 (ex Abbotsinch), coded 'E/138' (ex 802 Sqdn Lossiemouth). Engine No E4510. Downgraded to Class III at Culdrose 13.5.64 but used by the Air Command Driving School. To Predannack by 8.67 for fire-fighting practice, still coded 'E/138'.
A2525	SARO P.531-O/N	XN334	To Class II at Arbroath 13.9.62 (ex AIU Lee-on-Solent). Engine No E4511. Downgraded to Class III at R3.1.68. Still at Arbroath 7.68, coded '758' (ex 771 Sqdn Portland). To FAA Museum Yeovilton and stored in 1978. Open store at rear of Airwork hangars by 7.83. To Crawley Technical College 18.9.87 for restoration but this was not proceeded with. To FAAM store at Wroughton on 8.8.96.
A2526	Sea Hawk FGA.4	WV911	To Class I at Lee-on-Solent 3.9.59. Downgraded to Class II 31.10.62. Engine No E4513. At Lee-on-Solent to at least 6.67. At Fleetlands by 6.71. With AES Lee-on-Solent by 1974. Left by road 6.4.77 but returned to Lee-on-Solent by 25.6.77. Coded "C/115" (spurious) by 5.81. *Re-allocated A2626 [2] in 1988 (see later).*
A2527	Wessex HAS.1	XP107	To Class II at Lee-on-Solent 26.6.63 (ex Fleetlands). No engine. Reported on a lorry at Lee-on-Solent 8.63, coded 'A/D' (ex 845 Sqdn HMS Albion). At Lee-on-Solent by 3.64, still coded 'A/D'. Downgraded to Class III at Lee-on-Solent 23.3.71. To Predannack 11.9.86, uncoded minus boom. Last noted 5.88.
A2528	Gannet AS.1	XA363	To Class I at SAH Culdrose 13.9.63 (ex Abbotsinch), uncoded (ex MTPS). Downgraded to Class II 6.1.64. Engine No E4524, later E4534. Former code 'GN/550' painted out but still visible (ex 719 Sqdn Eglinton). MTPS badge also visible. Downgraded to Class III at SAH Culdrose 5.10.71. Taxayable. To Culdrose fire pits by 6.73 and badly burnt remains still 6.78. To Predannack for fire-fighting practice by 12.80.
A2529	VAS.508	VX133	To Class II at SAH Culdrose 7.1.64 (ex RAE Bedford), minus outer wings. Engine Nos E4524/4525. Downgraded to Class III 6.3.68. WFU by 11.68 and placed in open store to at least 1969. At Predannack by 1.8.70 for fire-fighting practice.
A2530	Sea Hawk FB.5	WM969	To Class II at SAH Culdrose 14.5.64 (ex Airwork FRU Hurn). Engine No E4526. Former code '036' (ex FRU) painted out but still visible. Allocated 'SAH-5' and by 7.64 marked '5' on the nose. This had become 'SAH-5' by 7.66. Taxayable. Was to have gone to Federal German Navy 8.76, but A2554 went instead. Still in use 3.75 but WFU soon after. To Imperial War Museum, Duxford 18.1.77 and under restoration 3.86. Current.
A2531	Dragonfly HR.5	WG718	To Class II at SAH Culdrose 18.2.65 (ex Fleetlands). Engine No E4531. Used by the Air Command Driving School. Downgraded to Class III 25.1.68. Allocated to FAA Museum 8.70 to replace WN493, to be refurbished to flying condition. To Yeovilton 24.2.71 (for parts to be used to restore WG719 to airworthiness) and in a derelict state by 7.72 to at least 8.78. To South Wales APS, Rhoose by 8.79 and repainted as '-/934'. Stored 8.91. To Long Marston, Warwicks by early 1992. To Elvington, N.Yorks 8.7.95. Current.

Gannet AS.1 A2466/WN364, ex 'GN/544' of No.719 Sqdn Eglinton, at Arbroath 6.59 (J.Chalmers vis C.H.Thomas)

Gannet AS.1 A2470/WN391, ex 'O/334' of No.824 Sqdn, at Lee-on-Solent 10.6.63. (MAP)

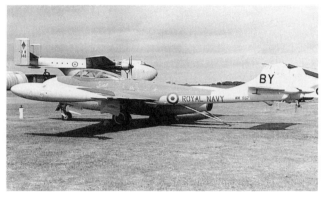

Sea Venom FAW.20 A2475/WM557, ex Airwork FRU Brawdy, at Arbroath in 1959. (MAP)

Sea Venom FAW.20 A2476/WM520 at Arbroath in 1959 (MAP)

Sea Venom FAW.20 A2478/WM512, ex Airwork FRU Brawdy, at Arbroath in 1959. (MAP)

D.H.110 prototype WG240 later became A2481 at Arbroath and then RNEC Manadon. (Hawker-Siddeley)

Sea Hawk FB.3 A2482/WM939, ex No.802 Sqdn HMS Eagle, at Arbroath in 1961. (N.D.Welch)

Sea Venom FAW.21 A2492/XG616, ex 'VL/736' of No.766 Sqdn Culdrose at Lee-on-Solent in 1961. (MAP)

'A' No.	AIRCRAFT TYPE	SERIAL	DETAILS
A2532	Sea Hawk FGA.6	WV826	To Class I at SAH Culdrose 27.2.62, coded 'LM/637' (ex 738 Sqdn Lossiemouth). Allocated 'SAH-2' and coded '2' by 7.64. Taxyable. Downgraded to Class II 29.1.65. Engine No E4532, later E4487. Painted black overall and recoded 'SAH-2' by 7.66, with original code 'LM/637' still visible under paint. WFU and derelict by 3.76. Allocated for Imperial War Museum but sold instead to South Wales APS in 1.77. Under restoration at Swansea in 1978. Preserved at Rhoose coded *"CU/147"* by 1.81, later *"Z/147"* and marked *"WV906"*. To Bruntingthorpe, Leics 2.2.96 and current, coded *"-/182"*.
A2533	Gannet AS.4	XA456	To Class I at SAH Culdrose 22.2.63 (ex Abbotsinch), coded 'E/283' (ex 814 Sqdn Culdrose). Downgraded to Class II 8.1.65. Coded 'E/283' (ex 814 Sqdn Culdrose). Engine No E4533. Downgraded to Class III at Culdrose 26.10.66. To Predannack for fire-fighting practice by 6.7.68.
A2534	Sea Hawk FGA.6	XE368	To Class I at HMS Ganges 20.9.62 (ex Lossiemouth), coded 'LM/631' (ex 738 Sqdn Lossiemouth) with spurious tail code *"G"* applied above 'LM' at HMS Ganges. Downgraded to Class II 28.5.66. Engine No E4543. To Culdrose 10.7.68, minus wings. Fitted with wings from WM915/A2523 by 5.69, still coded '-/651' with 'LM' and 'G' painted over but visible. Painted as *"A2555"* in error. Painted black overall and coded 'SAH-3' by 5.71. Taxyable. Repainted in 897 Sqdn marks as 'J/200' by 12.9.75 and towed to Cornwall Aeronautical Park, Helston in 1.76, coded 'J/200'. Current (now Flambards Village Theme Park).
A2535	Sea Vixen FAW.1	XJ484	To Class I at Arbroath 1.12.62 (ex Belfast). Downgraded to Class II 21.1.66. No engine. Downgraded to Class III 24.6.69. Derelict at Arbroath 7.68, coded 'V/208' (ex 892 Sqdn Yeovilton; no 'V' on starboard side).
A2536	Sea Hawk FGA.6	WV914	To Class I at Arbroath 15.7.59. Still at Arbroath 7.60, coded 'R/109' (ex 800 Sqdn Lossiemouth). Coded *"112"* (spurious) by 1965. Downgraded to Class II 21.1.66. Engine No E4544. Downgraded to Class III at Arbroath 30.6.67.
A2537	Whirlwind HAR.21	WV190	To Class I at Arbroath 15.6.58. Downgraded to Class II at Arbroath 1.66. Engine No E4545. Downgraded to Class III 30.6.67. Still at Arbroath 7.68, painted white overall and ex 781 Sqdn Lee-on-Solent.
A2538	Whirlwind HAR.3	XJ393	To Class I at Arbroath 15.2.61 (ex CS(A) charge at RRE/AD Pershore). Downgraded to Class II 1.66. Engine No E4546. Still at Arbroath 7.68. At Lee-on-Solent by 7.70. To Torbay Aircraft Museum, Higher Blagdon 3.72 and current 8.82. To Pulborough, West Sussex by 4.89 as an attraction for a cafeteria. By 12.91 the cafe burnt down and the Whirlwind was derelict. Gone by 5.93.
A2539	Gannet ECM.6	XG831	To Class II at SAH Culdrose 20.5.66 (ex 831 Sqdn Watton). Engine No E4548. Code 'SAH-8' allocated mid-1971 but not carried. Taxyable. WFU by 7.74 and repainted RAF blue grey overall for static display purposes. Sold to Cornwall Aeronautical Park, Helston 3.80 and towed there 11.5.80. Repainted in 831 Sqdn marks coded '-/396'. Current (now Flambards Village Theme Park).
A2540	Gannet ECM.6	WN464	To Class II at SAH Culdrose 20.5.66, uncoded (ex 831 Sqdn Watton). Engine No E4549. Allocated code 'SAH-9' by 3.73 but not carried. Taxyable. Current 1977 with 831 Sqdn crest below port side of pilot's cockpit. Towed to Cornwall Aeronautical Park, Helston 4.6.78 on permanent loan. Not restored and for sale 1988. Remained unsold and scrapped there (by then Flambards Triple Theme Park) in 12.88.
A2541	Whirlwind HAR.1	XA869	To Class II at Fleetlands 20.5.66 (ex Fleetlands), uncoded but in the black/orange scheme with the HMS Protector penguin badge on the nose (ex HMS Protector Ship's Flight). Engine No E4550. At SAH Culdrose by 7.66. Downgraded to Class III 16.1.68. To Predannack for fire-fighting practice by 1.8.70.

'A' No.	AIRCRAFT TYPE	SERIAL	DETAILS
A2542	Whirlwind HAR.1	XA862	To Class II at Fleetlands 25.5.66 (ex Fleetlands). Engine No E4551. To Lee-on-Solent 7.70. To Air Medical School, Seafield Park by 7.71. Returned to Lee-on-Solent 12.6.75. To Wroughton 12.1.76. To Midland Air Museum, Baginton 15.5.81 (ex Wroughton). Awaiting restoration 7.89. To IHM Weston-super-Mare on loan by 5.91 and current.
A2543	Whirlwind HAR.1	XA870	To Class II at Lee-on-Solent 18.5.66 (ex Fleetlands). Engine No E4552. Still at Lee-on-Solent 7.71. To Predannack early 1973 and stored in 626 VGS hangar. Transported to Culdrose late 1975 for repainting and sectioning. To Cornwall Aeronautical Park, Helston early 1976 (sectioned) and current (now Flambards Village Theme Park).
A2544	Sea Vixen FAW.1	XJ487	To Class I at Arbroath 1.12.62 (ex Belfast). Downgraded to Class II 15.7.66. No engine. Downgraded to Class III 24.6.68. At Arbroath 1968, coded 'V/215' (ex 892 Sqdn Yeovilton).
A2545	Sea Hawk FGA.6	WV836	To Class I at Arbroath 1.4.64 (ex Short Brothers, Belfast). Downgraded to Class II 15.7.66. Engine No E4553. Downgraded to Class III 3.1.68. Still at Arbroath 7.68, coded 'LM/639' (ex 738 Sqdn Lossiemouth).
A2546	Sea Hawk FGA.6	WV870	To Class I at Arbroath 1.4.64 (ex Short Brothers, Belfast). Downgraded to Class II 15.7.66. Engine No E4554. Downgraded to Class III 3.1.68. On Arbroath dump 7.68, coded 'LM/649' (ex 738 Sqdn Lossiemouth).
A2547	Sea Hawk FGA.6	WV860	To Class I at Arbroath 1.4.64 (ex Short Brothers, Belfast). Downgraded to Class II 15.7.66. Engine No E4555. Downgraded to Class III 3.1.68. Still at Arbroath 7.68, coded 'LM/635' (ex 738 Sqdn Lossiemouth).
A2548	Sea Hawk FGA.6	WV861	To Class I at Arbroath 1.4.64 (ex Short Brothers, Belfast). Downgraded to Class II 15.7.66. Engine No E4556. Downgraded to Class III 3.1.68. Still at Arbroath 7.68, coded 'LM/638' (ex 738 Sqdn Lossiemouth).
A2549	Sea Hawk FGA.6	WV909	To Class I at SAH Culdrose 7.7.65 (ex Lossiemouth), coded '-/983' (ex Lossiemouth Stn Flt). Downgraded to Class II 22.7.66. Engine No E4558, later E4616. Marked 'SAH-4' by 7.66 to at least 9.70. Downgraded to Class III 9.9.70. Wingless at Predannack by 4.71-7.71 (the wings having been fitted to WM983/A2511).
A2550	Whirlwind HAR.1	XA866	To Class I at Arbroath 19.5.66 (ex Fleetlands). Downgraded to Class II 7.2.67. Engine No E4561. Still at Arbroath 7.68, coded '448' (ex HMS Protector Ship's Flight). To Lee-on-Solent 11.8.70 on transfer of AES there. Sold to Donnington Car Museum by 1973 and scrapped there in 1985.
A2551	Whirlwind HAR.1	XA868	To Class I at Lee-on-Solent 17.5.66 (ex Fleetlands). Downgraded to Class II 1.67. Engine No E4562. SOC 7.4.67 but still at Lee-on-Solent 1968, coded '449' (ex HMS Protector Ship's Flight). To Crawley Technical College 4.7.73 and current 1981. To Arnold's scrapyard, Horsham, Sussex by 12.84.
A2552	Buccaneer S.1	XN932	To Class II at Lee-on-Solent 20.3.67 (ex Belfast). No engines. Carried 800 Sqdn marks. Derelict by 12.70.
A2553	Buccaneer S.1	XN924	To Class II at Arbroath 13.3.67 (ex NASU Lossiemouth). No engines. Downgraded to Class III 23.1.68. Still at Arbroath 7.68. Noted on the dump at Quarrywood 1971.
A2554	Sea Hawk FGA.6	WV865	To Class II at SAH Culdrose 14.3.67 (ex Airwork FRU Hurn), coded '038'. Engine No E4563. Allocated and coded 'SAH-7' by 3.68 still with code '038' on nose. Marked 'SAH-7' only by 5.71 and recoded 'SAH-1' by 7.71. Taxyable. WFU by 3.76 and refurbished at Culdrose in 7.76. To Luftwaffenmuseum, Uetersen 8.76 in exchange for Sea Fury T.20 WG655 for the FAA Historic Flight. Current at Uetersen 3.95 but due to move to the museum's new site at Berlin/Gatow 3/4.95.

'A' No.	AIRCRAFT TYPE	SERIAL	DETAILS
A2555	Sea Hawk FGA.6	XE330	To Class II at SAH Culdrose 13.3.67, coded '028' (ex Airwork FRU Hurn). Engine No E4564. Marked 'SAH-3' by 7.67-7.71, with code '028' on nose 10.68. Downgraded to Class III at Culdrose 14.10.69. To Predannack fire-fighting school by 1.8.70, but gone by 1977. Also reported at HMS Ganges but not confirmed. [NB XE368/A2534 was painted in error as A2555].
A2556	Sea Hawk FGA.6	XE327	To Class II at Belfast 9.6.67 (ex ADW at Short Brothers, Belfast). Engine No E4566. By road to Belfast harbour where embarked RFA Robert Dundas 27.4.71; presumed for 1 SoTT Halton but not taken up. On display at RN Air Stores Dept, Llangennech, Dyfed coded *"LH/644"* (spurious) until put up for disposal 3.88. Arrived at Trout Lake, Kings Langley, Herts 25.5.88 and current.
A2557	Sea Hawk FGA.6	WV798	To Class II at SAH Culdrose 10.5.67 (ex Airwork FRU Hurn), code '025' painted out but still visible. Engine No E4567. Allocated 'SAH-10' and marked 'SAH-10' by 3.68. Recoded 'SAH-4' by 5.71. Taxyable. To Thorpe Water Park, Chertsey, Surrey 16.5.75. To Second World War APS, Lasham by late 1981 and marked *"CU/026"* by 9.86. Current.
A2558	Sea Hawk FGA.6	WV831	To Class II at Arbroath 6.6.67 (ex Airwork FRU Hurn). Engine No E4568. Still at Arbroath 7.68-1969, coded '032' (ex FRU). To Fareham Technical College 11.70. Sold for scrap 12.81.
A2559	Sea Hawk FGA.6	WV792	To Class II at Arbroath 5.9.67 (ex Airwork FRU Hurn), coded '035'. Engine No E4569. Downgraded to Class III and scrap at Arbroath 15.10.69.
A2560	Hunter F.4	XF363	To Lee-on-Solent 22.11.62 (ex 19 MU St Athan). To Class I at RNEC Manadon 28.11.62. Downgraded to Class II 27.7.67. Engine No E4570. At Manadon 1968. Sold to Airwork Services and used in Saudi Arabia as an instructional airframe.
A2561	Hunter F.4	XF365	To Class I at Lee-on-Solent 14.11.62 (ex 19 MU St Athan). Downgraded to Class II 27.6.67. Engine No E4571. Sold to HSA and became G-9-297 (to Swiss Air Force as F.58A J-4109).
A2562	Scimitar F.1	XD226	To Class I at Arbroath 7.1.65 (ex AHU Lossiemouth). Downgraded to Class II 27.7.67. Engine Nos E4572/4573. Still at Arbroath 7.66-7.68, coded 'LM/615' (ex 736 Sqdn Lossiemouth). Downgraded to Class III at Arbroath 6.69.
A2563	Hunter F.4	WV405	To Class I at Arbroath 22.10.62 (ex 19 MU St Athan). Downgraded to Class II 27.7.67. Engine No E4574. Still at Arbroath 7.68. Sold to HSA and became G-9-316 (to Swiss Air Force as F.58A J-4106).
A2564	Hunter F.4	WV411	To Lee-on-Solent 19.2.63 (ex 19 MU St Athan). To Class I at Arbroath 22.2.63. Downgraded to Class II 27.7.67. Engine No E4575. Still at Arbroath 4.67, and coded *"115"* (spurious) in 1968. Sold to HSA and became G-9-314 (to Swiss Air Force as F.58A J-4108).
A2565	Hunter F.4	XF303	To Class I at Arbroath 30.3.63 (ex 5 MU Kemble). Downgraded to Class II 27.7.67. Engine No E4576. Still at Arbroath 1968. Sold to HSA and became G-9-315 (to Swiss Air Force as F.58A J-4105).
A2566	Hunter F.4	XF311	To Class I at Arbroath 30.3.63 (ex 5 MU Kemble), in 130 Sqdn markings. Downgraded to Class II 27.7.67. Engine No E4577. Sold to HSA in 1970 and to Singapore Air Force as instructional airframe 'SAFTECH.11'.
A2567	Hunter F.4	XF318	To Class I at Arbroath 30.3.63 (ex 5 MU Kemble). Downgraded to Class II 27.7.67. Engine No E4578. Still at Arbroath 1968. Sold to HSA and became G-9-328 (to Swiss Air Force as F.58A J-4110).
A2568	Hunter F.4	XF947	To Lee-on-Solent 19.2.63. To Class I at Arbroath 22.2.63 (ex 19 MU St Athan). Downgraded to Class II 27.7.67. Engine No E4579. Still at Arbroath 7.68. Sold to HSA and became G-9-317 (to Swiss Air Force as F.58A J-4104).

Sea Hawk FB.3 A2495/WM965 with the spurious code "104" at Arbroath some time after 1960. (N.D.Welch)

Sea Hawk FB.3 A2502/WM936, ex '035' of Airwork FRU Hurn, at Arbroath in 1961. (N.D.Welch)

Saunders-Roe P.531 O/N XN334, which became A2525 in 1962 at Arbroath. (MAP)

Gannet ECM.6 A2540/WN464 ex SAH Culdrose on display at Cornwall Aero Park 4.87 (Geoff Wakeham)

Whirlwind HAR.1 A2550/XA866, ex '448' of Ships Flight HMS Protector, at Arbroath in 1967. (MAP)

Sea Hawk FGA.6 A2557/WV798 marked 'SAH-10' with SAH Culdrose. (A.Mackay)

Whirlwind HAR.3 A2571/XG577 of the Imperial War Museum Collection, Duxford, seen at Cranfield 6.9.75

Scimitar F.1 A2574/XD332, ex '616' of No.764B Sqdn, at Culdrose 22.6.73. (G.Wakeham)

'A' No.	AIRCRAFT TYPE	SERIAL	DETAILS
A2569	Hunter F.4	XF976	To Lee-on-Solent 30.11.62. To Class I at Arbroath 7.12.62 (ex 19 MU St Athan). Downgraded to Class II 27.7.67. Engine No E4580. Still at Arbroath 1968. Sold to HSA and became G-9-329 (to Swiss Air Force as F.58A J-4112).
A2570	Hunter F.4	XF984	To Class I at Arbroath 7.12.62 (ex 19 MU St Athan), in 234 Sqdn markings. Downgraded to Class II 27.7.67. Engine No E4581. Still at Arbroath 7.68, coded 'ES-55' (ex 234 Sqdn Chivenor). Sold to HSA and became G-9-330 (to Swiss Air Force as F.58A J-4113).
A2571	Whirlwind HAR.3	XG577	To Class I at Arbroath 7.3.67 (ex NASU Culdrose). Downgraded to Class II 9.67. Engine No E4582. At Arbroath to at least 7.68. To Lee-on-Solent 30.6.70. To Imperial War Museum, Duxford 12.6.74. To Leicestershire & Loughborough Museum 22.5.80. Returned to Duxford 12.83. Preserved at 39 RE Rgt Barracks, Waterbeach, Cambs by 3.86 (probably since early-1984), unmarked in grey/green camo, and current 2.89. Returned to Duxford by 9.89 and stored. To Leconfield 10.90 and became 9050M.
A2572	Whirlwind HAR.3	XJ402	To Class I at RNEC Manadon 7.3.67 (ex Fleetlands). Downgraded to Class II 9.67. Engine No E4583. To FAA Museum Yeovilton by road 11.2.76, coded '61' (ex 705 Sqdn Culdrose). Current 1977. Stored outside in a compound between the FAAM hangars by 7.83 and ended up "boxed in" by new buildings. An attempt to lift it out by air was abandoned as impractical and it was scrapped on site between 1.88 and 3.88. Useful parts went to the FAA Museum store at Wroughton, other parts were dumped in the northeast area at Yeovilton and were current 3.90.
A2573	Scimitar F.1	XD215	To Class II at SAH Culdrose 6.10.67 (ex Lee-on-Solent), coded '-/614' (ex 764B Sqdn Lossiemouth). Engine Nos E4584/4585. Allocated 'SAH-18' but not carried. At Culdrose until at least 9.71 but to P&EE Foulness in 1972. Derelict at Foulness to at least 6.89. Rear fuselage to Mayer & Perry yard, Snailwell, Cambs 4.91 and scrapped. Nose to Barry Parkhouse at Ottershaw, Surrey 25.4.91 and on to Nick Parker at Cheltenham 19.2.94. Current 2.96.
A2574	Scimitar F.1	XD332	To Class II at SAH Culdrose 6.10.67 (ex Lee-on-Solent), coded '-/616' (ex 764B Sqdn Lossiemouth). Engine Nos E4586/4587. Allocated 'SAH-19' but not carried. Downgraded to Class III 5.10.71. Towed to Cornwall Aeronautical Park, Helston 6.7.76 and repainted in 736 Sqdn marks coded '-/612'. Repainted as *"C/194"* by 9.91 and current (now Flambards Village Theme Park).
A2575	Whirlwind HAR.3	XG574	To Class II at Lee-on-Solent 8.9.67 (ex Fleetlands). Engine No E4588. At Lee-on-Solent 6.68, coded 'PO/752' (ex 771 Sqdn Portland). Still at Lee-on-Solent with AES in 1974. To Wroughton 12.3.75 for FAA Museum storage. To FAA Museum, Yeovilton, arriving 21.1.88 (uncoded). Returned to FAAM store at Wroughton 15.7.94. Current.
A2576	Whirlwind HAR.21	WV198	To Class I at Arbroath 7.8.58. To Lee-on-Solent 15.1.60 for RN Recruitment Unit. At Culdrose 29.1.62 to 10.10.62 with RNRU on temporary loan. Downgraded to Class II 9.67 at Lee-on-Solent, being WOC 12.9.67. Engine No E4589. With Navy Recruiting Office, Lee-on-Solent by 3.69 to at least 1974. At Gosport 1977 with a Sea Scout company. Believed sold to a scrap merchant in the late 1970's. It was sighted being transported along the M27 early in 1980 to an unknown destination. However, it was acquired by Jim Wilkie of Carnforth, Lancashire (Helicopter Museum of Great Britain) in 5.81 and registered to him on 25.1.82 as G-BJWY for restoration to flying condition (which would have been a fitting tribute to *"the last of the line"*). Moved with the collection to Heysham, Lancs on 11.10.82, repainted as *"130191"* in USMC marks and later noted at the collection's workshop at Blackpool Airport. Disposed of to the National Fire School at Chorley, Lancs by 5.89 but rescued by The Helicopter Collection (Mr K Fern) and to Warmingham, Cheshire by 6.90 (in exchange for HAR.9

'A' No.	AIRCRAFT TYPE	SERIAL	DETAILS
A2576	Whirlwind HAR.21	WV198	(contd) XN298). To South Yorkshire Aviation Museum, at Firbeck for restoration late-1991. To Carlisle Airport 13.11.92 for continued restoration with Solway Aviation Society and current, coded 'K'.
A2577	Hiller HT.1	XB480	To Class I at RNEC Manadon 7.3.63 (ex Culdrose). Downgraded to Class II 9.67. Engine No E4590. Transferred to FAA Museum Yeovilton in 1972, coded '-/537' (ex 705 Sqdn Culdrose). To FAAM store at Wroughton 22.6.94.
A2578	Whirlwind HAR.3	XJ399	To Class II at Arbroath 7.9.67 (ex Fleetlands). Engine No E4591. At Arbroath 1968, coded *"AB/62"* (spurious, ex 705 Sqdn Culdrose). To Lee-on-Solent 10.4.70, coded '62'. With AES Lee-on-Solent 1974, still coded '62'. To RAE Farnborough (boom dumped there 9.78).
A2579	SARO P.531-O/N	XN332	To Class I at RNEC Manadon 7.5.63 (ex Portland). Downgraded to Class II 10.67. Engine No E4592. To FAA Museum, Yeovilton 7.10.71, coded '-/759' (ex 771 Sqdn Portland). Current 1977, to be used in a diving film. Left FAAM 8.4.87 for Wroughton store. To Finningley for BoB Show 21.9.91 and then to Yeovilton 24.9.91. Left 31.5.94 to Shepton Mallet (displayed at FAAM stand at Royal Bath and West Show), thence to FAAM store at Wroughton 6.6.94. Current.
A2580	Sea Hawk FGA.6	XE369	To Class II at Arbroath 29.11.67, coded '029' (ex Airwork FRU Hurn). Engine No E4593. Still at Arbroath 1970. To 1 SoTT Halton 30.12.70 as 8158M. [Later allocated A2633].
A2581	Buccaneer S.1	XK532	To Class I at RNEC Manadon 10.5.67 (ex NASU Lossiemouth), coded 'LM/632' (ex 736 Sqdn Lossiemouth). Downgraded to Class II 2.68. Engine Nos E4594 and E4639, although these were removed later. Still at Manadon 7.80. To RAF Lossiemouth in 1982 for preservation on the gate and allocated 8867M. For sale 3.92 and purchased by Kenneth Charleton. By road to Inverness 23.9.92 on loan to the Fresson Trust and stored for eventual static display. Current.
A2582	Buccaneer S.1	XK534	To Class I at Arbroath 22.9.66 (ex AHU Lossiemouth). Downgraded to Class II 2.68. No engines. At Arbroath 7.68, coded 'LM/633' (ex 736 Sqdn Lossiemouth).
A2583	Scimitar F.1	XD280	To Class I at Arbroath 14.8.66 (ex 800B Sqdn Lossiemouth), coded 'E/115'. Downgraded to Class II 14.2.68. Engine Nos E4596/4597. Downgraded to Class III at Arbroath 19.3.69.
A2584	Scimitar F.1	XD274	To Class I at Arbroath 12.10.66 (ex 803 Sqdn Lossiemouth). Downgraded to Class II 5.3.68. Engine Nos E4598/4599. Still at Arbroath 7.68, coded 'E/024' (ex 803 Sqdn).
A2585	Scimitar F.1	XD272	To Class I at Arbroath 8.11.66 (ex Lossiemouth). Downgraded to Class II 5.3.68. Engine Nos E4600/4601. Downgraded to Class III 6.69.
A2586	Scimitar F.1	XD278	To Class I at Arbroath 3.11.66 (ex 803 Sqdn Lossiemouth), coded 'R/061'. Downgraded to Class II 5.3.68. Engine Nos E4602/4603. Downgraded to Class III at Arbroath 6.69.
A2587	Scimitar F.1	XD275	To Class I at Lee-on-Solent 22.8.66 (ex Yeovilton), coded 'E/117' (ex 800B Sqdn Lossiemouth). Downgraded to Class II 27.2.68. Engine Nos E4604/4605. Transferred to MoD(Air) and to AWRE Foulness by road 21.9.70 after de-instrumentation at Fleetlands.
A2588	Scimitar F.1	XD243	To Class I at Lee-on-Solent 24.8.66 (ex 803 Sqdn Lossiemouth), believed coded 'E/025'. Engine Nos E4606/4607. Transferred to MoD(Air) and to AWRE Foulness by road 22.9.70 after de-instrumentation at Fleetlands. Current 2.80. Rear fuselage noted at P&EE Pendine Ranges, Dyfed 2.88 and current 3.94.
A2589	Scimitar F.1	XD271	To Class I at Lee-on-Solent 14.9.66 (ex Yeovilton), coded 'E/-' (ex 800B Sqdn Lossiemouth). Downgraded to Class II 27.2.68. Engine Nos E4608/4609. Preserved on the gate at Lee-on-Solent 6.68 to 7.69 at least. Transferred to MoD(Air) and to AWRE Foulness by road 25.9.70 after de-instrumentation at Fleetlands.

'A' No.	AIRCRAFT TYPE	SERIAL	DETAILS
A2590	Scimitar F.1	XD324	To Class I at Lee-on-Solent 14.10.66 (ex Yeovilton). Downgraded to Class II 27.2.68. Engine Nos E4610/4611. At Lee-on-Solent 1967/68, coded 'R/033' (ex 803 Sqdn Lossiemouth). Transferred to MoD(Air) and to AWRE Foulness by road 2.9.70 after de-instrumentation at Fleetlands. In Dowty-Rotol Ltd compound at Staverton by 1974. At PEE Foulness by 1977 and last noted 8.82.
A2591	Scimitar F.1	XD276	To Class I at Lee-on-Solent 21.10.66 (ex Yeovilton), coded 'R/017' (ex 803 Sqdn Lossiemouth). Downgraded to Class II 27.2.68. Engine Nos E4612/4613. Transferred to MoD(Air) and to AWRE Foulness by road 23.9.70 after de-instrumentation at Fleetlands.
A2592	Sea Hawk FGA.6	WV828	To Class II at Arbroath 4.3.68 (ex Airwork FRU Hurn), coded '037'. Engine No E4614. To Apprentices School, Lee-on-Solent 5.11.70. At AES Lee-on-Solent until to MARTSU 4.7.78 for Dutch International Aerospace Museum, Schiphol. Repainted in MLD marks as *"118/D"* and current 1989. To Valkenburg Museum by 6.92.
A2593	Sea Hawk FGA.6	WV825	To Class II at HMS Ganges 1.68 (ex Airwork FRU Hurn). Engine No E4615. Allocation cancelled and 'A' number re-allotted. Sold as scrap 5.68. Fuselage in Staravia yard at Lasham 8.70, coded '034' (ex FRU).
A2593	FR Pod Mk.20E	E.110	[Sea Vixen flight refuelling pod] To Class II at Arbroath 2.69 (ex Arbroath). Offered to RAF as training aid, but not taken up. To Lee-on-Solent 27.11.70. Later returned to stores.
A2594	Wessex HAS.3	XM920	To Class II at Arbroath 5.69 (ex Fleetlands, after heavy landing at Culdrose 1.11.68). No engine. At Lee-on-Solent 7.70, coded 'E/143' (ex 826 Sqdn Culdrose). To scrapyard of A. Brooks, Bordesley Green, Birmingham in mid-1974, still coded '43'.
A2595	Whirlwind HAS.7	XL868	To Class II at Arbroath 6.69 (ex AIU Lee-on-Solent, after damage in force-landing 20.6.69 while with 705 Sqdn Culdrose coded '57'). No engine. Presumably scrapped in 1970 when Arbroath closed and noted in scrapyard of J. Shackleton, Siddal, Halifax 10.73. Still present 10.86 but perished/buried circa 1989.
A2596	Wessex HU.5	XT448	To Class I at Arbroath 6.69 (ex Culdrose). No engine. To Fleetlands for PBM 1.7.70, completed 25.10.70. Returned to service and to 845 Sqdn Culdrose 27.4.72. Never in Class II although given an 'A' serial.
A2597	Wessex HU.5	XS509	To Class I at RNEC Manadon 27.8.69 (ex 848 Sqdn Culdrose), coded 'A/P'. To Fleetlands 13.7.70 for PBM and returned to service. Never in Class II although given an 'A' serial.
A2598	Sea Vixen FAW.1	XJ482	To Class I at Lee-on-Solent 9.2.67 (ex 766 Sqdn Yeovilton), coded 'VL/713'. Downgraded to Class II 3.8.69. No engines. Preserved on the gate at Lee-on-Solent 7.71. Downgraded to Class III 25.5.72. To Flight Refuelling Ltd, Wimborne Minster, Dorset by road 5.7.72, as a test rig in connection with the Sea Vixen drone programme. Left by road 23.11.79 for the Norfolk and Suffolk Air Museum at Flixton. Current, still coded 'VL/713'.
A2599	Sea Vixen FAW.1	XJ486	To Class I at Lee-on-Solent 9.10.62 (probably ex 893 Sqdn Yeovilton). Downgraded to Class II at Lee-on-Solent 3.8.69. No engines. Downgraded to Class III 14.3.72.

Hiller HT.1 A2577/XB480 '537' of the FAA Museum collection at Yeovilton Air Day on 17.7.93. (Bob Turner)

Pictured inside the FAA Museum on 23.10.86, Saro P.531-O/N A2579/XN332 '759' served at RNEC Manadon. (Bob Turner)

Scimitar F.1 A2589/XD271, ex No.800B Sqdn, at Arbroath in 1969. (MAP)

Scimitar F.1 A2591/XD276, ex 'R/017' of No.803 Sqdn HMS Ark Royal, at Arbroath in 1967. (MAP)

Buccaneer S.1 A2600/XN934, ex 'LM/632' of No.736 Sqdn Lossiemouth, seen at Fleetlands in 1969. (Peter G.Smith)

Sea Vixen FAW.2 A2611/XJ575, ex No.766 Sqdn Lossiemouth, marked 'SAH-13' at Culdrose on 2.6.76. (Geoff Wakeham)

Wessex HAS.3 A2615/XT256 of AES Lee-on-Solent in 1978. (MAP)

Kestrel FGA.1 A2619/XS695 '(SAH) 6' at Culdrose on 16.2.87. It is now in the RAF Museum store at Cardington. (Geoff Wakeham)

A2600 - A2699

This series continued at a slightly slower rate than the previous block and eventually spanned a period of 18 years. The basic types involved are largely similar to the previous block, but of later marks. Most of the aircraft were still in existence in the late-1970's, although many of them failed to bear their respective instructional serials and were therefore not readily recognisable as such. There were a few new types, including two Sioux, a Jet Provost, a Sea King, a Lynx, and the first two vertical take-off machines to grace the 'A' series, the P.1127 in anticipation of the Sea Harrier. Sea Vixen XN650 was the subject of some confusion, and succeeded in acquiring three 'A' serials, with A2612 and A2620 both being allocated before finally becoming A2639. It was during this series that Class II was superseded by Class GRB, and A2621 became the first issue after the change.

Reference is also made in this section to the re-allocations of numbers from A2600 in both 1988 and 1993 (see later). Other airframes were still extant during this period, as can be seen from the histories which follow, but no longer appeared in the official records.

'A' No.	AIRCRAFT TYPE	SERIAL	DETAILS
A2600	Buccaneer S.1	XN934	To Class I at Lee-on-Solent 15.5.68 (ex Belfast), coded 'LM/631' (ex 736 Sqdn Lossiemouth). Downgraded to Class II 7.69, but engines still graded Class I therefore given no 'E' numbers. At Lee-on-Solent coded "LS/631" (spurious) by 7.71. To SAH Culdrose 7.7.76 with no engines. Allocated to fire-fighting 3.10.79 and in open store by 12.80. Derelict near the fire pits by 12.81, minus wings/tail. To Predannack 28.6.83 as '-/631' (minus tail/wings) and last noted 8.95 (burnt).
A2601	Sea Vixen FAW.1	XJ477	To Class I at Arbroath 9.2.67 (ex NASU Yeovilton), coded 'VL/714' (ex 766 Sqdn Yeovilton). Downgraded to Class II 31.7.69, but engines still graded Class I therefore given no 'E' numbers. Allocated to Lee-on-Solent, but not required and scrapped 7.70. Remains at Arbroath until 3.75, coded "AB/714" (spurious) and preserved as gate guard by 1977. Intended for NEAM Sunderland in 1981 but proved too bulky to move. In poor condition at Arbroath 3.83 and the remains were noted in a scrapyard at Montrose by later that year.
A2602	Buccaneer S.1	XN925	To Class I with 803 Sqdn Lossiemouth 29.9.67 for ground armament instruction (ex NASU Lossiemouth), coded 'LM/640' (ex 736 Sqdn Lossiemouth - damaged by bird-strike 12.66). Downgraded to Class II at Lossiemouth 7.69. Engines still graded Class I therefore given no 'E' numbers. To RAF Catterick Fire School as 8087M by 8.70.
A2603	Whirlwind HAS.7	XK911	To Class I 13.11.69. Downgraded to Class II at Arbroath 26.1.70. Engine No E4618. To AES Lee-on-Solent 20.8.70, coded 'PO/519' (ex 771 Sqdn Portland). To Wroughton by road 6.12.79. Intended for Leeds Museum but not taken up. Remained in store until 29.8.92 when it left Wroughton by road to R J Everett, Ipswich, still 'PO/519'. Current.
A2604	Whirlwind HAS.7	XN259	To Class I 13.11.69. Downgraded to Class II at Arbroath 26.1.70 (or 27.8.70). Engine No E4619. At AES Lee-on-Solent by 7.71. Coded 'PO/518' (ex 771 Sqdn Portland) in 7.72. To RAE Farnborough 15.2.74 but returned to Lee-on-Solent 1.9.74, still coded 'PO/518'. Current 1977. To P&EE Foulness by 12.79, and still there 6.89 coded 'PO/518'. To London City Airport for FCR training by 11.90. Expired by 12.92.
A2605	Whirlwind HAS.7	XN308	To Class I 29.1.70. Downgraded to Class II at Arbroath immediately (or 27.8.70). Engine No E4620. At AES Lee-on-Solent from 1971, coded 'PO/510' (ex 771 Sqdn Portland). To Wroughton by road 27.11.80. To Lee-on-Solent 25.2.83 and used for BDR training 4.83. On the dump by 7.85. Left by road 30.6.86 for HMS Royal Arthur as a training aid. Arrived Yeovilton by road 22.7.87 for the dump. Lying on its side by 3.90. Current 7.92 but nearly burnt out by 12.93. Remains noted 1.94 but gone by 15.3.94.

'A' No.	AIRCRAFT TYPE	SERIAL	DETAILS
A2606	Whirlwind HAS.7	XN305	To Class II at Lee-on-Solent 5.3.70 (ex Fleetlands). Engine No E4621. With AES Lee-on-Solent by 7.70, coded 'PO/516' (ex 771 Sqdn Portland). To Wroughton by road 28.5.80 and in use for fire-fighting 6.80. Current 1982 but gone by 1984.
A2607	Whirlwind HAS.7	XK944	To Class II at Lee-on-Solent (or Arbroath) 5.3.70 (ex Fleetlands). Engine No E4622. With AES Lee-on-Solent by 7.70, coded *"PO/86"* (spurious - ex 'LM/86' Lossiemouth SAR Flt). Left Lee-on-Solent by road 5.4.78 and arrived at Brunel Technical College, Bristol 6.4.78 and believed still there 1984. To 617 Sqdn ATC at Malpas School, Cheshire by 2.87 (on 19.2.87 ?). Current.
A2608	Gannet ECM.6	XA459	To Class I at Lee-on-Solent 2.6.66, uncoded (ex 831 Sqdn Watton). To NASU Culdrose 10.7.68. Downgraded to Class II at SAH Culdrose 31.11.70. Engine No E4623, later E4664. Allocated 'SAH-7' in mid-1971 but not carried. Taxyable. Current 1977 but no engine. Dismantled by 23.11.78 and transported to South Wales APS at Rhoose 4.4.79. Left late-1989 for private owner in Gloucester area and damaged en route. Auctioned 8.11.90 and sold to private owner in Cirencester. Current.
A2609	Wessex HAS.1	XM329	To Class I at Arbroath 11.2.68 (ex 737 Sqdn Portland). To Fleetlands by 3.69. Downgraded to Class II at Lee-on-Solent 5.4.71. No engine. At AES Lee-on-Solent by 1974, coded 'PO/533' (ex 737 Sqdn). Current 5.86 but dumped at Lee-on-Solent by 19.7.86. To Predannack by 28.11.86 as 'PO/533'. Current as 'PO/33' 10.92, lying on its side, and only very burnt remains by 5.93.
A2610	Sea Vixen FAW.2	XN647	To Class I (ex NASU Yeovilton). Downgraded to Class II at SAH Culdrose 25.2.71, coded 'VL/707' (ex 766 Sqdn Yeovilton). Engine Nos E4624/4625. Marked 'SAH-10' and 'VL/-' with 766 Sqdn marks by 7.73 (taxyable). Derelict 1977. Sold to Cornwall Aeronautical Park, Helston and towed there 4.6.78 on permanent loan, restored as 'VL/707' with 766 Sqdn marks. Current (now Flambards Village Theme Park).
A2611	Sea Vixen FAW.2	XJ575	To Class I (ex NASU Yeovilton). Downgraded to Class II at SAH Culdrose 25.2.71, coded 'VL/713' (ex 766 Sqdn Yeovilton). Engine Nos E4626/4627. Marked 'SAH-13' by 7.74 and current 1977 marked 'VL/-' with 766 Sqdn markings. WFU near fire pits by 12.80. Sold to Cornwall Aero Park and towed there 23.10.83 as 'VL/-'. Scrapped at Flambards Triple Theme Park 12.88 and cockpit section preserved at Long Marston, Warwicks by 7.89 but moved on to Wellesbourne Mountford, Warwicks 24.3.90. Current.
A2612	Sea Vixen FAW.2 [1]	XN650	To Class II at Lee-on-Solent 11.70. Engine Nos E4628/4629, later re-allocated to replacement A2612. *[Note: A2620 and A2639 were also allocated to this aircraft].*
A2612	Sea Vixen FAW.2 [2]	XJ521	*[Number re-allocated after vacated by XN650]* To Class I at Lee-on-Solent 8.12.70. Downgraded to Class II 10.2.71. Engine Nos E4628/4629. Engine E4628 later exchanged with E4631 from A2613. Sold to Brunel University, Bristol 16.5.73. Engines sold to Marine Salvage, Fleetlands.
A2613	Sea Vixen FAW.2	XN706	To Class II at Lee-on-Solent 26.5.71, coded 'E/127' (ex 899 Sqdn Yeovilton). Engine Nos E4630/4631. E4631 later exchanged with E4628 from A2612. Flew to Farnborough 9.1.76 after restoration by an RAE team, on MoD(PE) charge for use in the Sea Vixen drone programme. Dumped at Farnborough by 9.84.
A2614	Whirlwind HAS.7	XN314	To Class I at Lee-on-Solent 26.3.65 (ex Fleetlands), and believed with AES by 1966, uncoded. Downgraded to Class II and SOC 6.2.70. Engine No E4632. To Wroughton by road 1.12.80. To Lee-on-Solent by road 29.11.83 for BDR training. Outside the old RNHU hangars by 1.84 and dumped by 3.85. Arrived Predannack by road 8.10.85, and last noted 5.88.

'A' No.	AIRCRAFT TYPE	SERIAL	DETAILS
A2615	Wessex HAS.3	XT256	To Class II at Lee-on-Solent 5.4.71 (ex MoD(PE) charge). Engine No E4633, later removed and fitted to A2618. To AES Lee-on-Solent 18.11.71 and current 1977 without engine. Engine No E4633 refitted 21.1.80 (ex A2618). To BDR training and derelict near dump by 9.2.87 but in 'Overlord' hangar 7.87. Sold in Sweden by 3.88, reportedly for the making of a film.
A2616	Sea Vixen FAW.2	XN651	To Class II at SAH Culdrose 29.7.71 and flown in that day from Yeovilton, coded 'VL/705' (ex 890 Sqdn Yeovilton). Engine Nos E4634/4635. Taxable. Marked 'SAH-11' and 'VL/-' by 7.73 and current 1977 with 890 Sqdn markings as 'VL/-'. Dismantled in early 1978 and dumped at SAH fire pits by 9.78, minus nose section, to at least 7.80 . To Predannack by 12.80. The nose was sold to the Winbolt Collection at Pucklechurch, near Bristol [date ?]. Current 10.93 but moved to Communications & Electronics Museum, Bletchley Park, Bucks by 3.96.
A2617	Buccaneer S.1	XN954	To Class II (ex NASU Yeovilton). Engine Nos E4636/4637. To SAH Culdrose 29.7.71, coded 'LM/631' (ex 736 Sqdn Lossiemouth). Engines transferred to XN967/A2627. Left for HMS Royal Arthur 18.4.74 and "accidentally" pushed of the stern of HMS Ark Royal for a flight safety film 4.74. [The date of this event was given as 14.4.74 in the original monograph but XN954 was seen leaving Culdrose on 18.4.74; the correct date of the Buccaneer's demise is not known].
A2618	Wessex HAS.3	XP116	To Class II at AES Lee-on-Solent 28.1.72, coded '-/520' (ex 737 Sqdn Portland). No engine but later fitted with E4633 from A2615; refitted to A2615 21.1.80. Authorised to be reduced to spares and produce 2.9.80 but still current 5.81. Noted 2.83 in the metalwork school, minus tail, and believed last noted there 7.85 but not confirmed.
A2619	Kestrel FGA.1	XS695	To Class II at RNEC Manadon, probably in 5.73. No engine. Rebuilt for RAF Museum, Hendon with wings of XS696 (ex HSA Brough). [Wings from XS695 to XP984/A2658 at RNEC Manadon]. To SAH Culdrose 11.4.78 on loan. Repainted in Sea Harrier type colour scheme by 7.79. Allocated 'SAH-6' and marked '6' on the tail by 7.83. Suffered nosewheel collapse 26.4.91 and allocated for return to RAF Museum. To open store in fire area on 18.6.91 but moved to inside store by 29.2.92. Left Culdrose by road 11.5.93 for Lee-on-Solent for work prior to moving to Cardington by 2.94 for restoration to static display. Current.
A2620	Sea Vixen FAW.2	XN650	[Formerly A2612] Allocation intended for use at Culdrose. Engine Nos E4645/4646. Became A2639 instead.
A2621	Sea Vixen FAW.2	XJ584	To Class GRB at SAH Culdrose 18.2.74 (ex Belfast). Engine Nos E4647/4648. Marked 'SAH-16' by 11.74 and current 1977. WFU near fire pits by 7.81. Sold to Cornwall Aero Park and towed there 23.10.83 for display in the car park. Scrapped at (what was by then) Flambards Triple Theme Park in 1.89.
A2622	Sea Vixen FAW.2	XJ602	To Class GRB at SAH Culdrose 28.9.73 (ex Belfast). Engine Nos E4649/4650. Allocated 'SAH-14' but not carried. Sold to Flight Refuelling Ltd for drone conversion and, after refurbishment, flown to Hurn 15.5.79. Scrapped 3.84.
A2623	Sea Vixen FAW.2	XN697	To Class GRB at SAH Culdrose 21.3.74 and flown in from Sydenham that day (ex Belfast), coded 'H/254' (ex 893 Sqdn Yeovilton). Engine Nos E4651/4652. Allocated 'SAH-15' but not carried (taxyable). Sold to Flight Refuelling Ltd for drone conversion and, after refurbishment, was flown to Hurn on 18.12.78. Scrapped 3.84.
A2624	Sea Vixen FAW.2	XN692	To Class GRB at SAH Culdrose 7.2.74 (ex Belfast), having been flown in from Belfast, uncoded. Engine Nos E4653/4654. Marked 'SAH-17' by 11.74. In use for snow melting 1.85! To Yeovilton 18.7.85 as a planned gate guardian and stored outside rear of FAA Museum. To dope shop and repainted as "E/125" in 899 Sqdn marks (spurious) by 3.5.88. Preserved outside FONAC (later FONA) HQ by 30.7.88.

'A' No.	AIRCRAFT TYPE	SERIAL	DETAILS
A2624	Sea Vixen FAW.2	XN692	(contd) Moved to fire station circa 26.7.93 and out on to airfield 7.10.93 for BDR use. Current 7.94 but for sale 11.94. Cut up for scrap and removed 15.2.95 to Hanningfield Metals, Stock, Essex (last noted 11.95).
A2625	Whirlwind HAS.7	XL846	To Class GRB at Lee-on-Solent 22.1.74 (ex Wroughton), coded '85' (ex Lossiemouth SAR Flt). Engine originally Class GRA and therefore given no 'E' number, but later downgraded to Class GRB and numbered E4696. Still at AES 7.80 but dumped by 9.80 and to Wroughton by road 1.12.80. Returned to Lee-on-Solent 19.2.83 for BDR training. Dumped by 3.84. Arrived Yeovilton by road 19.7.84 and dumped. To Predannack by road, arriving 19.2.86. Current 7.91 but expired by 10.92.
A2626	Whirlwind HAS.7	XL847	To Class GRB at AES Lee-on-Solent 23.1.74 (ex Wroughton), coded '83' (ex Lossiemouth SAR Flt). Engine originally Class GRA therefore given no 'E' number, but later downgraded to Class GRB and numbered E4697. Reported for sale in 1980 and on the dump at Lee-on-Solent later that year, still marked '-/(6)83'. At Middle Wallop by 2.81 and used by AETW for Battle Damage Repair training by 7.82. Dumped at Middle Wallop by 7.84 and still recognisable 9.95.
A2627	Buccaneer S.1	XN967	To Class I (later GRA) at Lossiemouth 27.11.69 (ex NASU Lossiemouth). Destined for Royal Scottish Museum, Edinburgh but not taken up. Downgraded to Class GRB at SAH Culdrose 2.5.74 on arrival from Lossiemouth. Engine Nos E4636/4637 removed. Allocated 'SAH-20' but not carried. Used by the Air Command Driving School. Towed to Cornwall Aeronautical Park, Helston 4.6.78 (later Flambards Village Theme Park) and painted as 'E/103' in 800 Sqdn marks. For sale 5.93 and scrapped on site 1.94, the cockpit section going to a private collector and the rest to a yard in Bodmin. Nose to Fleckney, Leics .94 and on to the Muckleburgh Collection, Weybourne, Norfolk by 8.95. Current.
A2628	Jet Provost T.4	XP558	To Class GRB at SAH Culdrose 22.5.74 (ex RAE Bedford), coded '20' on nose-wheel door (ex CAW, *"Macaws"* aerobatic team colour scheme). Engine No E4658. Allocated 'SAH-12' but not carried. To St Athan 19.3.79 and allocated 8627M (qv) with 4 SoTT.
A2629	Whirlwind HAS.7	XM667	To Class GRB at AES Lee-on-Solent 12.6.74, coded 'CU/56' (ex 705 Sqdn Culdrose). Engine originally Class GRA therefore given no 'E' number, but later downgraded to Class GRB and numbered E4694. To Wroughton by road 27.11.80. To Lee-on-Solent by road 1.12.83. Dumped by 7.84 and last noted 3.85. To Predannack as 'CU/56' 11.9.86. Last noted 5.88.
A2630	Whirlwind HAS.7	XL853	To Class GRB at AES Lee-on-Solent by road 12.6.74 (ex Wroughton), uncoded. Engine originally Class GRA therefore given no 'E' number, but later downgraded to Class GRB and numbered E4695. Dumped at Lee-on-Solent by 10.80. Marked 'LS/-' at some stage. To Middle Wallop for BDR training (authorised 20.2.81) and stored at Andover in 1984 for AAC Museum. To Southampton Hall of Aviation by 23.8.86 and on display at Ocean Village shopping centre, Southampton by 12.88. Preserved at Fleetlands Museum as 'LS/-' by 6.89 and current.
A2631	Sioux HT.2	XV312	To Class GRB at Fleetlands by road 6.11.74 for Apprentices Training School (ex Wroughton), uncoded (ex ARWF). Engine No E4662. To Milford Aviation 9.3.76. [See also 8430M]
A2632	Sea Hawk FGA.6	WV903	To 1 SoTT Halton 20.1.71 as 8153M (ex Belfast). To Class GRB at SAH Culdrose 17.12.74. Engine No E4666. Allocated 'SAH-3' and marked '3' by 3.75. Taxyable. Current as '3' 1977, with Halton instructional number 'I-228' on tail and still marked 8153M. Repainted as 'C/128' in 801 Sqdn marks by 7.81. Recoded '5' on the tail by 5.82 and '8' by 7.83. To Lee-on-Solent by road 9-10.5.85 and stored, still coded 'C/128' and '8'. For sale 11.94 but withdrawn, reportedly to be used in exchange for Sea Fury spares from Germany for the RNHF.

'A' No.	AIRCRAFT TYPE	SERIAL	DETAILS
A2632	Sea Hawk FGA.6	WV903	(contd) Loaded on to a lorry 24.5.95 and moved to BAe Dunsfold (for restoration of WV908/A2660). To Yeovilton 15.4.97, still 'C/128', and placed in storage compound. Current.
A2633	Sea Hawk FGA.6	XE369	[Previously A2580] To 1 SoTT Halton 30.12.70 as 8158M (ex Arbroath). To Class GRB at SAH Culdrose 17.12.74. Allocated 'SAH-5' and marked '5' by 3.75. Taxyable. Current as '5' 1977, with Halton instructional number 'I-223' on tail and still marked as 8158M. WFU for spares by 12.81 at least. Left Culdrose by road 22.2.83 for Lee-on-Solent and in use for BDR training 4.83. Parked near the dump by 12.83. To Yeovilton 7.5.85 as '5' and dumped that day. Badly burnt by 3.90 and burnt front fuselage only by 12.93. Current 1.94 but gone by 15.3.94.
A2634	Sea Hawk FGA.6	WV794	To 1 SoTT Halton 20.1.71 as 8152M (ex Belfast). To Class GRB at SAH Culdrose 17.12.74, with Halton instructional number 'I-227' on tail and still marked 8152M. Engine No E4668. Allocated 'SAH-1' by 7.76 but not carried. Taxyable. Reduced to spares (per letter 3.10.79). Sold to Airwork Services Training, Perth for GI on 22.10.80 and delivered to AST 10.80. Fate unknown.
A2635	Sea Hawk FGA.6	XE339	To 1 SoTT Halton 19.1.71 as 8156M (ex Fleetlands). To Class GRB at SAH Culdrose 17.12.74. Allocated 'SAH-6' and marked '6' by 1.76. Engine No E4669. Taxyable. Current as '6' 1977, with Halton instructional number 'I-224' on tail and still marked 8156M. Repainted as 'E/149' with 803 Sqdn marks by 7.77. Code '6' re-applied on the tail by 7.82 and '7' by 7.83. To Lee-on-Solent by road 6.6.85 (via Yeovilton) and stored, still coded 'E/149' and '7'. Withdrawn from sale 11.94 to be used as a spares source for RNHF. Noted 5.95 but to BAe Dunsfold by 10.6.95 (for restoration of WV908/A2660). To Yeovilton 17.4.97, still 'E/149', and placed in storage compound. Current.
A2636	Sea Hawk FGA.6	XE390	To 1 SoTT Halton 19.1.71 as 8157M (ex Fleetlands). To Class GRB at SAH Culdrose 6.2.75. Allocated 'SAH-4' and marked '4' by 1.76. Taxyable. Engine No E4670. Current as '4' 1977, with Halton instructional number 'I-225' on tail and still marked 8157M. WFU for spares by 12.81 at least. Left Culdrose by road 1.3.83 and arrived Lee-on-Solent 2.3.83 for BDR training. Used as spares for WV911 and in a poor state by 1.84. Dumped at Lee-on-Solent by 6.84 and last noted 7.84. Gone by 1985, having been sold in Canada.
A2637	Sea Hawk FGA.6	WV797	To 1 SoTT Halton 12.3.71 as 8155M (ex Belfast). To Class GRB at SAH Culdrose 6.2.75. Engine No E4671. Allocated 'SAH-2' by 7.76 but not carried. Taxyable. Current 1977, with Halton instructional number 'I-230' on tail and still marked 8155M. Reduced to spares by 3.10.79. Sold to Airwork Services Training at Perth on 22.10.80. To Midland Air Museum, Baginton 25.1.86 and current, coded '-/491'.
A2638	Sioux HT.2	XV317	To Class GRB at Wroughton 28.1.75, coded 'Z' (ex CFS). Engine No E4672. Current 1977 for mobile display purposes. Sold to a private buyer and left 13.11.78, later becoming G-WHIT.
A2639	Sea Vixen FAW.2	XN650	[Formerly A2612 and A2629, but new allocation given as previous issues were overlooked] Officially to Class II at SAH Culdrose 3.3.72, but actually flew into Culdrose from RNAY Belfast 28.9.73. Marked 'SAH-12' by 7.73, and used mainly for spares recovery. Engine Nos E4645/4646. Derelict by 1977 and used for spares. RNAY Belfast Stn Flt insignia of red hand of Ulster in white circle carried on tail. Dismantled by 23.11.78 and transported to Rhoose for South Wales APS 25.4.79 (the wings being noted at Lee-on-Solent 24.4.79). To Bruntingthorpe, Leics 15.2.96 and reduced to nose section. Current.
A2640	Wessex HAS.1	XP155	Ditched mid-1967 as '-/531' of 819 Sqdn Ballykelly. Salvaged and wreck to Arbroath for instructional purposes by 7.68. Coded "AB/31" (spurious). No engine. At Lee-on-Solent 7.71. To SAH Culdrose 28.2.72 and allocated 'SAH-21' but not carried. Used by the Air Command Driving School. Temporarily listed as Class DRB [see

'A' No.	AIRCRAFT TYPE	SERIAL	DETAILS
A2640	Wessex HAS.1	XP155	(contd) *Introduction - Airframe Classifications]*. WFU near fire pits by 12.80. To burning area of SAH fire pits by 2.82 but this was cancelled and instead to Lee-on-Solent 3.82 for airframe repair training; there are no subsequent reports of this aircraft.
A2641	Wessex HAS.1	XL729	Development aircraft for Wessex HAS.3; crashed 1967. With FAA Museum Yeovilton by 10.69. No engine. To SAH Culdrose 3.71. Allocated 'SAH-22' but not carried. Current 1977, being officially held for FAA Museum. Presumably surplus to requirements and dumped at the fire pits by 19.9.78. Very burnt by 7.80.
A2642	Whirlwind HAS.7	XL836	To Class GRB at Fleetlands 6.5.75 (ex Wroughton), coded *"FL/65"* (spurious - ex '65' 705 Sqdn Culdrose). No engine. Preserved on gate at Fleetlands by 7.76. Replaced by A2691 in 1980 but remained at Fleetlands. Loaned to Fareham Technical College on 5.11.81, but was vandalised and returned to Fleetlands in 1982. To Predannack as *"FL/65"* 2.8.83. Last noted 5.88.
A2643	Whirlwind HAR.9	XN311	To Class GRB at Fleetlands Apprentices Training School 18.9.75, with tail of HAS.7 XN297 and nose "cap" from HAR.9 XL880. Engine No E4698. Current 1977 but painted as *"XN297"* by 6.79. To Lee-on-Solent for BDR training by 7.84. Dumped by 7.85 but gone 5.86. To HMS Phoenix Fire School by 7.86. To Lee-on-Solent for BDR training and derelict near dump by 9.2.87. Broken up by 23.6.87. To HMS Royal Arthur, Corsham 7.7.87 (no engine). *Re-allocated A2760 as "XN297" in 1988 (see later)*.
A2644	Whirlwind HAS.7	XN358	To Class GRB at Air Medical School, Seafield Park 10.6.75 (ex Wroughton), for instruction of medical assistants in CASEVAC. No engine. [Parts reported on Fleetlands dump 6.76]. Dumped at Seafield Park by 6.80 (possibly in 1976). To Lee-on-Solent by 8.80 and dumped. To Yeovilton dump by 9.81. Burnt hulk last noted 7.82.
A2645	Sea Hawk F.1	WF225	To Culdrose for display purposes 4.6.58 (ex Airwork FRU Hurn). No engine. Mounted at Culdrose barrack main gate in 7.58, coded *"CU/-"* (spurious). Removed by 7.70 at the start of the airfield rebuild and stored. Class GRB in 1975. Remounted at airfield main gate by 7.81. Removed for repainting 4.3.83 and remounted by 6.83, coded 'CU/-' and with black fin bullet (ex 802 Sqdn). Current 9.90. Repainted without code 7.91 and current 9.91. *Re-allocated A2623 [2] in 1993 (see later)*.
A2646	Whirlwind HAR.10	XK988	[Originally a Mk.2] To Class GRB at AES Lee-on-Solent 5.6.75 (ex Wroughton, via Fleetlands), coded 'D' (ex 103 Sqdn Tengah). Engine No E4691. To Museum of Army Flying, Middle Wallop by 10.81 for possible reconversion to original Mk.2 standard, but not proceeded with. Loaned to Britannia Park at Ilkeston, Derby in 1985, but this venture failed. Returned to Middle Wallop in 1987. To Fleetlands Museum by 2.90 and current 10.91, still coded 'D'. To AAC Museum, Middle Wallop by 8.5.92 and current.
A2647	Wasp HAS.1	XS463	To Class GRB at AES Lee-on-Solent 24.6.75 (ex Wroughton, via Fleetlands). No engine. Stripped 11.80 for BDR training and placed outside. Allocated to British Rotorcraft Museum 30.12.80 and transferred to Fleetlands 19.6.81. To Predannack 26.1.82 minus tail boom, and last noted 8.83. Tail boom fitted to XT431 at Fleetlands and noted there 2.82 as 'XS463' coded *"RO/601"* (spurious). Delivered as such to the BRM (later IHM) at Weston-super-Mare 1.83 and current.
A2648	Wessex HAS.1	XS125	To Class I (later GRA) at AES Lee-on-Solent 14.12.71, coded 'PO/517' (ex 771 Sqdn Portland). Downgraded to Class GRB 2.7.75. Engine No E4692. Current 7.84 but dumped by 9.84, marked '-/517'. Left by road 5.9.85 to Yeovilton and dumped. To Predannack by road, arriving 21.2.86. Minus tail pylon by 12.86. Current 7.91 lying on its side, but expired by 10.92.

'A' No.	AIRCRAFT TYPE	SERIAL	DETAILS
A2649	Wessex HAS.1	XS869	To Class I (later GRA) at AES Lee-on-Solent 14.12.71 (ex Fleetlands), coded 'PO/508' (ex 771 Sqdn Portland). Downgraded to Class GRB 2.7.75. Engine No E4693. Current 1977. Engine removed and to Air Medical School at Seafield Park by 10.80 to at least 6.90. The AMS closed 9.91 - fate?
A2650	Wessex HAS.1	XP160	To Class GRB at SAH Culdrose 20.8.75, coded 'CU/521' (ex 771 Sqdn Culdrose). No engine. Allocated 'SAH-24' but not carried. Minus rotors and many panels by 1977. With Air Command Driving School, Culdrose by 9.81. Left by road 13.9.88 to AES Lee-on-Solent (received 22.9.88). Dumped by 6.91 and current 7.92. Arrived Predannack by road 20.10.92 and current 5.93, lying on its side. *Re-allocated A2628 [2] in 1993 (see later)*.
A2651	Whirlwind HAS.7	XG596	To Class GRB at Wroughton 31.7.75 (ex Wroughton). Engine No E4699. To British Rotorcraft Museum (later International Helicopter Museum), Weston-super-Mare by road 12.7.77. By road from IHM to Westlands, Yeovil 1.11.93 for survey and refurbishment by the craft apprentices. In open store at Yeovil by 10.96.
A2652	Whirlwind HAS.7	XN261	To Class GRB at AES Lee-on-Solent 15.11.75 (ex Wroughton), coded '61' (ex 705 Sqdn Culdrose). Engine No E4704. To open store outside MARTSU 10.80. Dumped by 11.83, minus boom. Last noted 7.84.
A2653	Whirlwind HAS.7	XK943	To Class GRB at AES Lee-on-Solent 13.11.75 (ex Wroughton), coded '57' (ex 705 Sqdn Culdrose). Engine No E4705. Current 1977. To open store outside MARTSU 10.80 to at least 11.82. To BDR training at Abingdon by 9.83, allocated 8796M.
A2654	Whirlwind HAS.7	XN302	To Class GRA at AES Lee-on-Solent 3.4.75 (ex NASU Culdrose), and used at first for vibration tests at Southampton University. Downgraded to Class GRB 11.75 at Lee-on-Solent. Engine No E4706. To FCR training at Lee-on-Solent fire station 22.5.80, marked *"LS/-"* (spurious) by 7.84. Transferred to the dump by 15.10.86. To HMS Royal Arthur, Corsham, Wilts on 7.7.87. *Re-allocated A2758 in 1988 (see later)*.
A2655	Buccaneer S.1	XN953	To Class GRB at SAH Culdrose 18.11.75 (ex 8182M at 4 SoTT St Athan, via Falmouth docks). Engine Nos E4710/4711. Allocated 'SAH-23' but not carried. Was to have gone to Abingdon in 1982, but allocated for sale (or fire pits) instead. WFU by 7.83 and placed in open store. Engines removed and placed in the fire pits by 1.7.87 but not burnt. Wings removed and airlifted to Predannack by 7 Sqdn Chinook HC.1 ZA712/ER on 23.8.88. Wings then refitted. Current for fire-fighting practice 5.93, newly burnt. Re-allocated A2600 [3] in 1993 *(see later)*.
A2656	Wasp HAS.1	XS476	To Class I at Culdrose 26.4.72 (ex Westland Aircraft) for Engineering Training Section. Downgraded to Class GRB at Engine Training School, Portland 12.75. Expired on Portland dump soon after 2.81. Boom to A2703/XT441 at Wroughton 9.83.
A2657	Lynx 1-07	XX469	To Class GRB at AES Lee-on-Solent 3.3.76 (ex Westland Aircraft, Cat.5 22.11.72). No engine. Hulk by dumped by 4.78 and gone by 1979. To Westland's Customer Training School, Sherborne by 1981. To Lancashire Fire Brigade HQ, Lancaster [date ?]. A planned swop for Lynx test rig RG-05 at the Helicopter Museum of Great Britain, Blackpool Airport in 1986 never transpired, although the registration G-BNCL was reserved in 1987. Assumed to have expired at Lancaster.
A2658	Hawker P.1127	XP984	To Class GRB at RNEC Manadon 12.2.76 (ex RAE Bedford). Engine No E4708. Fitted with wings from XS695/A2619. For disposal by 6.91 and noted 7.91 with damaged nose. Current 6.92. To Lee-on-Solent by 22.11.94 for sale by auction 26.11.94. Under restoration at BAe Dunsfold by 1.95. Current.
A2659	Sea King HAS.1	XV669	To Class GRB at Culdrose 29.9.76 for Engineering Training Section (ex AIU Lee-on-Solent, crashed 31.3.76), coded '-/410' (ex 820 Sqdn Culdrose). Engine Nos E4716/4717. Affectionately known as *"Mr*

'A' No.	AIRCRAFT TYPE	SERIAL	DETAILS
A2659	Sea King HAS.1	XV669	(contd) *Walter"* and refurbished 5.82 for weapons electrical training in the Duke of Cornwall building. Marked *"Mr Walter"* and coded '10' only by 3.87. The name stands for Mechanical Radio Weapons And Electrical Training Engineering Rig. Current.
A2660	Sea Hawk FGA.6	WV908	To 1 SoTT Halton 20.1.71 as 8154M (ex Belfast). To Class GRB at SAH Culdrose 28.10.76. Engine No E4719. Rebuilt to flying condition to TAE 22.5.78 and flew 23.5.78, coded 'A/188' (former 806 Sqdn code). To RN Historic Flight, Yeovilton 28.9.82. By road to BAe Dunsfold 17.5.95 for restoration. Flown back to RNHF at Yeovilton on 24.10.96, still 'A/188'. Grounded 7.97 with a cracked engine pipe. Current.
A2661	Sea Hawk FGA.6	WV795	To 1 SoTT Halton 20.1.71 as 8151M (ex Belfast). To Class GRB at SAH Culdrose 16.3.77. Engine No E4720. WOC 19.12.77 for spares and produce in support of WV908/A2660. Fuselage to South Wales APS at Rhoose 6.9.78. To Bob Poulter at Peasedown St John, Avon by 11.81. To Jet Heritage, Hurn 10.89 and under restoration 11.93 following sale to a new owner in Cyprus. Still at Hurn 3.95.
A2662	Sea Hawk FB.5	WF299	[Previously A2509] To Class GRB at Culdrose 6.77 (ex 8164M at Catterick) and probably arrived 8.77 via Topcliffe. Engine No E4718. Sold to St Agnes Model Village, Cornwall by 11.77 and there by 6.78. To Cornwall Aeronautical Park Ltd, Helston by road 20.10.83. Repainted by 9.88 as *"WN105"* in 738 Sqdn *"Red Devils"* aerobatic colours. For disposal 11.91 and to Graham Revill collection, Birlingham, Hereford & Worcester by 3.93. Current.
A2663	Whirlwind HAR.9	XN309	[Previously Class GRA - see earlier] To Class GRB at Wroughton 4.10.77 (ex Wroughton store), coded 'CU/590' (ex Culdrose Stn Flt). Delivered to SAH Culdrose 26.10.77. No engine. To Park Aviation, Faygate, Sussex by 27.5.80 (late 1979?). To Lasham 7.81 for Second World War Aircraft Preservation Society, still coded 'CU/590'. To Thatcham, Berkshire by 7.89. To Casement, Eire 8.3.90 and dumped. Possibly to the navy dockyard at Haulbowline, Cork for submergence training.
A2664	Sea King HAS.1	XV644	To Class GRB at AES Lee-on-Solent 18.10.77 (ex RAE Farnborough). Coded '-/664' (once 'PO/664' 737 Sqdn Portland). No engines. Allocated to spares and produce 9.80 but still at Lee-on-Solent 10.81. Sectioned by 6.88 and with Metalwork School 12.89. Hulk to dump by 23.10.91 and current 7.92. Arrived Predannack by road 28.10.92 and current 5.93 lying on its side. *[Note: XV644 was not officially listed in the 1988 re-allocations but was re-allocated A2615 [3] in 1993 (see later)].*
A2665	Whirlwind HAR.9	XL839	To Class GRA. To Class GRB at Lee-on-Solent 18.11.77 (ex Wroughton), coded 'CU/588' (ex Culdrose Stn Flt). Allocated for use with the FAA Touring Exhibition Team. No engine. Dumped at Lee-on-Solent by 10.82 as 'CU/588'. Remains only by 3.83 and perished by early 1984.
A2666	Wessex HAS.1	XS872	[Previously Class I for a time - see earlier] To Class GRB with Apprentices Training School, Fleetlands 19.1.78 (ex Electrical Research Association Ltd, Leatherhead for studies on aerial coupling). Once 'CU/572' 706 Sqdn Culdrose. No engine. Current 6.84 fitted with rear fuselage from HAS.3 XM331, with its own rear fuselage nearby. Almost certainly the aircraft marked *"XS873"* (see A2686) which arrived at Wroughton by road 29.4.85 for the dump. Rear fuselage of XS872 again noted at Fleetlands 6.85 and last noted 6.86.
A2667	Gannet AEW.3	XP226	To Lee-on-Solent 21.9.78 (ex Lossiemouth), coded 'LM/-'. Issued to HMS Dryad, Southwick 28.3.79 but allocated to the gate 9.6.79 and noted late-1979 coded 'E/073'. No engine. Removed to Lee-on-Solent 28.3.82 and awaiting sale 6.82. To Newark Air Museum by 17.11.82 and current, still 'E/073'.

'A' No.	AIRCRAFT TYPE	SERIAL	DETAILS
A2668	Wessex HAS.1	XS885	To Class GRB at SAH Culdrose 5.9.78 (ex NASU Culdrose), coded 'PO/512' (ex 772 Sqdn Portland). No engine. Minus serials by 3.87. Transferred to NASU Culdrose on 1.3.88 for preparation as replacement for XS888 (RNEF Roving Winching Display Aircraft). Completed and resprayed by 15.7.88, minus serials and spuriously marked "CU/12". Kept on SAH charge and used on dummy deck by 9.88. *Re-allocated A2631 [2] in 1993 (see later).*
A2669	Wessex HAS.1	XP149	To Class I (later GRA) at AES Lee-on-Solent 14.12.71, coded 'CU/574' (ex 706 Sqdn Culdrose). Downgrading to Class GRB requested 5.7.76. To Class GRB at AES Lee-on-Solent 7.79, to at least 12.82. No engine. Used for BDR training by 9.84 and dumped by 7.85. Left by road 2.5.86 and arrived Predannack 7.5.86, still 'CU/574' (ex 706 Sqdn Culdrose). Last noted 5.88 in burnt state.
A2670	Wessex HAS.1	XS128	To Class I (later GRA) at AES Lee-on-Solent 11.9.70 (ex Fleetlands), coded 'PO/437' (ex 737 Sqdn Portland). Downgrading to Class GRB requested 5.7.76. To Class GRB at AES Lee-on-Solent 9.78. No engine. "Despatch to 26.2.80" (sic). To Salisbury Plain by road 11.7.86 for explosive trials, returning 29.7.86 in overall grey colour scheme. To BDR training, but in the 846 Sqdn hangar at Yeovilton by 1.10.86. To Yeovilton BDR training compound 13.10.86 (minus rear fuselage) coded '-/437'. Moved to the dump on 5.11.92 and current, upside down. [NB Rear fuselage reported at HMS Gannet (Prestwick) by 16.11.87.] *Re-allocated A2690 [2] post-1993 (see later).*
A2671	Wessex HAS.1	XS867	To Class I (later GRA) at RNEC Manadon 19.11.70. Engine Class GRA (no 'E' number). To Class GRB 9.78 at RNEC Manadon. No engine. To SAH Culdrose 26.2.80. WFU by 30.1.82 and placed into open store beside fire pits. Cancelled and instead to Lee-on-Solent 3.82 for airframe repair training. Engine No E4726 fitted there. Dumped at Lee-on-Solent by 4.82 and gone by 11.83.
A2672	Wasp HAS.1	XS537	To Class I (later GRA) at Portland 12.2.72. Downgrading to Class GRB requested. To Class GRB at Portland 11.78, for use as Engineering Weapons Trainer on arming drills. No engine. Coded "-/582" but believed panel transferred as it did not serve with 706 Sqdn. To Portland dump by 7.86 and minus boom 11.86. Current 4.88 but removed by road sometime prior to 11.91.
A2673	Sea Prince T.1	WF122	To Class GRB at SAH Culdrose 1.79 for Dummy Deck, coded 'CU/575' (ex 750 Sqdn Culdrose). Engine Nos E4727/4728. With Air Command Driving School by 9.81, but found to be unsuitable and placed in storage. By 6.82 awaiting disposal and for sale. Towed to Cornwall Aeronautical Park, Helston 31.10.82 (now Flambards Village Theme Park). Current, still coded 'CU/575'.
A2674	Sea Prince T.1	WF125	To Class GRB at SAH Culdrose 1.79, coded 'CU/-' (ex 'CU/576' 750 Sqdn Culdrose). Flown out to Predannack 20.2.79 for crash rescue training, with code painted out but 'CU' on fin. Engines removed. Weathering revealed code but removed deckletters and noted 5.93 as '-/576'. Unmarked hulk last noted 5.94.
A2675	Wessex HAS.1	XS881	To FAA Museum Yeovilton 19.7.79, coded 'CU/046' (ex 771 Sqdn Culdrose but still with HMS Ark Royal SAR Flt code). Taken off RN charge 1.80. Engine No E4729. Left by road 21.1.88 for Wroughton store. Exchanged by FAA Museum for HU.5 A2766/XS508 (ex Lee-on-Solent) and allocated to ETS Lee-on-Solent. Re-allocated to BDR at Yeovilton and delivered by road from Wroughton on 29.6.93. Placed in the FCR reserve compound by 1.94, but to fire pits 6.96 still as 'CU/046'. *Re-allocated A2688 [2] post-1993 (see later).*
A2676	Gnat T.1	XR572	To Class GRB at SAH Culdrose 11.10.79 (ex "Red Arrows", flown in from Kemble 17.9.79). Engine No E4732. Allocated 'SAH-3' and marked '3' on fin by 11.79. Taxyable. WFU by 23.4.86 and put into open storage near fire pits. Sold to Arnold Glass and left by road 28.10.87 for Leavesden. To USA and registered N572XR.

'A' No.	AIRCRAFT TYPE	SERIAL	DETAILS
A2677	Gnat T.1	XR993	To Class GRB at SAH Culdrose 11.10.79 (ex *"Red Arrows"*, flown in from Kemble 17.9.79). Engine No E4733. Allocated 'SAH-4' and marked '4' on fin by 11.79. Taxable. WFU by 23.4.86 and put into open storage near fire pits. Moved back to 'A' site 3.2.87, dismantled and departed in crates 20.2.87 for the USA (tail section noted in shipping agents yard in Southall, London 15.2.88). Registered N3XR, w/o 10.1.91. *[Also allocated 8878M for display at RAF Museum but not taken up].*
A2678	Gnat T.1	XR955	To Class GRB at SAH Culdrose 11.10.79 (ex *"Red Arrows"*, flown in from Kemble 17.9.79). Engine No E4731. Allocated 'SAH-2' and marked '2' on fin by 11.79. Taxable. WFU by 23.4.86 and put into open storage near fire pits. Sold to Arnold Glass and left by road 29.10.87 for Leavesden (the tail leaving on 17.11.87). Nothing further known.
A2679	Gnat T.1	XP535	To Class GRB at SAH Culdrose 11.10.79 (ex *"Red Arrows"*, flown in from Kemble 17.9.79). Engine No E4730. Allocated 'SAH-1' and marked '1' on fin by 11.79. Taxable. WFU by 23.4.86 and stored in SAH hangar. Put into open storage near fire pits on 3.2.87. Sold to Arnold Glass and left by road 3.11.87 to Leavesden. Registered to Ruanil Investments Ltd as G-BOXP and flown to Cranfield 5.8.88. To USA and registered N8130N, later N1CW.
A2680	Wessex HAS.1	XP157	To Class GRB at AES Lee-on-Solent 7.12.79 (ex Wroughton), uncoded. Engine No E4734. *Re-allocated A2780 in 1988 (see later).*
A2681	Wessex HAS.1	XP117	To Class GRA at Aircrewmens Engineering Training School, Culdrose, coded '-/521' (ex 771 Sqdn Culdrose). To Class GRB at SAH Culdrose 12.2.80. Engine No E4735. To fire pits by 11.10.85 (no engine) and expired by 1987.
A2682	Wessex HAS.1	XM845	To Class GRB at AES Lee-on-Solent 1.5.80, coded 'CU/530' (ex 771 Sqdn Culdrose). Involved in a collision en route to Lee-on-Solent by road, rolled over and badly damaged. Engine No E4739, removed and fitted to A2706. Airframe WOC and to fire pits at Lee-on-Solent by 6.81, marked '-/530'. Lying on its side 3.83. Left by road 5.9.85 to Yeovilton and dumped there, lying on its side 11.85. Badly burnt remains last noted 7.89.
A2683	Wessex HAS.1	XS878	To Class GRB at AES Lee-on-Solent 5.3.80, coded 'CU/527' (ex 771 Sqdn Culdrose). Engine No E4740. Uncoded by 1.6.81. Transferred to fire drill 4.8.89 and on the dump by 7.89 to 6.90, but gone by 25.8.90.
A2684	Wessex HAS.1	XP151	To Class GRB at AES Lee-on-Solent 14.3.80, coded 'R/047' (ex 771 Sqdn SAR detachment HMS Ark Royal). Engine No E4741. Current 7.87 but dumped near the fire pits for BDR training by 17.12.87. Transfer to fire training requested 30.11.90. Current 11.92 as 'R/047', lying almost on its port side. By road to Culdrose 3.5.94 and on to Predannack 4.5.94. Current 8.95 as 'R/047' but expired by 6.96.
A2685	Wessex HAS.1	XS886	To Class GRB at AES Lee-on-Solent 1.5.80, coded 'CU/527' (ex 771 Sqdn Culdrose). Engine No E4742. To 492 ATC Sqdn Shirley, West Midlands by 10.9.87, still 'CU/527'. To Evesham Sea Cadets (HMS Explorer) 26.6.92.
A2686	Wessex HAS.1	XS873	To Class GRB at AES Lee-on-Solent 14.3.80, coded 'CU/525' (ex 771 Sqdn Culdrose). Engine No E4743. To Predannack by road 5.12.86 as 'CU/525'. Current 10.92 but only very burnt remains by 5.93. *[Note: the aircraft marked "XS873" on Wroughton dump in the mid-1980's is almost certainly A2666/XS872 qv]*
A2686	Wessex HAS.1	XS868	Allocated to Class GRB at SAH Culdrose 5.80 (ex Wroughton), coded 'CU/526' (ex 771 Sqdn Culdrose). Engine Class GRA therefore given no 'E' number. Instead to Fleetlands 5.6.80 for gate guardian duties and repainted in red/white/blue colour scheme. Placed on the gate 13.5.81. Stored by 3.10.94. Replaced on the gate by Wessex HU.5 A2603[2]/XT480 and arrived at AES Lee-on-Solent 24.11.94 for BDR

'A' No.	AIRCRAFT TYPE	SERIAL	DETAILS
A2686	Wessex HAS.1	XS868	(contd) training. Placed outside by 5.95 (gutted) and noted 9.95 with 760 Sqdn. To new AESS facility at HMS Sultan, Gosport by 6.96 for BDR training. To 760 Sqdn building by 2.97 and current.
A2687	Wessex HAS.1	XS877	To Class GRB at AES Lee-on-Solent by road 29.5.80 (ex Wroughton), coded 'PO/516' (ex 772 Sqdn Portland). To SAH Culdrose by 10.80. No engine. Transferred to ETS by 9.6.88. Moved to the fire pits area at Culdrose 29.4.92. To Predannack by road 18.1.94. Current 8.95 as 'PO/516' but expired 6.96.
A2688	Wessex HAS.1	XP158	To Class GRB at SAH Culdrose by road 2.6.80 (ex Wroughton), coded 'CU/522' (ex 771 Sqdn Culdrose). Engine initially Class GRA but later Class GRB allocated E4766. Used by the Air Command Driving School. By road 13.9.88 to AES Lee-on-Solent (received 22.9.88) for airframe repair training and current 11.92. To ETS Culdrose by road 15.12.92, still 'CU/522' (in exchange for XT760). Moved to fire pits area 1.6.93 minus tail as '-/522'. To Predannack by road on 14.5.96, but current 9.97.
A2689	Wessex HAS.1	XM874	To Class GRB at SAH Culdrose by road 2.6.80 (ex Wroughton), coded 'CU/521' (ex 771 Sqdn Culdrose). Engine initially Class GRA but later Class GRB allocated E4765. Left by road 12.7.88 for AES Lee-on-Solent (received 13.7.88). To dump by 8.90 for BDR training (engine removed, probably at this time). Arrived Predannack by road 20.10.92, still 'CU/521'. Noted 5.93 lying on its side. *Re-allocated A2629 [2] in 1993 (see later).*
A2690	Wessex HAS.1	XS887	To Class GRB at SAH Culdrose by road 29.5.80 (ex Wroughton), coded 'PO/514' (ex 772 Sqdn Portland). Engine initially Class GRA but later Class GRB allocated E4764. Towed to Flambards Triple Theme Park, Helston 1.8.87 and current 8.90. Restored as 'FI/403' by 6.92 and current (now Flambards Village Theme Park).
A2691	Wessex HAS.1	XS868	Allocated to Class GRB at SAH Culdrose 5.80 (ex Wroughton), coded 'CU/526' (ex 771 Sqdn Culdrose). Engine Class GRA therefore given no 'E' number. Instead to Fleetlands 5.6.80 for gate guardian duties and repainted in red/white/blue colour scheme. Placed on the gate 13.5.81. Stored by 3.10.94. Replaced on the gate by Wessex HU.5 A2603[2]/XT480 and arrived at AES Lee-on-Solent 24.11.94 for BDR training. Placed outside by 5.95 (gutted) and noted 9.95 with 760 Sqdn. To new AESS facility at HMS Sultan, Gosport by 6.96 for BDR traning. Re-allocated A2686[2] post-1993 (see later).
A2692	Wessex HAS.1	XM917	To Class GRB at AES Lee-on-Solent 29.8.80, coded 'CU/528' (ex 771 Sqdn Culdrose). Engine No E4747. Marked 'PO/528' by 7.86. To BDR training and placed near the dump by 7.1.87. Current 6.87 but resprayed olive drab overall, minus all marks, by 7.87. Either this or XS865/A2694 was still on the dump 9.88 but had gone by 7.89, the other Wessex going to HMS Phoenix Fire School by 24.7.88.
A2693	Wessex HAS.1	XM843	[Previously Class I for a time]. To Class GRB at AES Lee-on-Solent 5.8.80, coded 'CU/527' (ex 771 Sqdn Culdrose). Engine No E4748. Current 7.86 but positioned outside Lee-on-Solent Fire Station by 14.10.86, marked *"LS/527"*. Current 9.87 but placed by the slipway 9.88, and on the gate 7.89 for the Air Day only. Current 1.93 for airframe repair training as '-/527'. *Re-allocated A2625 [2] in 1993.*
A2694	Wessex HAS.1	XS865	To Class GRB at AES Lee-on-Solent 11.8.80, coded 'CU/529' (ex 771 Sqdn Culdrose). Engine No E4749. To BDR training near the dump by 7.1.87. Current 6.87 but resprayed olive drab overall, minus all marks, by 7.87. Either this or XM917/A2692 was still on the dump 9.88 but had gone by 7.89, the other going to HMS Phoenix Fire School by 24.7.88.
A2695	Wessex HAS.1	XS876	To Class GRB at AES Lee-on-Solent 6.8.80, coded '-/523' (ex 771 Sqdn Culdrose). Engine No E4750. To SAH Culdrose by road 12.7.88 for the Air Command Driving School and current 7.92, still '-/523'. *Re-allocated A2626 [3] in 1993 (see later).*

'A' No.	AIRCRAFT TYPE	SERIAL	DETAILS
A2696	Wessex HAS.1	XS882	To Class GRB at AES Lee-on-Solent 18.9.80, coded 'CU/524' (ex 771 Sqdn Culdrose). Engine No E4751. To HMS Phoenix Fire School, Portsmouth by 9.4.87, coded '-/524'. Noted aboard HMS Naiad in Portsmouth harbour by 3.8.88 and burnt 10.88 during trials of new shipborne fire-fighting equipment.
A2697	Wessex HAS.1	XS870	To Class GRB at AES Lee-on-Solent 12.9.80 (ex Wroughton by road), coded 'PO/-' (tail probably from another aircraft). Engine No E4752. To BDR training by 9.88. Disposal requested 28.2.91 and allocated to RNEC Manadon 13.6.91. Re-allocated to fire training 18.6.91 and remained at Lee-on-Solent. Current 4.92. To Portland fire pits by 10.12.92 and current 9.97.
A2698	Wessex HAS.3	XP105	To Class GRB at AES Lee-on-Solent 11.8.78, coded 'CU/03' (ex HMS Devonshire Flt; fitted with the rear fuselage from XS150). No engine. Reduced to spares and produce 9.80. Stored outside MARTSU circa 4.82 and dumped by 3.83. Front fuselage only by 12.83, last noted 3.85.
A2699	Wasp HAS.1	XS570	To Class GRB at AES Lee-on-Solent 17.9.80, coded 'AP/470' (ex 829 Sqdn HMS Apollo Ships Flt). Engine No E4753. Current 7.81 marked 'P' only. Allotted to Warship Preservation Trust [WPT] 8.5.89, initially for return by 30.11.89, and placed on board preserved frigate HMS Plymouth at Millbay Docks, Plymouth 2.6.89 to at least 10.89. At Rosyth in 1990. Marked *"P/445"* (spurious) by 2.91 when moored at Glasgow. Still on AES charge 6.91 but donated to WPT 4.12.91 as a gift. Moved to Birkenhead 11.91 and current.

Former Red Arrows '1', Gnat T.1 A2679/XP535 at SAH Culdrose on 22.2.87. Later that year it was sold for civil use and is now in the USA. (Geoff Wakeham)

Sea Prince T.1 A2673/WF122, ex 'CU/575' of No.750 Sqdn, with SAH Culdrose for Dummy Deck training in 1979. It is still extant nearby at Flambards Village Theme Park, Helston. (MAP)

Wessex HAS.3 A2669/XP149, ex 'CU/574' of No.706 Sqdn Culdrose, at Lee-on-Solent in 1978. (MAP)

Wessex HAS.1 A2687/XS877, ex 'PO/517' of No.772 Sqdn, with SAH Culdrose on 4.12.90. (Geoff Wakeham)

A2700 - A2770

This series spans an eight year period up to 1988 and the increase in allocations to Wasp HAS.1's and Wessex HU.5's marks the withdrawal of these types from front-line service. The significant feature is that in 1988 the long-established sequential allocation was discarded and a re-organisation of the system was carried out. This is more fully explained in the next section but here it should be noted that the last sequential allocation cannot be determined. An educated guess suggests A2770 but there are several anomalies.

It will be seen from the following details that A2755 and A2756 arrived at Lee-on-Solent in 1986 but follow A2754 which did not arrive at Culdrose until 1987. It is possible that the former pair were Class GRA initially, albeit for a short period, but it is equally likely that the 'A' numbers were not issued until 1987. Similarly, most of the allocations after A2756 were 1988 arrivals, but A2770 reached Lee-on-Solent in early 1987 so it is surmised that the allocations occurred in 1988. These apparently out-of-sequence allocations were probably made following the receipt by FONA of the bi-annual census returns. However, the first known use of A2757 is not until 1991, while the first known allocations of A2758/2759/2760/2764 follow the 1988 re-organisation and these are all included in the next section.

The sequential allocation of engine numbers is the main factor in determining A2770 as the last in this section, Wessex HU.5 A2770/XS513 being allocated E4836/4837. Although SH-3D A2771/XV370 was allocated E4838/4839 (see next section), it did not arrive at Lee-on-Solent until 1990 by which time the allocations were far more arbitrary.

Once again reference is also made in this section to the re-allocations in 1988 and 1993 (see later) and there were airframes which were still extant during this period but which no longer appear in the official records.

'A' No.	AIRCRAFT TYPE	SERIAL	DETAILS
A2700	Hawker P.1127	XP980	To Class GRB at SAH Culdrose 10.10.80 (ex Flight Refuelling Ltd, Tarrant Rushton, where already fitted with wings of Harrier GR.3 XV751). Engine No E4746. Repainted in Sea Harrier type colour scheme by 11.81. Left by road 6.3.89 and arrived at the FAA Museum, Yeovilton 9.3.89. Current.
A2701	Gannet AEW.3	XL500	Flown in from Lossiemouth 21.11.78. To Class GRB at SAH Culdrose by 7.80, coded 'LM/-' (ex 849 Sqdn HQ Flt Lossiemouth). Engine No E4755. Believed never actually used due to reconstruction of the dummy deck. Placed in LTS by 12.81. Moved to 705 Sqdn hangar 26.5.83 and returned to airworthy state, first flew 19.9.83 prior to six months loan to Dowty-Rotol for propeller noise tests [loan presumably extended as noted at Yeovilton 4.8.84]. To Lee-on-Solent 28.2.85 (still airworthy) and stored as 'LM/-'. Noted 24.5.95 being prepared for a move to Culdrose and arrived there 5.7.95 for restoration and respray prior to display outside the 849 Sqdn hangar. Displayed in front of the public viewing enclosure 18.7-29.8.96 and again from 23.6.97. [This aircraft was a possible candidate for the Historic Flight at one time but was not taken on board]
A2702	Wasp HAS.1	XS545	To Class GRB at AES Lee-on-Solent 7.12.80 (ex Wroughton), coded '-/635' (ex 703 Sqdn Portland). Engine No E4756. To BDR training by 9.88 and current 4.92, although listed for disposal by 13.11.91 and gone by 1.6.92.
A2703	Wasp HAS.1	XT441	[Previously Class I for a time]. To Class GRB at Wroughton 4.6.79. Engine No E4757. Coded '-/337' but marked '465' on the nose. SOC 22.10.82. Dumped at Wroughton by 9.83 for the fire section, fitted with boom from A2656/XS476. To SAH Culdrose by road 14-15.7.86 for fire pits. To Predannack by 24.4.87, still marked '-/337' and '465'. Last noted 5.88 in burnt state.
A2704	Wasp HAS.1	XT438	To Class GRB at Wroughton 1980 for battle damage repair training. No engine. Left by road 21.6.84 en route 71 A/c Workshops, Detmold, coded '-/465'. To BDR training at AAC 1 Rgt Hildesheim by 12.85 (minus boom). No subsequent sightings recorded.

'A' No.	AIRCRAFT TYPE	SERIAL	DETAILS
A2705	Wessex HAS.1	XS866	To Class GRB at AES Lee-on-Solent 5.10.81 (ex Wroughton), coded 'CU/520' (ex 771 Sqdn Culdrose). No engine. Used for basic training. Engine No E4762 listed by 1988 [but see A2711/XW179!]. To SAH Culdrose by road 21-22.6.88 for the Air Command Driving School and current 7.92, still 'CU/520'. *Re-allocated A2627 [2] in 1993 (see later)*.
A2706	Wessex HAS.1	XM868	To Class GRB at AES Lee-on-Solent 5.10.81 (ex Wroughton, left 23.9.81), coded 'PO/517' (ex 772 Sqdn Portland). Engine No E4739 from A2682/XM845. Allocated to sheet metal repair 5.6.91 and for disposal 2.9.91. To BDR training area near dump by 6.6.92 but not seen 11.7.92. Arrived Predannack by road 28.10.92 and current 5.93, lying on its side. *Re-allocated A2630 [2] in 1993 (see later)*.
A2707	Wessex HAS.3	XS122	To Class GRA at RNEC Manadon by road 19.3.76 (ex Wroughton), coded 'PO/655' (ex 737 Sqdn Portland). Downgraded to Class GRB 9.81 at RNEC Manadon. No engine. Still 'PO/655' 7.89 and current 6.92, marked '-/655'. To AES Lee-on-Solent by 4.11.93. *Re-allocated A2632 [2] in 1993 (see later)*.
A2708	Gnat T.1	XR540	To Class GRB at SAH Culdrose 11.12.81 (ex 8636M RAFC Engineering Wing, Cranwell), still in *"Red Arrows"* colour scheme. Engine No E4758. Allocated 'SAH-5' and marked '5' by 7.83. Taxyable. WFU by 23.4.86 and put into open storage near fire pits (engine removed). Moved back to 'A' site 3.2.87, dismantled and departed in crates 20.2.87 (reported for USA/Canada). Tail section noted in shipping agents yard in Southall, London 15.2.88. Nothing further known.
A2709	Gnat T.1	XR991	To Class GRB at SAH Culdrose 27.1.82 (ex 8637M RAFC Engineering Wing, Cranwell), still in *"Red Arrows"* colour scheme. Engine No E4759. Allocated 'SAH-6' and marked '6' by 7.83. Taxyable. WFU by 23.4.86 and stored in an SAH hangar. Moved to open storage near fire pits on 3.2.87. Sold to Arnold Glass and left by road 10.11.87 to Leavesden for restoration to flying condition. Registered to Ruanil Investments as G-BOXO. To USA and registered N1CL.
A2710	Lynx DB	XW839	Allocated to Class GRB at AES Lee-on-Solent 7.6.82 (ex Rolls-Royce, Filton). No engine. Still at Filton 9.82 (on ground runs for digital engine control trials) and retained there. A2710 was apparently not taken up as XW839 was unsuitable, being fitted with skids not wheels. *[Allocated A2657 [2] circa 1991 - see later]*
A2711	Sioux AH.1	XW179	To Class GRA at Wroughton 21.9.79, coded 'A' (ex 662 Sqdn). Downgraded to Class GRB in 1982. Engine No E4762. To Middle Wallop by road 23.2.83 as spare a/c for Historic Flt. To Wessex Aviation Society, Stapehill, Wimborne 23.3.83 and used in the restoration of XT242 (both were noted there 4.85). *[XT242 is now with The Helicopter Collection/K.Fern]*.
A2712	Whirlwind HAR.9	XN359	[Previously Class I for a time] To Class GRB at Wroughton 1982, coded 'ED/34' (ex 829 Sqdn HMS Endurance Ships Flt). No engine. By road to Lee-on-Solent 2.12.83 for BDR training. Derelict near the slipway by 1.84 to 3.85 and dumped by 7.85. Lying on its side by 7.87 and remains only by 9.88. *Re-allocated A2759 in 1988 (see later)*.
A2713	Whirlwind HAR.9	XN386	To Class GRB at Wroughton 1982, coded 'ED/35' (ex 829 Sqdn HMS Endurance Ship's Flt). No engine. Left by road 26.2.87 as 'ED/-' on sale to Mr Sanderson, Radcliffe, Nottingham and with Helicopter Museum of Great Britain, Blackpool Airport by 3.87. Current 1.93 but for sale and not noted since.
A2714	Whirlwind HAR.9	XL880	To Class GRB at Wroughton 1982, coded 'ED/35' (ex 829 Sqdn HMS Endurance Ships Flt). To Lee-on-Solent by road 30.11.83 for BDR training. To dump area for BDR training by 6.90, minus boom. Current as '35' 11.92. Arrived Predannack by road 10.3.94 for FCR training and unburnt hulk current 8.95, still '35'. Expired by 6.96.

'A' No.	AIRCRAFT TYPE	SERIAL	DETAILS
A2715	Wasp HAS.1	XS568	To Fleetlands apprentices 18.5.83 (ex AIU Lee-on-Solent ?), coded '-/441' (ex 829 Sqdn HMS Falmouth Flt, ditched 28.10.82) and fitted with boom from XS539. Engine No E4767. Correctly marked XS568 by 6.85. Current 6.92. *Re-allocated A2637 [2] in 1993 (see later).*
A2716	Wasp HAS.1	XT780	To Class GRB with Fleetlands apprentices 15.8.83 (arrived by road 17.8.83 ex Wroughton), coded '-/636' (ex 829 Sqdn Portland). Engine No E4768. Current 6.92. *Re-allocated A2638 [2] in 1993 (see later).*
A2717	Wasp HAS.1	XS569	To Class GRB with Fleetlands apprentices 15.8.83 (arrived by road 16.8.83 ex Wroughton), uncoded. Engine No E4769. Current 6.92. *Re-allocated A2639 [2] in 1993 (see later).*
A2718	Wessex HAS.3	XM916	To Class GRB at Wroughton 9.84, coded 'PO/666'. Engine No E4770? (guess). Placed on the dump at Wroughton 5.86. In poor condition by 1991 and expired.
A2719	Wessex HAS.3	XP150	To Class GRB at AES Lee-on-Solent by road 8.8.84 (ex Wroughton), coded 'AN/406' (ex 737 Sqdn HMS Antrim Flt). Engine No E4771. *Re-allocated A2764 in 1988 (see later).*
A2720	Wessex HAS.3	XP142	From Portland to Yeovilton 26.7.82 for FAA Museum, uncoded (ex 737 Sqdn HMS Antrim Flt), named *"Humphrey"*. To Class GRB at Yeovilton 7.84. Engine No ?? To FAAM store at Wroughton 6.9.94. To Lee-on-Solent 23.6.95 for a reunion 8.95. Still present 9.95 but returned to Wroughton by 1.11.95.
A2721	Lynx HAS.2	XZ249	Wreck to RNEC Manadon 8.84, named *"Purdy"* (ex 'AG/341' 815 Sqdn HMS Avenger Flt, w/o 4.5.83). No engine. Cabin hulk to Predannack by 6.90. Current 10.92 but expired by 1.5.93.
A2722	Wessex HU.5	XT757	To Class GRB at AES Lee-on-Solent (left Wroughton by road 7.8.84), coded '-/XH' (ex 847 Sqdn Yeovilton). Engine Nos ?? In 'Overlord' hangar 7.85, and also 7.86 minus all marks and serials. To Predannack by road 15.10.86. Last noted 5.88.
A2723	Wessex HU.5	XT487	To Class GRB at AES Lee-on-Solent (left Wroughton by road 25.7.84 (ex 781 Sqdn Lee-on-Solent, *"Green Parrot"* scheme). Engine Nos ?? In metalwork shop 7.85 and derelict in BDR training area by 5.86. Last noted on the dump 7.86 and gone by 1.87.
A2724	Wasp HAS.1	XV623	To Class GRB at Portland 1985? Certainly WFU at Portland by 11.86, coded '-/601' (ex 829 Sqdn HQ Flt Portland). Engine No E4774. Dumped by 5.87 (minus boom) and current 4.88; believed last noted 11.91.
A2725	Wasp HAS.1	XS538	To Class GRB at AES Lee-on-Solent 1985. To BDR training by 2.86, coded '-/451' and marked 'FIR2' on nose (ex 829 Sqdn FIR and HMS Lowestoft Flt). Engine No E4775. Cabin hulk dumped by 6.90 and derelict by north fence 8.90-6.91. On the dump for BDR training by 9.91. Arrived SAH Culdrose fire pits by road 12.10.93, still '-/451' and 'FIR2'. To Predannack by 22.11.93 and current 8.94, but gone by 8.95.
A2726	Wasp HAS.1	XT786	To Class GRB for BDR training at Portland 1985 (ex Wroughton by road 13.4.85), minus boom coded '-/441' (ex 829 Sqdn HMS Falmouth Flt). Engine No E4776. To the dump by 7.86 and current 5.87. Remains only by 4.88.
A2727	Wessex HAS.3	XM328	To Class GRB at SAH Culdrose 9.5.85 (arrived by road 22.4.85 ex Wroughton), uncoded. Engine No E4777. Marked *"The Sow"* (with nose artwork) by 7.87. Current 7.93. *Re-allocated A2644 [2] in 1993 (see later).*
A2728	Wessex HAS.3	XP110	To Class GRB with Fleetlands apprentices by road 25.4.85 (ex Wroughton), coded 'PO/655' (ex 737 Sqdn Portland). Engine No probably E4778? (guess). Marked *"FL/55"* (spurious) by 6.86. *Re-allocated A2714 in 1988 (see later).*
A2729	Hunter T.7	XL600	To Class GRB at Fleetlands apprentices 9.4.85 (arrived by road 12.3.85 from Scampton), coded 'Y' (ex 12 Sqdn). Engine No E4779. Marked *"FL"* on starboard side of fin in place of 'Y' by 6.85. For disposal by 30.8.91. Left by road 5.6.92 for Southall (reportedly sold in the USA) and still in store there 12.93.

'A' No.	AIRCRAFT TYPE	SERIAL	DETAILS
A2730	Hunter GA.11	WV382	To Class GRB at AES Lee-on-Solent by road 5.2.85 (ex Shawbury), coded '-/830' (ex FRADU Yeovilton). Engine No E4780. To BDR training area by 9.88. *Re-allocated A2724 in 1988 (see later).*
A2731	Hunter GA.11	WT711	To Class GRB at SAH Culdrose 18.9.85 (arrived 23.9.85 ex Shawbury), coded '-/837' (ex FRADU Yeovilton). Engine No E4781. Taxyable. Recoded 'DD/833' by 16.5.86 for dummy deck training. Engine No E5117 by 8.88. *Re-allocated A2645 [2] in 1993 (see later).*
A2732	Hunter GA.11	WT804	To Class GRB at SAH Culdrose 22.10.85 (ex Shawbury), coded 'VL/831' (ex FRADU Yeovilton). Engine No E4782. Taxyable. Recoded 'DD/831' by 28.5.86 for dummy deck training. Engine No E5090 by 8.88. Current 6.92. *Re-allocated A2646 [2] in 1993 (see later).*
A2733	Hunter GA.11	XE668	To Class GRB at SAH Culdrose 8.2.85, coded 'VL/832' (ex FRADU Yeovilton). Engine No not known but allocated E5105 by 8.88. Taxyable. Recoded 'DD/832' by 30.5.85 for dummy deck training. To Predannack by road 11.8.93. *Re-allocated A2647 [2] in 1993 (see later).*
A2734	Hunter T.7	XF321	To Class GRB at RNEC Manadon 2.5.85 (ex RAE Bedford in r/w/b scheme; damaged in belly landing at Bedford 27.7.84). Engine No E4784. Current 6.92. *Re-allocated A2648 [2] in 1993 (see later).*
A2735	Wasp HAS.1	XV625	To Class I (later GRA) at RNEC Manadon 15.10.71 (ex Fleetlands), coded '-/471' (ex 829 Sqdn Phoebe Flt). Engine class GRA (no 'E' number allotted). Marked 'HMS Thunderer' on nose by 6.81. Downgraded to Class GRB circa 1985 with Engine No E4785. At 7.91 airframe serviceable with 456 hours 10 minutes, able to be ground run. Noted at Portland 3.93 for disbandment of 829 Sqdn. *Re-allocated A2649 [2] in 1993 (see later).*
A2736	Hunter GA.11	XE682	Front fuselage and wings to Class GRB at SAH Culdrose 22.11.85 (ex Shawbury), coded '-/835' (ex FRADU Yeovilton). Used for spares recovery. Forward fuselage to fire pits by 28.11.86. Burnt hulk noted 7.87-1.91 and gone by 7.91.
A2737	Hunter GA.11	WV267	To Class GRB at SAH Culdrose 6.2.86, coded 'VL/836' (arrived by road 21.1.86, ex FRADU Yeovilton; SOC as Cat.5(GI) after bird-strike 29.11.85). Engine No not known but allocated E5092 by 8.88. Taxyable. Recoded 'DD/836' by 11.11.86 for dummy deck training. *Re-allocated A2650 [2] in 1993 (see later).*
A2738	Hunter T.7	XX466	To Class GRB at SAH Culdrose 15.5.86 (ex Shawbury), coded 'VL/879' (arrived 14.5.86, ex FRADU Yeovilton, white codes on RAF camouflage scheme). Engine No not known but allocated E5116 by 8.88. Taxyable. Recoded 'DD/830' (white codes) for dummy deck training on 24.7.86 and used for training of taxy "pilots". Moved 22.3.93 to 820 Sqdn hangar for storage. To Predannack by road 10.8.93. *Re-allocated A2651 [2] in 1993 (see later).*
A2739	Wessex HU.5	XS516	To Class GRB at AES Lee-on-Solent 3.7.86, coded '(Y)Q' (ex 845 Sqdn Yeovilton, believed flown in 11.4.86). Engine Nos E4788/4789. Current 1.93. *Re-allocated A2652 [2] in 1993 (see later).*
A2740	Wessex HU.5	XS514	To Class GRB at AES Lee-on-Solent 3.7.86, coded '(Y)L' (ex 845 Sqdn Yeovilton, flown in 7.7.86). Engine Nos E4790/4791. Current 1.93. *Re-allocated A2653 [2] in 1993 (see later).*
A2741	Wessex HU.5	XT455	To Class GRB at AES Lee-on-Solent 3.7.86, coded '(Y)U' (ex 845 Sqdn Yeovilton, believed flown in 10.4.86). Engine Nos E4792/4793. Current 1.93. *Re-allocated A2654 [2] in 1993 (see later).*
A2742	Wessex HU.5	XT484	To Class GRB at AES Lee-on-Solent 3.7.86, coded '(Y)H' (ex 845 Sqdn Yeovilton, flown in 24.6.86). Engine Nos E4794/4795. Current 1.93. *Re-allocated A2655 [2] in 1993 (see later).*

'A' No.	AIRCRAFT TYPE	SERIAL	DETAILS
A2743	Wasp HAS.1	XS529	To Class GRB at AES Lee-on-Solent 14.10.86, coded '-/461' (ex 829 Sqdn HMS Galatea Flt). Engine No E4796. Coded '-/430' with 760 Sqdn 10.91, still with HMS Galatea badge (see XT778), but marked '-/461' again by 4.92. Departed by 1.6.92, apparently to RNEC Manadon (not noted there) from whence it was delivered to Culdrose on 28.3.95 and placed in the fire pits area for BDR training. To Predannack for FCR training by 7.10.96. [*Note that no new 'A' number was allocated in 1988 or 1993; subsequently re-allocated A2696 [2] post-1993 (see later)*].
A2744	Wessex HU.5	XT460	To Class GRB at AES Lee-on-Solent 31.10.86, coded '(Y)K' (ex 845 Sqdn Yeovilton). Engine Nos E4797/4798. Arrived Wroughton by road 17.3.87 for storage. To AES Lee-on-Solent 24-25.6.91 by road, still coded '(Y)K'. No engines. In use for airframe repair by 11.92, minus serials. Current 1.93. *Re-allocated A2668 [2] in 1993 (see later).*
A2745	Wessex HU.5	XT482	To Class GRB at AES Lee-on-Solent by road 17-18.11.86 (ex Wroughton), coded 'VL/ZM' (ex 707 Sqdn Yeovilton). Engine Nos E4799/4800. Noted 11.92 marked '19' on starboard door. Current 1.93. *Re-allocated A2656 [2] in 1993 (see later).*
A2746	Wessex HU.5	XS483	To Class GRB at AES Lee-on-Solent by road 24.11.86 (ex Wroughton by road 18.11.86), coded '(Y)T' (ex 845 Sqdn Yeovilton). Engine Nos E4801/4802. With 760 Sqdn by 10.91. To the dump for BDR training by 6.92 and current 1.93 as 'VL/(Y)T'. *Re-allocated A2657 [3] in 1993 (see later).*
A2747	Wessex HU.5	XS515	To Class GRB at AES Lee-on-Solent 6.11.86, coded '(Y)N' (ex 845 Sqdn Yeovilton, flown in 31.10.86). Engine Nos E4803/4804. Current 1.93. *Re-allocated A2658 [2] in 1993 (see later).*
A2748	Wasp HAS.1	XT795	[Previously Class GRA for a time] To Class GRB at AES Lee-on-Solent 3.9.86 (by air from Portland), coded 'LE/476' (ex 829 Sqdn HMS Leander Flt; named *"Willy the Wasp"* in dayglo strip on nose, *"Lt B Gordon USN"* on cockpit side). Engine No E4805. To store at Wroughton, arriving by road 16.1.89. Left Wroughton by road 5.8.92 for Fleetlands, coded 'LE/476' (ex 829 Sqdn HMS Leander Flt). By road to Harwich and left 19.4.93 aboard MV *Koningen Beatrix* en route to De Kooy, Netherlands for preservation.
A2749	Wessex HU.5	XS520	[Previously Class GRA for a time] To Class GRB at AES Lee-on-Solent 2.10.86, coded '(Y)F' (ex 845 Sqdn Yeovilton, flown in 5.9.86). Engine Nos E4806/4807. Current 1.93. *Re-allocated A2659 [2] in 1993 (see later).*
A2750	Wessex HU.5	XS511	To Class GRB at AES Lee-on-Solent 22.9.86, coded '(Y)M' (ex 845 Sqdn Yeovilton, flown in 18.9.86). Engine Nos E4808/4809. Current 1.93. *Re-allocated A2660 [2] in 1993 (see later).*
A2751	Wessex HU.5	XT762	To Class GRB at AES Lee-on-Solent by road 25.11.86 (ex Wroughton), uncoded in r/w/b scheme (ex RAE Bedford). Engine Nos E4810/4811. To SAH Culdrose by road, arriving 28.7.87 (engines removed and retained at AES; re-allocated E4614/4615 in 1988). Current 7.93. *Re-allocated A2661 [2] in 1993 (see later).*
A2752	Wessex HU.5	XT449	To Class GRB at AES Lee-on-Solent 1.12.86 (ex Wroughton by road 5.11.86), coded '(Y)C' (ex 845 Sqdn Yeovilton). Engine Nos E4812/4813. With 760 Sqdn by 10.91. To the dump for BDR training by 6.92 and current 1.93. *Re-allocated A2662 [2] in 1993 (see later). Engine E4812 to Manadon and re-allocated E4603 in 1993.*
A2753	Wessex HU.5	XS522	To Class GRB at AES Lee-on-Solent 1.12.86 (ex Wroughton by road 7.11.86), coded 'VL/ZL' (ex 707 Sqdn Yeovilton). Engine Nos E4814/4815. Probably in use for BDR training by 7.89 and noted 11.92 marked '-/ZL'. Current 1.93. *Re-allocated A2663 [2] in 1993 (see later).*

'A' No.	AIRCRAFT TYPE	SERIAL	DETAILS
A2754	Hunter GA.11	WW654	Wings and front fuselage to Class GRB at SAH Culdrose by road 11.2.87, coded '-/833' (ex FRADU Yeovilton, overall grey scheme with black markings), together with a rear fuselage from XF368 (still current with FRADU at the time). The rear fuse left by road on 2.3.87 but returned on 19.3.87 (to where and why ?). The parts were mated to form one aircraft at SAH by 24.4.87 and by 29.9.87 the aircraft was repainted in grey/white scheme with serial WW654 and recoded 'DD/83<u>4</u>' for dummy deck training (to avoid conflict with A2731/WT711. Engine No E5121 by 8.88. Moved 22.3.93 to 820 Sqdn hangar for storage. *Re-allocated A2664 [2] in 1993 (see later).*
A2755	Wessex HU.5	XT765	To Class GRB at AES Lee-on-Solent 13.10.86, coded '(Y)J' (ex 845 Sqdn Yeovilton, flown in 2.10.86). Engine Nos E4818/4819. Current 1.93. *Re-allocated A2665 [2] in 1993 (see later).*
A2756	Wessex HU.5	XT453	To Class GRB at AES Lee-on-Solent 21.7.86, coded '(Y)A' (ex 845 Sqdn Yeovilton SAR detachment at Lee-on-Solent). Engine Nos E4816/4817. To Yeovilton (13?).9.93 for 846 Sqdn 50th Anniversary and noted outside paint shop 29.9.93. Returned to AES marked "-/VL" and "846 Naval Air Squadron 1943-1993". *Re-allocated A2666 [2] in 1993 (see later).*
A2757			*Original allocation (if any) not known - see later.*
A2758			*Original allocation (if any) not known - see later.*
A2759			*Original allocation (if any) not known - see later.*
A2760			*Original allocation (if any) not known - see later.*
A2761	Wessex HU.5	XT771	To Class GRB at AES Lee-on-Solent 11.4.88, coded 'PO/620' (ex 772 Sqdn Portland). Engine Nos E4820/4821. Current 1.93. *Re-allocated A2673 [2] in 1993 (see later).*
A2762	Wessex HU.5	XS507	To Class GRB at AES Lee-on-Solent 11.4.88, coded 'PO/627' (ex 772 Sqdn Portland). Engine Nos E4822/4823. Current 1.93. *Re-allocated A2674 [2] in 1993 (see later).*
A2763	Wessex HU.5	XS496	Transferred from Lee-on-Solent SAR Detachment to Class GRB at AES Lee-on-Solent 24.3.88, coded 'PO/625' (ex 772 Sqdn Portland). Engine Nos E4824/4825. Current 1.93. *Re-allocated A2675 [2] in 1993 (see later).*
A2764			*Original allocation (if any) not known - see later.*
A2765	Wessex HU.5	XS510	[Previously Class I for a time] Transferred from Lee-on-Solent SAR Detachment to Class GRB at AES Lee-on-Solent 24.3.88, coded 'PO/626' (ex 772 Sqdn Portland). Engine Nos E4826/4827. Current 1.93. *Re-allocated A2676 [2] in 1993 (see later).*
A2766	Wessex HU.5	XS508	To Class GRB at AES Lee-on-Solent 14.4.88, uncoded in SAR colour scheme (ex NASU Yeovilton). Engine Nos E4828/4829. To FAA Museum Yeovilton 28.6.93. *Re-allocated A2677 [2] in 1993 (see later).*
A2767	Wessex HU.5	XT761	To Class GRB at AES Lee-on-Solent by road 12.4.88 (ex Wroughton), uncoded in SAR colour scheme. Engine Nos E4830/4831. Current 1.93. *Re-allocated A2678 [2] in 1993 (see later).*
A2768	Wessex HU.5	XT458	To Class GRB at AES Lee-on-Solent 23.3.88, coded '-/622' (ex 772 Sqdn Portland). Engine Nos E4832/4833. Current 1.93. *Re-allocated A2679 [2] in 1993 (see later).*
A2769	Wessex HU.5	XT485	To Class GRB at AES Lee-on-Solent 23.3.88, coded 'PO/621' (ex 772 Sqdn Portland). Engine Nos E4834/4835. Current 1.93. *Re-allocated A2680 [2] in 1993 (see later).*
A2770	Wessex HU.5	XS513	To Class GRB at AES Lee-on-Solent 14.3.87, coded 'PO/419' (ex 'A' Flt 772 Sqdn Portland). Engine Nos E4836/4837. In use for BDR training by 9.88 and current 1.93. *Re-allocated A2681 [2] in 1993 (see later).*

Wasp HAS.1 A2715/XS568, ex '441' of No.829 Sqdn HMS Falmouth Flight, seen in use for Fleetlands apprentices on 6.6.87. Under the 1993 re-allocation it became A2637 [2].

Hawker P.1127 A2700/XP980 at SAH Culdrose on 5.6.85 in the original Sea Harrier scheme. (Bob Turner)

Wasp HAS.1 A2716/XT780 '-/636' (later A2638 [2]) with the Fleetlands Apprentice Training Centre on 7.6.86. (Bob Turner)

Wessex HU.5 A2762/XS507 (later A2674 [2]), 'PO/627' of No.772 Sqdn Portland, at the Lee-on-Solent Air Day on 22.7.89. (Bob Turner)

Lynx HAS.2 A2772/XX510 "LS/69" outside Yeovilton spray shop on 24.1.92 after respray in the medium sea grey scheme for preservation at Lee-on-Solent. (Bob Turner)

CLASS GR(2) AIRFRAMES 1988 - 1993

As noted in the previous section the sequential issues of 'A' numbers was discarded in 1988. There is no requirement to mark 'A' numbers and 'E' numbers on the airframes and ECU's and it seems reasonable to assume that the receiving station involved in the transfer of an airframe effectively had no record of its allocated 'A' or 'E' numbers. As with any 'new' arrivals, these would be listed as *"not known"* in the half-yearly returns provided by each station. Furthermore, it was noted in the introduction to this book that there is no permanent cross-referencing of serials and 'A' numbers. New numbers were therefore issued to the airframes and ECU's recorded as *"not known"*. Faced with this apparent chaos it was undoubtedly difficult for any officer taking charge of the records to resist the temptation to re-organise the system. In 1988 the decision was made to use only the block A2600 to A2799 for airframes and E4600 to E4899 for ECU's, and the vacant numbers in this range were re-issued in an arbitrary fashion. The reason for engine numbers in the range from E5000 for the Avon engines of the Hunters at Culdrose is not known. A new list of instructional numbers was issued by FONA in September 1988 for use in all subsequent records and correspondence. It is also evident that by this time reference is made to Class GR(1) and GR(2) in place of Class GRA and GRB respectively.

Features of the allocations which follow are, therefore, the re-allocation of previously issued 'A' numbers from A2600, allocations of a second serial to airframes which already had an 'A' number, and re-allocations to airframes for which the original 'A' number fell outside of the chosen block of numbers to be used. There are also a number of airframes (A2704/2710-2713/2718/2719/2730) delivered between 1983 and 1986 for which the original allocation is not known - they may, of course, have been Class GRA initially. This naturally creates problems for the researcher. For example, Sea Hawk FGA.4 A2526/WV911 was re-allocated A2626 presumably to fall within the chosen sequence, but the reason for Wessex HAS.1 A2680/XP157 being re-allocated A2780 is uncertain. Typing error must be a possibility as the engine number remained unchanged! Reflecting the movement of airframes, Whirlwind HAS.7 A2654/XN302 and HAR.9 A2643/XN311 moved to HMS Royal Arthur in July 1987 and in 1988 were re-allocated A2758/A2760 respectively. However, HAS.7 A2712/XN359 was re-allocated A2759 despite continuing to serve at Lee-on-Solent! A2758/XN302 also received a new engine number, whereas Wessex HAS.3 A2719/XP150 (another airframe which did not move) was re-allocated A2764 but retained the same engine number. Lynx XX510 further defies any theories; having been issued with the second allocation of A2601 in 1989 it was then re-allocated A2772 in 1991, and the engine numbers were also amended. Further speculation may be purely academic as in late 1993 the entire system was re-organised yet again!

This section also refers back to the previous allocations which were still current from the A2600 to A2770 series covered in the previous sections. Note that A2759 and A2760 were subsequently re-issued in 1991. A number of other airframes were still extant during this period, although mostly relegated to fire drills. A surprising omission is Sea King HAS.1 A2664/XV644 which escaped attention until the 1993 re-organisation when it was re-issued A2615 [3]. Among the continuing allocations to Hunters, Wasps and Wessex are a number of former RAF Harrier GR.3's for various training connected with Sea Harrier operations.

'A' No.	AIRCRAFT TYPE	SERIAL	DETAILS
A2600 [2]	Harrier GR.1	XV277	To Class GR(2) at ETS Yeovilton 28.11.88 (arrived 30.11.88, ex Rolls-Royce, Filton). Engine No E4686. *Re-allocated A2602 [3] in 1993 (see later)*.
A2601 [2]	Lynx HAS.2	XX510	To Class GR(2) at AES Lee-on-Solent 10.10.89 (ex P&EE Foulness). Engine Nos E4619/4620 *(but see A2602 [2] and A2606 [2])*. First noted 20.7.91 and on the field by 10.91. *Re-allocated A2772 and Engine Nos E4628/ 4629 by 8.91 (see later)*.
A2602 [2]	Harrier GR.3	XZ129	To Class GR(2) at ETS Yeovilton by road 24.4.91 (ex CIT, Cranfield), coded '3C' (ex 233 OCU Wittering). Engine No E4619 *(but see A2601[2]/XX510)*. Repainted in RN scheme by 18.7.92, with 899 Sqdn marks and 'ETS' in place of code (dark sea grey with black markings). *Re-allocated A2604 [3] in 1993 (see later)*.
A2603	Whirlwind HAS.7	XK911	*Current in 1988 (see earlier)*.
A2604 [2]	Harrier GR.3	XV755	To Class GR(2) at ETS Yeovilton by road 22.5.91 (ex St Athan), coded 'M' (ex 233 OCU Wittering). No engine. In use for BDR training by 7.92 and marked 'Royal Navy' on tail by 2.10.92. *Re-allocated A2606 [3] in 1993 (see later)*.

'A' No.	AIRCRAFT TYPE	SERIAL	DETAILS
A2605			*Not re-allocated. Whirlwind HAS.7 A2605/XN308 was not listed in 1988 but was still extant (see earlier).*
A2606 [2]	Harrier GR.3	XV806	To Class GR(2) at SAH Culdrose by road 17.4.91 (received 18.4.91, ex Cosford), coded 'E' (ex 4 Sqdn Gutersloh). Engine No E4620 *(but see A2601 [2]).* Current 7.92 in store. Moved 22.3.93 to 820 Sqdn hangar for further storage. *Re-allocated A2607 [3] in 1993 (see later).*
A2607 [2]	Harrier GR.3	XV741	To Class GR(2) at SAH Culdrose by road 24.4.91 (received 25.4.91, ex Cosford), uncoded with 233 OCU marks. Engine No E4621. Current 7.93 for taxy training. *Re-allocated A2608 [3] in 1993 (see later).*
A2608 [2]	Harrier GR.3	XV783	To Class GR(2) at SAH Culdrose by road 1.5.91 (received 2.5.91, ex Cosford), coded 'N' (ex 233 OCU Wittering). Engine No E4622. Left Culdrose by road 10.8.93 for AES Lee-on-Solent. *Re-allocated A2609 [3] in 1993 (see later).*
A2609			*Not re-allocated. Wessex HAS.1 A2609/XM329 was not listed in 1988 but was still extant (see earlier).*
A2609 [2]	Harrier GR.3	XW919	To Class GR(2) at SAH Culdrose by road 8.5.91 (received 9.5.91, ex Cosford), coded 'W' (ex 4 Sqdn Gutersloh, with special tail marks). Engine No E4623. Current 7.92 in store. *Re-allocated A2610 [3] in 1993 (see later).*
A2610 [2]	Harrier GR.3	XZ969	To Class GR(2) at RNEC Manadon 24.4.91 (ex St Athan), coded 'D' (ex 4 Sqdn Gutersloh, with special tail marks). Engine No E4624. Current 6.92. *Re-allocated A2612 [3] in 1993 (see later).*
A2611 [2]	Lynx HAS.3	XZ243	Wreck allocated for possible use by AES Lee-on-Solent 2.89 (shell only, ex AIU Lee-on-Solent and 'PO/635' 702 Sqdn Portland, ditched 10.3.88). To AMG Portland by 9.89, minus all marks and serials. Refurbished for instructional use by 2.11.90 (resprayed in the Medium sea grey scheme). Probably to Class GR(2) in 1991, no engine. Current 10.93. *Re-allocated A2613 [3] in 1993 (see later).*
A2612			*Not re-allocated [Note: already allocated twice - see earlier]*
A2613 [2]	Sea King HAS.2A	XV642	To Class GR(2) at AES Lee-on-Solent by road 19.3.91 (received 20.3.91, ex Westlands, Yeovil), having been repainted in Medium sea grey scheme. Engine Nos E4625/4626. Current 1.93 with 760 Sqdn. *Re-allocated A2614 [3] in 1993 (see later).*
A2614 [2]	Harrier GR.3	XV760	To Class GR(2) at SAH Culdrose by road 30.5.91 (ex St Athan), coded 'K' (ex 3 Sqdn Gutersloh). No engine. Left 29.9.92 by road to Yeovilton. Repainted in RN scheme as *"VL/-"* 899 Sqdn (spurious; dark sea grey with black markings) and placed on main gate 20.11.92. *Re-allocated A2605 [2] in 1993 (see later).*
A2615 [2]	Harrier GR.3	XV786	To Class GR(2) at SAH Culdrose by road 5.6.91 (ex St Athan), coded 'S' (ex 3 Sqdn Gutersloh). No engine. Current 7.92 in store. Moved 22.3.93 to 820 Sqdn hangar for further storage. Moved to the fire pits area 25.6.93 for FCR training and dismantled by 22.11.93. *Re-allocated A2611 [3] in 1993 (see later).*
A2616 [2]	Wessex HAS.1	XS888	Allocated for disposal 14.6.91 at Wroughton (ex RNEF), coded '-/521' (ex ?). To Class GR(2) at AES Lee-on-Solent by road 7.7.92, still coded '-/521'. No engine. Near the dump 7.92 but outside the BDR training hangar by 23.11.92. To Guernsey Airport 19.4.93 for FCR training as an underslung load by 7 Sqdn Chinook HC.1 ZA683/EW. Current on the fire dump.
A2617 [2]	Wessex HU.5	XT480	To Class GR(2) with Fleetlands apprentices by road 12-13.12.90 (ex Wroughton), coded '-/XQ' (ex 847 Sqdn Yeovilton). Engine Nos E4635/4636. Current 6.92. *Re-allocated A2603 [3] in 1993 (see later).*
A2618 [2]	Wessex HU.5	XS523	To Class GR(2) with Fleetlands apprentices by road 11.12.90 (ex Wroughton), coded 'CU/824' (ex 771 Sqdn Culdrose). Engine Nos E4637/4638. Current 6.92. To AES Lee-on-Solent by 4.11.93 (engines removed and retained at Fleetlands; *re-allocated E4616/4617 in 1993). Re-allocated A2670 [2] in 1993 (see later).*

'A' No.	AIRCRAFT TYPE	SERIAL	DETAILS
A2619	Kestrel FGA.1	XS695	*Current in 1988 (see earlier).*
A2620			*Not re-allocated.*
A2621			*Not re-allocated.*
A2622			*Not re-allocated.*
A2623			*Not re-allocated.*
A2624			*Not re-allocated. Sea Vixen FAW.2 A2624/XN692 was not listed in 1988 but was still extant (see earlier).*
A2625			*Not re-allocated.*
A2626 [2]	Sea Hawk FGA.4	WV911	Formerly A2526; new 'A' number allocated in 1988. With AES Lee-on-Solent marked *"C/115"* (spurious). Engine No E4513. Stored by 10.91 and current 11.93. *Re-allocated A2623 [2] in 1993 (see later).*
A2627			*Not re-allocated.*
A2628			*Not re-allocated.*
A2629			*Not re-allocated.*
A2630			*Not re-allocated.*
A2631			*Not re-allocated.*
A2632			*Not re-allocated.*
A2633	Sea Hawk FGA.6	XE369	*Not re-allocated. Sea Hawk FGA.6 A2633/XE369 was not listed in 1988 but was still extant (see earlier).*
A2634			*Not re-allocated.*
A2635			*Not re-allocated.*
A2636			*Not re-allocated.*
A2637			*Not re-allocated.*
A2638			*Not re-allocated.*
A2639			*Not re-allocated.*
A2640			*Not re-allocated.*
A2641			*Not re-allocated.*
A2642			*Not re-allocated.*
A2643			*Not re-allocated.*
A2644			*Not re-allocated.*
A2645	Sea Hawk F.1	WF225	*Current in 1988 (see earlier). Re-allocated A2623 [2] in 1993 (see later).*
A2646			*Not re-allocated.*
A2647			*Not re-allocated.*
A2648			*Not re-allocated.*
A2649			*Not re-allocated.*
A2650	Wessex HAS.1	XP160	*Current in 1988 (see earlier). Re-allocated A2628 [2] in 1993 (see later).*
A2651			*Not re-allocated.*
A2652			*Not re-allocated.*
A2653			*Not re-allocated.*
A2654			*Not re-allocated.*
A2655	Buccaneer S.1	XN953	*Current in 1988 (see earlier). Re-allocated A2600 [3] in 1993 (see later).*
A2656			*Not re-allocated.*
A2657 [2]	Lynx DB	XW839	[Previously A2710 for a time]. To Class GR(2) at RNEC Manadon 1.11.88 (ex storage at Rolls-Royce, Filton; orange colour scheme). No engines. Current 6.92. Repainted in the medium sea grey scheme (date ?). *Re-allocated A2624 [2] in 1993 (see later).*
A2658	Hawker P.1127	XP984	*Current in 1988 (see earlier).*
A2659	Sea King HAS.1	XV669	*Current in 1988 (see earlier).*
A2660			*Not re-allocated.*
A2661			*Not re-allocated.*
A2662			*Not re-allocated.*
A2663			*Not re-allocated.*
A2664			*Not re-allocated. Sea King HAS.1 A2664/XV644 was not listed in 1988 but was still extant (see earlier). However, it was re-allocated A2615 [3] in 1993 (see later).*
A2665			*Not re-allocated.*

'A' No.	AIRCRAFT TYPE	SERIAL	DETAILS
A2666			*Not re-allocated.*
A2667			*Not re-allocated.*
A2668	Wessex HAS.1	XS885	*Current in 1988 (see earlier). Re-allocated A2631 [2] in 1993 (see later).*
A2669			*Not re-allocated.*
A2670			*Not re-allocated. Wessex HAS.1 A2670/XS128 was not listed in 1988 but was still extant (see earlier). It was re-allocated A2690 [2] post-1993 (see later).*
A2671			*Not re-allocated.*
A2672	Wasp HAS.1	XS537	*Current in 1988 (see earlier).*
A2673			*Not re-allocated.*
A2674			*Not re-allocated. Sea Prince T.1 A2674/WF125 was not listed in 1988 but was still extant (see earlier).*
A2675			*Not re-allocated. Wessex HAS.1 A2675/XS881 was not listed in 1988 but was still extant (see earlier). It was re-allocated A2688 [2] post-1993 (see later).*
A2676			*Not re-allocated.*
A2677			*Not re-allocated.*
A2678			*Not re-allocated.*
A2679			*Not re-allocated.*
A2680			*Not re-allocated.*
A2681	Wessex HAS.1	XP117	*Current in 1988 (see earlier).*
A2682			*Not re-allocated.*
A2683	Wessex HAS.1	XS878	*Current in 1988 (see earlier).*
A2684	Wessex HAS.1	XP151	*Current in 1988 (see earlier).*
A2685			*Not re-allocated.*
A2686			*Not re-allocated. Wessex HAS.1 A2686/XS873 was not listed in 1988 but was still extant (see earlier).*
A2687	Wessex HAS.1	XS877	*Current in 1988 (see earlier). A2688 Wessex HAS.1 XP158 Current in 1988 (see earlier).*
A2689	Wessex HAS.1	XM874	*Current in 1988 (see earlier). Re-allocated A2629 [2] in 1993 (see later).*
A2690	Wessex HAS.1	XS887	*Current in 1988 (see earlier).*
A2691			*Not re-allocated. Wessex HAS.1 A2691/XS868 was not listed in 1988 but was still extant (see earlier). It was re-allocated A2686 [2] post-1993 (see later).*
A2692	Wessex HAS.1	XM917	*Current in 1988 (see earlier).*
A2693	Wessex HAS.1	XM843	*Current in 1988 (see earlier). Re-allocated A2625 [2] in 1993 (see later).*
A2694	Wessex HAS.1	XS865	*Current in 1988 (see earlier).*
A2695	Wessex HAS.1	XS876	*Current in 1988 (see earlier). Re-allocated A2626 [3] in 1993 (see later).*
A2696	Wessex HAS.1	XS882	*Current in 1988 (see earlier).*
A2697	Wessex HAS.1	XS870	*Current in 1988 (see earlier).*
A2698			*Not re-allocated.*
A2699	Wasp HAS.1	XS570	*Current in 1988 (see earlier).*
A2700	Hawker P.1127	XP980	*Current in 1988 (see earlier).*
A2701			*Not re-allocated.*
A2702	Wasp HAS.1	XS545	*Current in 1988 (see earlier).*
A2703			*Not re-allocated.*
A2704 [2]	Wessex HAS.3	XS153	*[Original allocation, if any, not known]* To Class GRB at AES Lee-on-Solent by road 13.9.83 (ex Wroughton), coded 'PO/662' (ex 737 Sqdn Portland). To RNEC Manadon by 28.7.87. No engine. Declared surplus to requirements 14.2.89 and allocated to Army charge 21.3.89. Departed by 1.6.89, reportedly for Lee-on-Solent but probably en route to Sennelager ranges, Germany where noted by 25.10.91 and still recognisable as 'PO/662'. Scrapped 3.96.
A2705	Wessex HAS.1	XS866	*Current in 1988 (see earlier). Re-allocated A2627 [2] in 1993 (see later).*

'A' No.	AIRCRAFT TYPE	SERIAL	DETAILS
A2706	Wessex HAS.1	XM868	*Current in 1988 (see earlier). Re-allocated A2630 [2] in 1993 (see later).*
A2707	Wessex HAS.3	XS122	*Current in 1988 (see earlier). Re-allocated A2632 [2] in 1993 (see later).*
A2708			*Not re-allocated.*
A2709			*Not re-allocated.*
A2710 [2]	Wessex HAS.3	XP137	*[Original allocation, if any, not known]* To Class GRB at AES Lee-on-Solent by road 27.9.83 (ex Wroughton), coded 'PO/665' (ex 737 Sqdn Portland). No engine. Remained as such until repainted dark grey overall with white serials and deckletters 'CU' only (fitted with tail pylon from another a/c) and arrived SAH Culdrose by road 13.9.88. Placed in open store at 'A' site by 31.3.93. With ETS Culdrose by 23.11.93 (probably by 6.93 as replacement for A2688/ XP158). *Re-allocated A2633 [2] in 1993 (see later).*
A2711 [2]	Wessex HAS.3	XS862	*[Original allocation, if any, not known]* To Class GRB at AES Lee-on-Solent by road 19.9.83 (ex Wroughton), coded 'PO/650' (ex 737 Sqdn Portland). Marked '-/650' by 2.87. Last noted 27.9.88. Transferred to the Nuclear, Biological and Chemical Defence Centre, Winterbourne Gunner 30.8.89 and current 3.94.
A2712 [2]	Wessex HAS.3	XM870	*[Original allocation, if any, not known]* To Class GRB at AES Lee-on-Solent by road 28.11.83 (ex Wroughton), coded 'PO/652' (ex 737 Sqdn Portland). No engine. Marked '-/652' by 2.87. Remained as such until repainted dark grey overall with white serials and deckletters 'PO' only (fitted with tail pylon from another aircraft) and arrived SAH Culdrose by road 13.9.88. Placed in open store at 'A' site by 31.3.93. Left Culdrose for AES Lee-on-Solent by road 27.7.93. *Re-allocated A2634 [2] in 1993 (see later).*
A2713 [2]	Wessex HAS.3	XM836	*[Original allocation, if any, not known]* To Class GRB with Fleetlands apprentices by road 20.11.84 (ex Wroughton) for apprentices, coded 'PO/651' (ex 737 Sqdn Portland). No engine. Marked '-/651' by 6.85. To Culdrose and arrived by road 16.4.91, marked '-/651. Dumped on its side in the fire pits. Hulk removed 11.12.91 by local scrap dealer.
A2714			*Whirlwind HAR.9 A2714/XL880 was not listed in 1988 but was still extant (see earlier).*
A2714 [2]	Wessex HAS.3	XP110	Formerly A2728; new 'A' number allocated in 1988. Engine re-allocated E4604. With Fleetlands apprentices, marked *"FL/55"* (spurious). Current 6.92. To AES Lee-on-Solent by 4.11.93, minus engine. *Re-allocated A2636 [2] in 1993 (see later).*
A2715	Wasp HAS.1	XS568	*Current in 1988 (see earlier). Re-allocated A2637 [2] in 1993 (see later).*
A2716	Wasp HAS.1	XT780	*Current in 1988 (see earlier). Re-allocated A2638 [2] in 1993 (see later).*
A2717	Wasp HAS.1	XS569	*Current in 1988 (see earlier). Re-allocated A2639 [2] in 1993 (see later).*
A2718 [2]	Wasp HAS.1	XS539	[Previously Class GRA for a time - see earlier] *[Original allocation, if any, not known]* To Class GRB at AES Lee-on-Solent 24.6.86 (flown in 19.6.86), coded '-/435' (ex 829 Sqdn HMS Endurance Flt). Engine No E4774. To Fleetlands apprentices 7.1.92 as '-/435' and current 6.92. *Re-allocated A2640 [2] in 1993 (see later).*
A2719 [2]	Wasp HAS.1	XS567	*[Original allocation, if any, not known]* To Class GRB at AES Lee-on-Solent 3.6.86 (flown in 5.6.86), coded 'E/434' (ex 829 Sqdn HMS Endurance Flt). Engine No E4775. With NBC School at Lee-on-Solent 9.88. To Imperial War Museum, Duxford 8.92 and current as 'E/434'.
A2720 [2]	Wasp HAS.1	XT429	[Previously Class GRA for a time - see earlier] To Class GRB at AES Lee-on-Solent by 27.9.88, coded 'PLY/445' (ex 829 Sqdn HMS Plymouth Flt). Engine No E4771. To Wroughton store, arriving by road 16.1.89. Left by road 10.8.92 en route Malaysian Navy.

'A' No.	AIRCRAFT TYPE	SERIAL	DETAILS
A2721 [2]	Wasp HAS.1	XT437	To Class GRB at AES Lee-on-Solent 23.3.88, coded '-/423' (ex 829 Sqdn HMS Diomede Flt). Engine No E4782. With 760 Sqdn 10.91 and current 1.93. *Re-allocated A2641 [2] in 1993 (see later).*
A2722 [2]	Wasp HAS.1	XT778	[Previously Class GRA for a time - see earlier] To Class GRB at AES Lee-on-Solent 23.3.88, coded '-/430' (ex 829 Sqdn HMS Achilles Flt). Engine No E4783. Marked '-/461' (see XS529) and *"Sleezebag"* on nose by 10.91 with 760 Sqdn. Marked '-/430' only again by 4.92 and current as such with 760 Sqdn 1.93. *Re-allocated A2642 [2] in 1993 (see later).*
A2723 [2]	Wasp HAS.1	XT434	To Class GRB at AES Lee-on-Solent 23.3.88, coded '-/455' (ex 829 Sqdn HMS Ariadne Flt). Engine No E4786. To Fleetlands apprentices 7.1.92 and current 6.92. *Re-allocated A2643 [2] in 1993 (see later).*
A2724 [2]	Hunter GA.11	WV382	Formerly A2730; new 'A' number allocated 1988. With AES Lee-on-Solent for BDR training, coded '-/830'. Engine No E4780 removed by 8.88. Derelict on the north side for BDR training by 9.88 and for sale 4.89. To Staravia yard at Smethwick mid 1989.
A2725			*Not re-allocated. Wasp HAS.1 A2725/XS538 was not listed in 1988 but was still extant (see earlier).*
A2726			*Not re-allocated.*
A2727	Wessex HAS.3	XM328	*Current in 1988 (see earlier). Re-allocated A2644 [2] in 1993 (see later).*
A2728			*Not re-allocated.*
A2729	Hunter T.7	XL600	*Current in 1988 (see earlier).*
A2730 [2]	Hunter GA.11	XE712	[Original allocation, if any, not known] To Class GRB at AES Lee-on-Solent by road 5.3.85 for BDR training (ex Shawbury), coded '-/708' (no fin, ex Yeovilton Stn Flt). No engine. To Predannack by road arriving 9.2.88, still '-/708'. Current 5.93. *Re-allocated A2620 [2] in 1993 (see later).*
A2731	Hunter GA.11	WT711	*Current in 1988 (see earlier). Re-allocated A2645 [2] in 1993 (see later).*
A2732	Hunter GA.11	WT804	*Current in 1988 (see earlier). Re-allocated A2646 [2] in 1993 (see later).*
A2733	Hunter GA.11	XE668	*Current in 1988 (see earlier). Re-allocated A2647 [2] in 1993 (see later).*
A2734	Hunter T.7	XF321	*Current in 1988 (see earlier). Re-allocated A2648 [2] in 1993 (see later).*
A2735	Wasp HAS.1	XV625	*Current in 1988 (see earlier). Re-allocated A2649 [2] in 1993 (see later).*
A2736	Hunter GA.11	XE682	*Current in 1988 (see earlier).*
A2737	Hunter GA.11	WV267	*Current in 1988 (see earlier). Re-allocated A2650 [2] in 1993 (see later).*
A2738	Hunter T.7	XX466	*Current in 1988 (see earlier). Re-allocated A2651 [2] in 1993 (see later).*
A2739	Wessex HU.5	XS516	*Current in 1988 (see earlier). Re-allocated A2652 [2] in 1993 (see later).*
A2740	Wessex HU.5	XS514	*Current in 1988 (see earlier). Re-allocated A2653 [2] in 1993 (see later).*
A2741	Wessex HU.5	XT455	*Current in 1988 (see earlier). Re-allocated A2654 [2] in 1993 (see later).*
A2742	Wessex HU.5	XT484	*Current in 1988 (see earlier). Re-allocated A2655 [2] in 1993 (see later).*
A2743	Wasp HAS.1	XS529	*Current in 1988 (see earlier). Re-allocated A2696 [2] post-1993 (see later).*
A2744	Wessex HU.5	XT460	*Current in 1988 (see earlier). Re-allocated A2668 [2] in 1993 (see later).*
A2745	Wessex HU.5	XT482	*Current in 1988 (see earlier). Re-allocated A2656 [2] in 1993 (see later).*
A2746	Wessex HU.5	XS483	*Current in 1988 (see earlier). Re-allocated A2657 [3] in 1993 (see later).*

'A' No.	AIRCRAFT TYPE	SERIAL	DETAILS
A2747	Wessex HU.5	XS515	*Current in 1988 (see earlier). Re-allocated A2658 [2] in 1993 (see later).*
A2748	Wasp HAS.1	XT795	*Current in 1988 (see earlier).*
A2749	Wessex HU.5	XS520	*Current in 1988 (see earlier). Re-allocated A2659 [2] in 1993 (see later).*
A2750	Wessex HU.5	XS511	*Current in 1988 (see earlier). Re-allocated A2660 [2] in 1993 (see later).*
A2751	Wessex HU.5	XT762	*Current in 1988 (see earlier). Re-allocated A2661 [2] in 1993 (see later).*
A2752	Wessex HU.5	XT449	*Current in 1988 (see earlier). Re-allocated A2662 [2] in 1993 (see later).*
A2753	Wessex HU.5	XS522	*Current in 1988 (see earlier). Re-allocated A2663 [2] in 1993 (see later).*
A2754	Hunter GA.11	WW654	*Current in 1988 (see earlier). Re-allocated A2664 [2] in 1993 (see later).*
A2755	Wessex HU.5	XT765	*Current in 1988 (see earlier). Re-allocated A2665 [2] in 1993 (see later).*
A2756	Wessex HU.5	XT453	*Current in 1988 (see earlier). Re-allocated A2666 [2] in 1993 (see later).*
A2757	Wessex HU.5	XT468	To Class GR(2) at AES Lee-on-Solent by road 24/25.6.91 (ex Wroughton), coded 'PO/628' (ex 772 Sqdn Portland). No engines. Noted 11.92 for airframe repair training as '-/628'. Current 1.93. *Re-allocated A2667 [2] in 1993 (see later).*
A2758	Whirlwind HAS.7	XN302	Formerly A2654; allocated new 'A' number in 1988. Engine re-allocated No E4601. To HMS Royal Arthur, Corsham, Wilts 7.7.87 (ex Lee-on-Solent dump). To RAF Finningley by 5.90 allocated 9037M.
A2759	Whirlwind HAS.7	XN359	Formerly A2712; allocated new 'A' number in 1988. No engine. Remains on Lee-on-Solent dump for BDR training last noted 9.88.
A2759 [2]	Harrier GR.3	XW630	To Class GR(2) at AES Lee-on-Solent 15.5.91 (ex St Athan), coded 'T' (ex 3 Sqdn Gutersloh). Engine No E4627. Repainted in Dark sea grey Sea Harrier scheme by 23.10.91, uncoded. Current 1.93. *Re-allocated A2671 [2] in 1993 (see later).*
A2760	Whirlwind HAR.9	XN311	Formerly A2643; allocated new 'A' number in 1988. *[Note that this aircraft is given as "XN297" in official lists - see A2643 earlier].* To HMS Royal Arthur, Corsham 7.7.87 (ex Lee-on-Solent dump), no engine. Noted in a scrapyard in the Hull area by mid-9.88 and for sale 11.88. Remains moved onto Birmingham area around 27.1.89.
A2760 [2]	Harrier GR.3	XV751	To Class GR(2) at AES Lee-on-Solent 16.5.91 (ex St Athan), coded 'U' (ex 3 Sqdn Gutersloh). No engine. Noted 11.92 for airframe repair, repainted in the Dark sea grey Sea Harrier scheme minus marks and serials. Current 1.93. *Re-allocated A2672 [2] in 1993 (see later).*
A2761	Wessex HU.5	XT771	*Current in 1988 (see earlier). Re-allocated A2673 [2] in 1993 (see later).*
A2762	Wessex HU.5	XS507	*Current in 1988 (see earlier). Re-allocated A2674 [2] in 1993 (see later).*
A2763	Wessex HU.5	XS496	*Current in 1988 (see earlier). Re-allocated A2675 [2] in 1993 (see later).*
A2764	Wessex HAS.3	XP150	Formerly A2719; allocated new 'A' number in 1988. With AES Lee-on-Solent, coded 'AN/406' (ex 737 Sqdn HMS Antrim Flt). Engine No E4771. Noted on field 8.91. Current 7.92, outside BDR training hangar, minus marks with many damage repair panels. BDR use by the fire pits by 11.92, marked *"XP15"* and spuriously coded *"LS/-"*. To the Home Office Fire and Emergency Training Centre, Moreton-in-Marsh, Gloucs by 25.1.93. Current 2.97. *[Tail possibly to A2780/XP157, and may have acquired the tail section of A2693/XM843, hence the "LS" marking].*
A2765	Wessex HU.5	XS510	*Current in 1988 (see earlier). Re-allocated A2676 [2] in 1993 (see later).*

'A' No.	AIRCRAFT TYPE	SERIAL	DETAILS
A2766	Wessex HU.5	XS508	*Current in 1988 (see earlier). Re-allocated A2677 [2] in 1993 (see later).*
A2767	Wessex HU.5	XT761	*Current in 1988 (see earlier). Re-allocated A2678 [2] in 1993 (see later).*
A2768	Wessex HU.5	XT458	*Current in 1988 (see earlier). Re-allocated A2679 [2] in 1993 (see later).*
A2769	Wessex HU.5	XT485	*Current in 1988 (see earlier). Re-allocated A2680 [2] in 1993 (see later).*
A2770	Wessex HU.5	XS513	*Current in 1988 (see earlier). Re-allocated A2681 [2] in 1993 (see later).*
A2771	SH-3D Sea King	XV370	To Class GR(2) at AES Lee-on-Solent 8.1.90 (ex ETPS in r/w/b scheme, WFU 8.89). Engine Nos E4838/4839. To Yeovil by road 31.1.90 and repainted in Medium sea grey scheme. Returned to Lee-on-Solent by road 22.2.90. With 760 Sqdn by 11.92. Current 1.93. *Re-allocated A2682 [2] in 1993 (see later).*
A2772	Lynx HAS.2	XX510	Formerly A2601 [2] with Engine Nos E4619/E4620. Allocated new 'A' number by 8.91, together with new Engine Nos E4628/4629. Preserved (?) on the field at Lee-on-Solent. To Yeovilton by road 13.1.92 for respray and noted in Medium sea grey scheme by 21.1.92 marked *"LS/69"* (spurious). To Lee-on-Solent by road 27.1.92 and displayed near the Lynx Training School. Current 6.94. *Re-allocated A2683 [2] in 1993 (see later).*
A2773			*No known allocation.*
A2774			*No known allocation.*
A2775			*No known allocation.*
A2776			*No known allocation.*
A2777			*No known allocation.*
A2778			*No known allocation.*
A2779			*No known allocation.*
A2780	Wessex HAS.1	XP157	Formerly A2680; allocated new 'A' number in 1988. AES Lee-on-Solent, uncoded. Engine No E4734. Last noted 27.9.88. Transferred to HMS Royal Arthur 28.8.89. Arrived Yeovilton by road 3.11.92 for FCR training, marked *"AN/-" [the tail section marked "AN" is believed to be from A2719/XP150].* Part burnt by 12.94. *[Not listed in new allocations in 1993 but subsequently re-allocated A2689 [2] - see later].*

Former RAE Canberra B(I).6 WT308 at Predannack on 13.10.92 following its arrival 1.10.92. It was subsequently allocated A2601 [3].
(Geoff Wakeham)

CLASS GR(2) AIRFRAMES 1993 - 1997

In 1993 it was decided to re-allocate 'A' numbers in the range from A2600 to A2700 and engine numbers from E4700, with the range from E4600 used for ECU's not fitted to an airframe. The following list was correct at 4 November 1993 with subsequent additions and contains some surprises. Some but by no means all of the fire training airframes at Predannack which had previously been overlooked in the 1988 re-organisation now appear in the list. Indeed, FCR airframes at other establishments, notably Yeovilton, have been allocated 'A' numbers post-1993. There are other airframes known to be extant during this period which have escaped the re-allocations. The reader is referred to the previous sections and also, for the purposes of researching a particular type or serial, to the cross-reference section (see later). 'New' allocations in this section include more Hunters, Harrier GR.3s, a Wessex HU.5, a Canberra, a Sea King HAS.6 and a Jetstream T.2. Note that the SAH was renamed the School of Flight Deck Operations (SFDO) in November 1995. The AES had completed its relocation to a new facility at HMS Sultan, Gosport by June 1996, becoming the Air Engineering and Survival School (AESS).

'A' No.	AIRCRAFT TYPE	SERIAL	DETAILS
A2600 [3]	Buccaneer S.1	XN953	Formerly A2655. No engines. FCR training Predannack. Newly burnt by 5.93 and burnt hulk current 8.95, but expired by 6.96.
A2600 [4]	Sea King HAS.5	XV657	To ETS Culdrose by road 5.7.94 (ex Fleetlands store), coded '-/132' (ex 826 Sqdn Culdrose) and fitted with tail boom from HAS.6 ZA135. No engines. Current as "ZA135".
A2601 [3]	Canberra B(I).6	WT308	[Former allocation, if any, not known] Allocated to Culdrose 30.5.90 (ex RAE) for ground rescue training but remained at Farnborough until delivered to Predannack 1.10.92 by road for FCR training (ex DRA Farnborough store). Presumably Class GR(2). No engines. Current 9.97.
A2602 [3]	Harrier GR.1	XV277	Formerly A2600 [2]. Engine re-allocated No E4700. ETS Yeovilton. Sold to R J Everett, Ipswich and left by road 9.1.96. Current.
A2603 [2]	Wessex HU.5	XT480	Formerly A2617 [2]. Engines re-allocated Nos E4702/4703. Fleetlands apprentices, coded '-/XQ'. Current 3.94 but stored by 6.94. Replaced Wessex HAS.1 A2691/XS868 on the gate by 3.11.94, coded 'PO/-' (no engines). Repainted in sand/spinach camouflage and coded 'RG/468' by 6.4.95. Current.
A2604 [3]	Harrier GR.3	XZ129	Formerly A2602 [2]. Engine re-allocated No E4704. ETS Yeovilton, repainted in RN scheme with 899 Sqdn marks and 'ETS' in place of a code. Current.
A2605 [2]	Harrier GR.3	XV760	Formerly A2614 [2]. No engine. Yeovilton gate guard in RN scheme as "VL/-" (spurious). Removed from the gate 12.10.94 to the ETS hangar. Allocated for FCR training by 6.95. Left by road 6.3.96 to BAe Dunsfold to assist in rebuild of Sea Harrier FRS.1 XZ493 for FAA Museum. Current.
A2606 [3]	Harrier GR.3	XV755	Formerly A2604 [2]. No engine. BDR training Yeovilton coded 'M' and marked 'Royal Navy' on tail, parked near south dispersal. Moved to the FCR area 4.96. Current.
A2607 [3]	Harrier GR.3	XV806	Formerly A2606 [2]. Engine re-allocated No E4705. SAH Culdrose, coded 'E' (ex 4 Sqdn). Stored in 820 Sqdn hangar, but possibly with Air Command Driving School by 4.94. Put on display in front of the public enclosure at Culdrose on 10.5.95. Returned to SFDO dummy deck 6.96. Current but due to depart mid-1997.
A2608 [3]	Harrier GR.3	XV741	Formerly A2607 [2]. Engine re-allocated No E4706. SAH Culdrose, uncoded (233 OCU marks). Used for taxi training and coded '1' in white on fin by 28.4.94 for dummy deck training. Fin flash overpainted in white and black code '5' applied 8.95. Current with SFDO.
A2609 [3]	Harrier GR.3	XV783	Formerly A2608 [2]. Engine re-allocated No E4708. AES Lee-on-Solent, coded 'N' (ex 233 OCU). Current 10.95. Moved to new AESS facility at HMS Sultan, Gosport (date?). Arrived SFDO Culdrose on 24.4.96. Current.

'A' No.	AIRCRAFT TYPE	SERIAL	DETAILS
A2610 [3]	Harrier GR.3	XW919	Formerly A2609 [2]. Engine re-allocated No E4709. SAH Culdrose, coded 'W' (ex 4 Sqdn, special tail marks). Stored in 820 Sqdn hangar, but with Air Command Driving School by 4.94. Left by road 3.6.97 for gate guard duties at RMCS Shrivenham. Current
A2610 [4]	Harrier T.4	XZ145	To SFDO Culdrose by road 29.5.97 (ex Shawbury), coded 'T' (20[R] Sqdn marks). Engine No E4709. Current.
A2611 [3]	Harrier GR.3	XV786	Formerly A2615 [2]. No engine. SAH Culdrose, coded 'S' (ex 3 Sqdn). Dismantled in fire pits. Noseless fuselage and wings taken to Predannack 10.2.94 and current 9.97. [Cockpit section retained at Culdrose for FCR training and mounted on a trailer 2.94. Noted at Predannack 14.6.96 but back to Culdrose by 28.6.96.]
A2611 [4]	Jetstream T.2	XX479	Arrived Culdrose by road 18.2.97 (ex St.Athan store) and on to Predannack 19.2.97, coded 'CU/563' (ex 750 Sqdn Culdrose). No engines. Current 9.97.
A2612 [3]	Harrier GR.3	XZ969	Formerly A2610 [2]. Engine re-allocated No E4710. RNEC Manadon, coded 'D' (ex 4 Sqdn, special tail marks). Arrived SAH Culdrose 17.5.95 for dummy deck training and current with SFDO.
A2613 [3]	Lynx HAS.3	XZ243	Formerly A2611 [2]. No engines (later E4791/4892). Wreck refurbished for instructional use at AMG Portland (resprayed in the Medium sea grey scheme). Current 10.93 but dumped by 5.97 and current 9.97. However, fitted with Engine Nos E4791/E4792 by 6.97 and due to transfer to AESS, HMS Sultan, Gosport 9.97.
A2614 [3]	Sea King HAS.2A	XV642	Formerly A2613 [2]. Engines re-allocated Nos E4711/4712. AES Lee-on-Solent (760 Sqdn), repainted in Medium sea grey scheme. Current 9.95 with 760 Sqdn. To new AESS facility at HMS Sultan, Gosport by 6.96 and current with 760 Sqdn.
A2615 [3]	Sea King HAS.1	XV644	Formerly A2664. No engines. FCR training Predannack, coded '-/664'. Noted 5.93 lying on its side and burnt hulk last noted 5.94.
A2616 [3]	Hunter PR.11	WT723	[Former allocation, if any, not known] To Class GR(2) at SAH Culdrose 19.3.93, coded 'VL/866' (by air ex FRADU Yeovilton). Engine No E4713. Also coded '3' in white on fin by 28.4.94 for dummy deck training. Listed 6.95 for disposal and stored. Auctioned 2.97 but not sold. Sold later and flown to Exeter 12.9.97 as N723WT to be fitted with long-range tanks for its flight to the USA.
A2617 [3]	Hunter T.7	XL601	[Former allocation, if any, not known] To Class GR(2) at SAH Culdrose 25.3.93, coded 'VL/874' (by air ex FRADU Yeovilton). Engine No E4714. Also coded '4' in white on fin by 28.4.94 for dummy deck training. Current with SFDO and put on display in front of the public enclosure at Culdrose on 18.6.96. Sold 2.97 to Barry Pover and moved back to the dummy deck 6.3.97, leaving by road 23.5.97 for Exeter. Current
A2617 [4]	Wessex HU.5	XT466	[Formerly 8921M (q.v.)] Ex 8921M with Duke of Wellington's Regt at Weeton Barracks, Preston for de-emplaning exercises. To AESS HMS Sultan, Gosport c.6.97, coded '-/XV' (ex 847 Sqdn Yeovilton). Engine Nos E4714/4715. Current.
A2618 [3]	Hunter T.7	XF310	[Former allocation, if any, unknown] To Class GR(2) at SAH Culdrose 25.3.93, coded 'VL/869' (by air ex FRADU Yeovilton). Engine No E4715. Also coded '2' in white on fin by 28.4.94 for dummy deck training. Sold 2.97 and being dismantled 21.3.97 for shipment by road; left 19.5.97 for Tilbury Docks en route to Tasmania. Current.
A2619 [2]	Hunter T.7	WV372	[Former allocation, if any, not known] To Class GR(2) at SAH Culdrose 19.3.93, coded 'VL/877' (by air ex FRADU Yeovilton). Engine No E4716. Also coded '1' in white on fin by 29.4.94 for dummy deck training. Current with SFDO and put on display in front of the public enclosure at Culdrose on 2.9.96. Sold 2.97 and moved back to the Dummy Deck on 6.3.97 for preparation for one flight; flown to North Weald on 23.5.97. Current.
A2620 [2]	Hunter GA.11	XE712	Formerly A2730 [2]. No engine. FCR training Predannack, coded '-/708'. Badly burnt by 8.94 and current 8.95, but expired by 6.96.

'A' No.	AIRCRAFT TYPE	SERIAL	DETAILS
A2620 [3]	Wessex HU.5	XT766	[Formerly 9054M (q.v.)] To AESS HMS Sultan, Gosport by 10.4.97 (ex St.Athan?), coded 'CU/822' (ex 771 Sqdn Culdrose). Engines allocated E4717/4718. Current.
A2621 [2]	Sea King HAS.6	ZD631	[Former allocation, if any, not known] Fuselage Class GR(2) with ETS Yeovilton by 7.92 (ex Fleetlands), coded '-/(2)66' (ex 814 Sqdn Culdrose, w/o 10.9.91). No engines. Removed by road 19.1.95 and noted in the Bristow Helicopter's hangar at Lee-on-Solent 5.95 (for instructional use ?). To new AESS facility at HMS Sultan, Gosport by 2.97 for airframe repair training. Current.
A2622 [2]	Sea Hawk FGA.4	WV911	Formerly A2626 [2] [and also A2526]. Engine re-allocated No E4717. Stored Lee-on-Solent, marked *"C/115"* (spurious). Current 11.94 but moved to AES hangar by 3.5.95. To BAe Dunsfold by 24.5.95 and current.
A2623 [2]	Sea Hawk F.1	WF225	Formerly A2645. No engine. Gate guard Culdrose, coded 'CU/-'. Removed from the gate 5.10.94 as the area was re-designed due to work on the new Merlin simulator. Remounted on display adjacent to the barrack area main gate on 24.5.95 in virtually the same position it first occupied 37 years earlier. Removed for respray 20.4-1.6.97.
A2624 [2]	Lynx DB	XW839	Formerly A2657 [2] [and also A2710]. No engines. RNEC Manadon (medium sea grey scheme). Allocated for FCR training at Yeovilton late-1994 and arrived 28.3.95 to be placed in the FCR reserve compound. To IHM Weston-super-Mare 11.1.96 (in exchange for XW837 and Lynx test rig RG-05). Current.
A2624 [3]	Wessex HU.5C	XT463	To AESS HMS Sultan, Gosport by 2.97 with 760 Sqdn (ex Shawbury store and 84 Sqdn, Ace of Clubs marks), fitted with rear fuselage of HC.2 XR508/B and tail section marked 'PO'. No engines. Current for BDR training.
A2625 [2]	Wessex HAS.1	XM843	[Previously Class I for a time]. Formerly A2693. Engine re-allocated No E4718. AES Lee-on-Solent for airframe repair training, coded '-/527'. To the BDR compound by 24.5.95, but scrapped 11.95.
A2625 [3]	Wessex HU.5C	XS517	To AESS HMS Sultan, Gosport by 2.97 in outside store (ex Shawbury store and 84 Sqdn, Ace of Diamonds marks), fitted with rear fuselage of HC.2 XS679/WG. No engines. Current.
A2626 [3]	Wessex HAS.1	XS876	Formerly A2695. Engine re-allocated No E4719. SAH Culdrose Air Command Driving School, coded '-/523'. Current 8.94 but moved to the fire pits by 6.95. Transferred to new AESS facility at HMS Sultan, Gosport by road on 14.5.96 for BDR training minus tail pylon. Arrived SFDO Culdrose by road on 12.8.97. Current.
A2627 [2]	Wessex HAS.1	XS866	Formerly A2705. Engine re-allocated No E4720. SAH Culdrose (later SFDO) Air Command Driving School, coded 'CU/520'. Left by road 19.9.96 to new AESS facility at HMS Sultan, Gosport for BDR training. Noted 2.97 in outside store, marked '-/520'. Returned by road to SFDO Culdrose 7-10.4.97. Current.
A2628 [2]	Wessex HAS.1	XP160	Formerly A2650. No engine. FCR training Predannack, coded 'CU/521'. Noted 5.93 lying on its side and current 9.97, still 'CU/521'.
A2629 [2]	Wessex HAS.1	XM874	Formerly A2689. No engine. FCR training Predannack, coded 'CU/521'. Noted 5.93 lying on its side and noted 6.96, still 'CU/521'. Believed current 9.97.
A2630 [2]	Wessex HAS.1	XM868	Formerly A2706. No engine. FCR training Predannack, coded 'PO/517'. Noted 5.93 lying on its side and noted 6.96 as '-/517'. Current 9.97.
A2631 [2]	Wessex HAS.1	XS885	Formerly A2668. No engine. SAH Culdrose, coded *"CU/12"* (spurious), for dummy deck training. Current with SFDO.
A2632 [2]	Wessex HAS.3	XS122	Formerly A2707. No engine. AES Lee-on-Solent, coded '-/655'. Placed outside by 5.95, coded 'PO/655' ("new" tail), and current 9.95 with 760 Sqdn. No engine. To new AESS facility at HMS Sultan, Gosport by 2.97 for Air Medical School. Current outside in use for medivac exercises.

'A' No.	AIRCRAFT TYPE	SERIAL	DETAILS
A2633 [2]	Wessex HAS.3	XP137	Formerly A2710 [2]. No engine. ETS Culdrose, coded 'CU/-' (dark grey overall with white markings). Current 11.93 but replaced by Sea King HAS.5 XV657 and moved to storage in the old A.R.E. hangar by 5.94. To the fire pits on 27.3.95 for BDR training but returned to Dummy Deck 9.96. Current.
A2634 [2]	Wessex HAS.3	XM870	Formerly A2712 [2]. No engine. AES Lee-on-Solent, coded 'PO/-' (dark grey overall with white markings). Current 3.5.95 (gutted) but noted outside by 24.5.95. To BDR compound by 9.95 (uncoded) and current 10.95. To new AESS facility at HMS Sultan, Gosport and current 6.96 for BDR training. To Culdrose 25.11.96 and on to Predannack next day for FCR training. Curren 9.97, lying on its side.
A2635 [2]	*Listed as Wessex HAS.3 "XT308" at SAH Culdrose - true identity uncertain.*		
A2635 [3]	Wessex HU.5C	XS485	To AESS HMS Sultan, Gosport by 2.97 (ex Shawbury store and 84 Sqdn, Ace of Hearts marks), fitted with rear fuselage of HC.2 XR503, and stored for BDR training. No engines. Current.
A2636 [2]	Wessex HAS.3	XP110	Formerly A2714 [2] [and also A2728]. No engine. AES Lee-on-Solent, coded *"FL/55"* (spurious). Current 9.95 for BDR training. To new AESS facility at HMS Sultan, Gosport by 2.97 for airframe repair training and current.
A2637 [2]	Wasp HAS.1	XS568	Formerly A2715. Engine re-allocated No E4721. Fleetlands apprentices, coded '-/441'. Last noted 6.92 and subsequently stored, initially in 'C' shop. To 'B' shop store by 3.97 and current.
A2638 [2]	Wasp HAS.1	XT780	Formerly A2716. Engine re-allocated No E4722. Fleetlands apprentices, coded '-/636'. Current.
A2639 [2]	Wasp HAS.1	XS569	Formerly A2717. Engine re-allocated No E4723. Fleetlands apprentices, uncoded. Current.
A2640 [2]	Wasp HAS.1	XS539	[Previously Class GRA for a time - see earlier] Formerly A2718 [2]. Engine re-allocated No E4724. Fleetlands apprentices, coded '-/435'. Current.
A2641 [2]	Wasp HAS.1	XT437	Formerly A2721 [2]. Engine re-allocated No E4725. AES Lee-on-Solent (760 Sqdn), coded '-/423'. Current 11.94 but gone by 9.95. To Boscombe Down by 6.96.
A2641 [3]	Wessex HU.5C	XS498	To AESS HMS Sultan, Gosport by 2.97 (ex Shawbury store and 84 Sqdn. Joker playing card marks), fitted with rear fuselage of HC.2 XS677/WK, and stored for BDR training. No engines. Current.
A2642 [2]	Wasp HAS.1	XT778	[Previously Class GRA for a time - see earlier] Formerly A2722 [2]. Engine re-allocated No E4726. AES Lee-on-Solent (760 Sqdn), coded '-/430' and marked *"HMS Achilles"* on the nose. Current 6.94, but departed by 22.11.94 to the School of Petroleum, Royal Logistics Corps, West Moors, Dorset in 10.94. Current?
A2643 [2]	Wasp HAS.1	XT434	Formerly A2723 [2]. Engine re-allocated No E4727. Fleetlands apprentices, coded '-/455'. Current 6.94. Subsequently stored in 'C' shop, and later moved to 'B' shop store by 2.97. Current.
A2644 [2]	Wessex HAS.3	XM328	Formerly A2727. Engine re-allocated No E4728. SAH Culdrose, uncoded (marked *"The Sow"*) for dummy deck training. Current with SFDO.
A2645 [2]	Hunter GA.11	WT711	Formerly A2731. Engine re-allocated No E4729. SAH Culdrose, coded 'DD/833'. Sold to Harry Pound, Portsmouth and due to leave 1.94 but still at Culdrose 8.94. Put on display in front of the public enclosure at Culdrose on 10.5.95 for the summer and current 8.95, but tendered for sale 6.95. Purchased by Air Atlantique and moved to Coventry Airport by road 23/24.11.95.
A2646 [2]	Hunter GA.11	WT804	Formerly A2732. Engine Re-allocated No E4730. SAH Culdrose, coded 'DD/831'. Left by road 11.5.94 on an RAF transporter for fire-fighting duties at the Home Office Fire and Emergency Training Centre, Moreton-in-Marsh, Gloucs. Current 2.97.
A2647 [2]	Hunter GA.11	XE668	Formerly A2733. Engine re-allocated No E4731, although it was probably removed at Culdrose. FCR training Predannack, coded 'DD/832'. Current 9.97.

'A' No.	AIRCRAFT TYPE	SERIAL	DETAILS
A2648 [2]	Hunter T.7	XF321	Formerly A2734. Engine re-allocated No E4732. RNEC Manadon (RAE r/w/b scheme). Current 10.94. Allocated for FCR training at Yeovilton late-1994. To Yeovilton 19.5.95 and placed on south dispersal. Wings and undercarriage refitted 30.8.95. Moved into former FRADU hangar 21.3.96. For sale 5.96 but still current at Yeovilton.
A2649 [2]	Wasp HAS.1	XV625	Formerly A2735. Engine re-allocated No E4733. RNEC Manadon, coded '-/471' and marked 'HMS Thunderer' on the nose. Arrived Culdrose by road 1.3.95 for 706 Sqdn 50th anniversary 7.3.95. Noted on a lorry at Yeovilton 9.3.95, probably en route AES Lee-on-Solent where it had arrived by 3.5.95. Marked 'HMS Daedalus' by 9.95 and current 10.95. To new AESS facility at HMS Sultan, Gosport by 2.97, when reported marked 'HMS Thunderer' once again. Marked 'HMS Sulan' by 7.97 when it appeared at the Culdrose Air Day. Current.
A2650 [2]	Hunter GA.11	WV267	Formerly A2737. Engine re-allocated No E4734. SAH Culdrose, coded 'DD/836'. Sold and left by road 13.1.94 for North Weald en route to California 2.96.
A2651 [2]	Hunter T.7	XX466	Formerly A2738. Engine re-allocated No E4735, although it was probably removed at Culdrose. FCR training Predannack, coded 'DD/830'. To fire pits 6.96.
A2652 [2]	Wessex HU.5	XS516	Formerly A2739. Engines re-allocated Nos E4736/4737. AES Lee-on-Solent, coded '(Y)Q'. To BDR training by 11.94(?) and current 9.95. Engies removed by 6.96. To new AESS facility at HMS Sultan, Gosport by 2.97 for airframe repair training and current.
A2653 [2]	Wessex HU.5	XS514	Formerly A2740. Engines re-allocated Nos E4738/4739. AES Lee-on-Solent, coded '(Y)L'. Fitted with red/white/blue rear fuselage (no tail) from HC.2 XR503 by 3.5.95 and noted outside by 24.5.95. Inside by 9.95 with correct rear fuselage refitted (that of XR503 had moved to BDR, marked "XS514" !). To new AESS facility at HMS Sultan, Gosport by 6.96 as 'PO/(Y)L' and current.
A2654 [2]	Wessex HU.5	XT455	Formerly A2741. Engines re-allocated Nos E4740/4741. AES Lee-on-Solent, coded '(Y)U'. Placed outside by 9.95 with 760 Sqdn and current 10.95. To new AESS facility at HMS Sultan, Gosport by 2.97. Current.
A2655 [2]	Wessex HU.5	XT484	Formerly A2742. Engines re-allocated Nos E4742/4743. AES Lee-on-Solent, coded '(Y)H'. Current 11.94, but gone by 9.95. To new AESS facility at HMS Sultan, Gosport by 6.96 and current.
A2656 [2]	Wessex HU.5	XT482	Formerly A2745. Engines re-allocated Nos E4744/4745. AES Lee-on-Solent, coded 'VL/ZM'. To FAA Museum Yeovilton by 23.2.94.
A2657 [3]	Wessex HU.5	XS483	Formerly A2746. Engines re-allocated Nos E4746/4747. Dumped at Lee-on-Solent for BDR training, coded 'VL/(Y)T'. Removed to the BDR compound by 4.94 and current 5.95, but scrapped by 9.95.
A2658 [2]	Wessex HU.5	XS515	Formerly A2747. Engines re-allocated Nos E4748/4749. AES Lee-on-Solent, coded '(Y)N'. Placed outside by 9.95 with 760 Sqdn and current 10.95. To new AESS facility at HMS Sultan, Gosport by 6.96 and current.
A2659 [2]	Wessex HU.5	XS520	[Previously Class GRA for a time - see earlier] Formerly A2749. Engines re-allocated Nos E4750/4751. AES Lee-on-Solent, coded '(Y)F'. Placed outside by 9.95 with 760 Sqdn and current 10.95. To new AESS facility at HMS Sultan, Gosport by 6.96 and current.
A2660 [2]	Wessex HU.5	XS511	Formerly A2750. Engines re-allocated Nos E4752/4753. AES Lee-on-Solent, coded '(Y)M'. Placed outside by 9.95 with 760 Sqdn and current 10.95. To new AESS facility at HMS Sultan, Gosport by 6.96 and current.
A2661 [2]	Wessex HU.5	XT762	Formerly A2751. No engines. SAH Culdrose, uncoded (RAE r/w/b scheme), for dummy deck training. Current with SFDO.

Initially allocated A2602 [2] and later A2604 [3], Harrier GR.3 XZ129 at Yeovilton 4.6.94 in the dark sea grey scheme with No.899 Sqdn marks and the initials 'ETS' applied as a code to reflect its use with the Engineering Training School. (Bob Turner)

Seen here on 20.7.91, following respray in the medium sea grey scheme at Yeovil, former Westland's trials Sea King HAS.2A XV642 was delivered to AES Lee-on-Solent on 19.3.91, initially allocated A2613 [2] and later A2614 [3]. (Bob Turner)

'A' No.	AIRCRAFT TYPE	SERIAL	DETAILS
A2662 [2]	Wessex HU.5	XT449	Formerly A2752. Engines re-allocated Nos E4754/4755. Derelict at Lee-on-Solent for BDR training, coded '(Y)C'. Last seen 11.92 and possibly moved inside as next noted 9.95 in the BDR compound. To new AESS facility at HMS Sultan, Gosport and current 6.96 for BDR training (engines removed by this date). To Culdrose 25.11.96 and on to Predannack next day for FCR training. Hulk not positively identified 9.97.
A2663 [2]	Wessex HU.5	XS522	Formerly A2753. Engines re-allocated Nos E4756/4757. AES Lee-on-Solent, coded '-/ZL'. BDR training. Engines remoced circa 6.96. Current 9.95. To new AESS facility at HMS Sultan, Gosport by 2.97 for airframe repair training and current.
A2664 [2]	Hunter GA.11	WW654	Formerly A2754. Engine re-allocated No E4758. SAH Culdrose, coded 'DD/834'. Sold to Harry Pound, Portsmouth and left Culdrose by road 15.12.93.
A2665 [2]	Wessex HU.5	XT765	Formerly A2755. Engines re-allocated Nos E4759/4760. AES Lee-on-Solent, coded '(Y)J'. Current 10.95. To new AESS facility at HMS Sultan, Gosport by 6.96 and current without engines.
A2666 [2]	Wessex HU.5	XT453	Formerly A2756. Engines re-allocated Nos E4761/4762. AES Lee-on-Solent, coded "-/VL" and marked "846 Naval Air Squadron 1943-1993" (see earlier). To Yeovilton and into the dope shop 7.11.94, emerging 15.11.94 coded 'A/B' in sand/spinach camouflage with 848 Sqdn marks (unit reformed 9.2.95). Still present 8.95 but noted on a lorry in Fareham 22.5.96. To new AESS facility at HMS Sultan, Gosport and current.
A2667 [2]	Wessex HU.5	XT468	Formerly A2757. No engines. AES Lee-on-Solent for airframe repair training, coded '-/628'. To new AESS facility at HMS Sultan, Gosport by 2.97 for airframe repair training, fitted with rear fuselage from XT460/A2668 [3]. Current.
A2668 [2]	Wessex HU.5	XT460	Formerly A2744. No engines. AES Lee-on-Solent for airframe repair training, coded '(Y)K' minus serials. To the BDR compound by 24.5.95, but scrapped 11.95. See A2667 [2]/XT468 above.
A2669 [2]	Wessex HU.5	XT760	[Former allocation, if any, not known. Listed 1.93 with no 'A' number officially allocated.] Allotted to Class GR(2) at AES Lee-on-Solent 28.2.91 for BDR training. Re-allocated to RNEC 18.6.91 and left RNAY Wroughton by road 25.6.91 for Manadon, coded '-/418' with Union Jack on nose (ex 'PO/418' 'A' Flt 772 Sqdn Portland). Arrived ETS Culdrose by road 6.5.92. To AES Lee-on-Solent 16.12.92 (in exchange for A2688/XP158) for BDR training. No engines. Current 9.95 (uncoded). To new AESS facility at HMS Sultan, Gosport by 2.97 for airframe repair training, fitted with a rear fuselage from HC.2 XT604. To RN Diving School, Horsey Island in lieu of A2691/XS868.
A2670 [2]	Wessex HU.5	XS523	Formerly A2618 [2]. No engines. AES Lee-on-Solent, coded 'CU/824'. Current 6.94 in BDR compound but gone by 5.95. To HMS Excellent and awaiting tender 4.96.
A2671 [2]	Harrier GR.3	XW630	Formerly A2759 [2]. Engine re-allocated No E4763. AES Lee-on-Solent, uncoded in dark sea grey Sea Harrier scheme. Current 10.95. To new AESS facility at HMS Sultan, Gosport by 6.96 and on display by 2.97. Current.
A2672 [2]	Harrier GR.3	XV751	Formerly A2760 [2]. No engine. AES Lee-on-Solent for airframe repair training, repainted in the Dark sea grey Sea Harrier scheme minus marks and serials. Reported as due to be scrapped 10.95 but moved to the Peter Vallance Collection, Charlwood, Surrey by 12.95.
A2673 [2]	Wessex HU.5	XT771	Formerly A2761. Engines re-allocated Nos E4764/4765. AES Lee-on-Solent, coded 'PO/620'. Placed outside by 9.95 with 760 Sqdn and current 10.95. To new AESS facility at HMS Sultan, Gosport by 2.97 and current.
A2674 [2]	Wessex HU.5	XS507	Formerly A2762. Engines re-allocated Nos E4766/4767. AES Lee-on-Solent, coded 'PO/627'. Current 10.95, marked '-/(6)27'. To new AESS facility at HMS Sultan, Gosport by 6.96, uncoded. Current.

'A' No.	AIRCRAFT TYPE	SERIAL	DETAILS
A2675 [2]	Wessex HU.5	XS496	Formerly A2763. Engines re-allocated Nos E4768/4769. AES Lee-on-Solent, coded 'PO/625'. Current 10.95. To new AESS facility at HMS Sultan, Gosport by 6.96 and reported uncoded 2.96. Current.
A2676 [2]	Wessex HU.5	XS510	[Previously Class I for a time] Formerly A2765. Engines re-allocated Nos E4770/4771. AES Lee-on-Solent, coded 'PO/626'. Noted 5/9.95 (but reported at Warton 4.6.95 ?). Current at Lee-on-Solent 10.95. To new AESS facility at HMS Sultan, Gosport by 6.96 and in outside store 2.97. Current.
A2677 [2]	Wessex HU.5	XS508	Formerly A2766. Engines re-allocated Nos E4772/4773. AES Lee-on-Solent, uncoded (SAR colour scheme). To FAA Museum Yeovilton 28.6.93 and current.
A2678 [2]	Wessex HU.5	XT761	Formerly A2767. Engines re-allocated Nos E4774/4775. AES Lee-on-Solent, uncoded (SAR colour scheme). Current 10.95. To new AESS facility at HMS Sultan, Gosport by 6.96 and current.
A2679 [2]	Wessex HU.5	XT458	Formerly A2768. Engines re-allocated Nos E4776/4777. AES Lee-on-Solent, coded '-/622'. Current 11.94, but gone by 9.95. To new AESS facility at HMS Sultan, Gosport by 6.96 and current.
A2680 [2]	Wessex HU.5	XT485	Formerly A2769. Engines re-allocated Nos E4778/4779. AES Lee-on-Solent, coded 'PO/621'. Placed outside by 9.95 (uncoded) with 760 Sqdn and current 10.95. To new AESS facility at HMS Sultan, Gosport by 6.96, coded 'PO/-'. Current.
A2681 [2]	Wessex HU.5	XS513	Formerly A2770. Engines re-allocated Nos E4780/4781. AES Lee-on-Solent, coded 'PO/419', for BDR training. Current 9.95, uncoded. To new AESS facility at HMS Sultan, Gosport by 6.96 for BDR training. To main AESS hangar by 2.97, when reported as 'CU/419'. Engines removed by 7.97 (at least). Current.
A2682 [2]	SH-3D Sea King	XV370	Formerly A2771. Engines re-allocated Nos E4782/4783. AES Lee-on-Solent (760 Sqdn), uncoded (repainted in Medium sea grey scheme). Current 9.95 with 760 Sqdn. To new AESS facility at HMS Sultan, Gosport by 6.96 and current with 760 Sqdn.
A2683 [2]	Lynx HAS.2	XX510	Formerly A2601 [2] and A2772. Engines re-allocated E4784/4785. Preserved on field at Lee-on-Solent, with spurious code "LS/69" (repainted in Medium sea grey scheme). Current 9.95. To new AESS facility at HMS Sultan, Gosport by 6.96 (engines disposed of by thsi date) and noted uncoded 2.97 with 760 Sqdn, but listed as BDR airframe by 7.97. Due to go to Westlands for underwater trials.
A2684 [2]	Harrier GR.3	ZD667	[Former allocation, if any, not known] To Class GR(2) and flown to SAH Culdrose 30.7.93, coded '3B' (ex 20[R] Sqdn with 1417 Flt marks). Engine No E4701. Used for taxy training and recoded '3' in white on fin by 28.4.94 for dummy deck training. Fin flash overpainted white and black code '2' applied 8.95. Current with SFDO.
A2685 [2]	Harrier GR.3	XZ996	[Former allocation, if any, not known] To Class GR(2) at SAH Culdrose by road w/c 19.7.93, coded 'F' (ex-Wittering, 1417 Flt marks). Engine No E4707. Used for taxy training and recoded '2' in white on fin by 28.4.94 for dummy deck training. Fin flash overpainted in white and black code '3' applied 8.95. Current with SFDO.
A2686 [2]	Wesex HAS.1	XS868	Formerly A2691 (new number allocated post-1993 but by 5.97 at least). With AESS at HMS Sultan, Gosport by 6.96 for BDR training (red/white/blue/colour scheme). No engine. To 760 Sqdn building by 2.97 and current.
A2687 [2]	Harrier GR.3	XV808	To SAH Culdrose by road 11.7.94 (ex 9076M 1 SoTT Halton), coded '3J' (ex 233 OCU Wittering). Engine No E4790. For dummy deck training. Fin flash overpainted in white and black code '6' applied 8.95. Current with SFDO.
A2688 [2]	Wessex HAS.1	XS881	Formerly A2675; new number allocated post-1993. FCR reserve compound at Yeovilton, coded 'CU/046'). No engine. Moved to the fire pits by 5.97. To Predannack by road 30.9.97 and current.

'A' No.	AIRCRAFT TYPE	SERIAL	DETAILS
A2689 [2]	Wessex HAS.1	XP157	Formerly A2780; allocated new number post-1993. No engine. At Yeovilton for FCR training, marked "AN/-" (see earlier entries). Part burnt by 12.94. Current
A2690 [2]	Wessex HAS.1	XS128	Formerly A2670; new number allocated post-1993. At Yeovilton for FCR training, coded '-/437' (minus rear fuselage). No engine. Current upside down.
A2691 [2]	Harrier GR.3	XV753	To SAH Culdrose by road 12.7.94 (as '9075M' ex 1 SoTT Halton), coded '3F' (ex 233 OCU Wittering). Engine No E4786. For dummy deck training. Fin flash overpainted in white and black code '4' applied 8.95. Current with SFDO.
A2692 [2]	Harrier T.4	XW271	To SAH Culdrose by road 3.11.94, coded 'X' (ex 20[R] Sqdn Wittering) For dummy deck training. Engine No E4787. Fin flash over-painted in white and black code '1' applied 8.95. Current with SFDO.
A2693 [2]	Buccaneer S.2c	XV359	Flown to Culdrose 30.3.94 from Lossiemouth (ex 208 Sqdn) for FCR traiing at Predannack. Engine Nos E4788/4789. Current 9.97. Due to be airlifted by RAF Chinook to Culdrose for preservation.
A2694			*Not yet re-allocated*
A2695			*Not yet re-allocated*
A2696 [2]	Wasp HAS.1	XS529	Formerly A2743; new number allocated post-1993. At Predannack for FCR training by 7.10.96, coded '-/461'. Gutted shell (no engine). Current lying on its side 9.97.
A2697			*Not yet re-allocated*
A2698 [2]	Sea King HAS.6	XV654	To AESS HMS Sultan, Gosport by 2.97 with 760 Sqdn (ex Fleetlands), coded '705' (ex 819 Sqdn Prestwick, crashed 21.7.93). No engines. BDR training by 7.97. Current.
A2699 [2]	SH-3D Sea King	XV371	To AES at HMS Sultan, Gosport by road 12.10.95 (ex DRA, wfu at Boscombe Down 31.3.95), red/white/blue colour scheme. No engines. Current 6.96 but to Fleetlands by 9.96 for paint trials. Returned to AESS circa 5.97 in standard RN medium sea grey scheme. Current.
A2700 [2]	Harrier GR.1	XV280	Cockpit arrived Yeovilton by road 1.11.90 (ex Foulness) for ground instructional duties. Mounted on a trailer and moves around the airfield. Spuriously marked "XV880" by 9.91. Current.

Harrier GR.3 XZ969 at RNEC Manadon in 10.94 became A2610 [2] and later A2612 [3]. (Keith A.Saunders)

Hunter GA.11 A2730 [2]/XE712, ex '708' of Station Flight Yeovilton, at Predannack 17.2.88. (Geoff Wakeham)

Hunter T.7 A2617 [3]/XL601, ex FRADU 'VL/874' at Culdrose 4.5.94 with SAH marking '4' on the fin. (Geoff Wakeham)

Hunter PR.11 A2616 [3]/WT723, ex FRADU 'VL/866' at Culdrose 20.5.93. (Geoff Wakeham)

UNIDENTIFIED CLASS II AIRFRAMES

PART 1 - BY TYPE

There are numerous FAA aircraft which are known or believed to have become instructional airframes, but for which 'A' or 'M' numbers have not yet been traced. A few of these are undoubtedly Class I or Class III, but the vast majority are in the Class II category, and must therefore have been allocated 'A' numbers. Either they never carried them or all record of them has been lost. Readers are invited to pit their wits against the following list, and we would be delighted to learn of any 'A' number identities the reader can supply to help complete the record. Provision is made in the list for the insertion of such numbers.

AIRCRAFT TYPE	SERIAL	'A' No.	DETAILS
Albacore	X9112		At HMS Ariel, Culcheth 1943.
Attacker prototype	TS416		To instructional at St Merryn 21.5.54 (ex CS(A) charge. To RNEC Manadon by 8.56 with '2' in a yellow disc on the nose. On Culdrose dump by 7.58.
Attacker F.1	WA470		To Class II 19.5.52 (ex CS(A) at Vickers-Armstrong)
	WA472		To Class II 7.9.53 (ex Yeovilton).
	WA509		To Class II 25.2.52, coded 'FD/056' (ex 703 Sqdn Ford). To at least 6.55.
Attacker FB.1	WA483	A23__?	To instructional at Arbroath 10.2.53 (ex CS(A) charge at RAE Farnborough). Possibly A2312 or A2314.
	WA516		At Bramcote by 11.58.
	WA518		At Bramcote by 11.58.
	WA529		To Class II at Abbotsinch 27.10.54 (probably ex Abbotsinch). To Ford 21.6.58. Scrapped at Ford.
Attacker FB.2	WK329		[w/o 25.8.52] At Arbroath 3.55, coded "J/119" (spurious).
Avenger I	FN758		At 5 SoTT Locking 8.45.
	FN827		To 10 SoTT Kirkham 28.3.44 (ex Abbotsinch). SOC RN 1.8.44.
	JZ129		To instructional at Ford 25.5.50 (ex CS(A) charge at RAE Farnborough).
Avenger III	KE437		Believed at Bramcote, coded 'M' (ex 703 Sqdn).
Avenger AS.4	XB317	A22__?	WOC 3.54 after force-landing 25.1.54. At Worthy Down 6.56. Engine No. E3279.
Balliol prototype	VL892		To instructional at Arbroath 5.4.54 (ex CS(A) charge after crash-landing at Boscombe Down 18.1.54).
Barracuda II	P9857		At HMS Ariel, Culcheth 1943.
	BV722		To 12 SoTT Melksham 1.4.45 (ex RN Easthaven).
	DR139		At 5 SoTT Locking 9.45.
	LS676		At HMS Ariel, Culcheth by 4.47 to at least 4.48.
	LS870		At 5 SoTT Locking 8.45.
	MX888		At HMS Ariel, Culcheth by 4.47 to at least 4.48.
	MX903		At HMS Ariel, Culcheth by 4.47 to at least 4.48.
	PM779		At HMS Ariel, Culcheth by 4.47 to at least 4.48.
Barracuda III	ME123		At Bramcote 3/4.48 (ex 'D' 703 Sqdn Thorney Island). Probably instructional.
	RJ963		At HMS Ariel, Culcheth by 4.47 to at least 4.48.
	RJ964		At HMS Ariel, Culcheth by 4.47 to at least 4.48.
Corsair II	JT207		At 5 SoTT Locking 9.45.
	JT221		At 5 SoTT Locking 9.45.
	JT601		At 5 SoTT Locking 8-9.45, coded '12V9' (ex 1848 Sqdn).
	JT681		At 5 SoTT Locking 8.45.

AIRCRAFT TYPE	SERIAL	'A' No.	DETAILS
Dragonfly HR.5	VZ962		To instructional at Dartmouth 20.7.64. At RNEC Manadon 6.68 and 7.72. At Norton Helicopter Station, Dartmouth for BRNC in 1974 and still there early 1979. Owned by FAA Museum. Loaned to Cornwall Aero Park, Helston 7.81. From Flambards Triple Theme Park to British Rotorcraft Museum, Weston-super-Mare 14.1.88, coded '-/904'. Current 12.93.
Firebrand TF.II	DK376		At Bramcote 3/4.48. Probably instructional.
Firebrand TF.III	DK404		At HMS Ariel, Culcheth by 4.47 to at least 4.48, coded 'FD-Z' (painted over '3F-1', ex 708 Sqdn Ford).
Firebrand TF.IV	EK605		To instructional at Culdrose 8.9.47 (ex A&AEE Boscombe Down). At Yeovilton by 7.50.
	EK630		To instructional at Bramcote 13.1.48 (ex A&AEE Boscombe Down), to at least 4.48.
	EK720		At Bramcote 3/4.48. Probably instructional.
Firebrand TF.5	EK779		To instructional 14.10.49 and at Bramcote circa 1952, coded 'C/911' (ex Ships Flight HMS Implacable). Burnt 30.1(?).53 by Warwick County Fire Brigade at Pingle Fields, Nuneaton at 5th Annual Review.
	EK783		To instructional at Gosport 22.3.50 (ex Anthorn).]
	EK792		At Anthorn 1.49. SOC 14.6.69. Possibly instructional. Burnt at Anthorn display 2.6.51.
	EK795		At Bramcote 6.53. SOC 29.8.53. Almost certainly instructional.
	EK843		To instructional at Bramcote 8.6.53, coded '124' (ex 827 Sqdn) [NB believe should be '127'].
	EK844		SOC 8.6.53. Burnt at Bramcote display 6.53, coded '120'. Probably instructional.
Firebrand TF.5A	EK728		To instructional 6.4.50. Scrapped at Bramcote 1956.
Firefly F.1	Z1865		To 4 SoTT St Athan 2.3.46 (ex NAS Lee-on-Solent).
	Z1868		To 4 SoTT St Athan 2.3.46 (ex NAS Lee-on-Solent).
	Z1899		To Class II at Bramcote 11.10.49 (ex Yeovilton). Instructional at Bramcote until at least 10.50, coded 'VL/204' (ex 767 Sqdn Yeovilton).
	Z1901		SOC 9.3.49. At Bramcote 6.49-6.51, coded 'MV/203' (ex 767 Sqdn Milltown). Probably instructional.
	Z1907		SOC 8.11.49. At Bramcote 6.53 and probably instructional. Still at Bramcote 1956 for fire-fighting purposes.
	Z1942		At Yeovilton 7.50.
	Z1972		At Yeovilton 7.50.
	Z1986		At Yeovilton 7.50, coded 'Y2J' (ex 700 Sqdn Yeovilton).
	Z2097		At Yeovilton 7.50.
	Z2099		To instructional at Arbroath 21.3.50 (ex 737 Sqdn Eglinton).
	Z2103		To instructional at Arbroath 21.3.50, coded 'JR/221' (ex 737 Sqdn Eglinton). On Gosport dump 7.55, coded "916" (spurious local code).
	DK416		To 12 SoTT Melksham 19.6.45 (ex Lee-on-Solent).
	DK420		To instructional at Arbroath 21.3.50 (ex 737 Sqdn Eglinton).
	DK496		To instructional at Arbroath 31.1.50 (ex Fairey Aviation). Reported on Balado dump 3.53, coded '216' (ex Lossiemouth, and therefore presumed ex 766 Sqdn).
	DK510		SOC 10.3.49 at Abbotsinch. Probably instructional. Reported at Bramcote 6.49, coded 'AC/296', but this code seems improbable. Later reported at Bramcote 10.50, coded 'LM/296' (ex 766 Sqdn Lossiemouth).
	DV119		To Class II at Anthorn 26.9.50 (ex Anthorn), coded 'R/274'. At Bramcote 6.51. On Gosport dump 7.55.
	DV130		SOC 17.3.49. At Bramcote 10.50, coded 'MV/210' (ex 767 Sqdn Milltown). Probably instructional.

AIRCRAFT TYPE	SERIAL	'A' No.	DETAILS
Firefly FR.1	MB401		SOC 19.7.49. At Bramcote 10.50, coded 'VL/200' (ex 767 Sqdn Yeovilton). Probably instructional.
	MB413		To instructional at Yeovilton by 7.50, coded 'VL/203' (ex 700 Sqdn Yeovilton).
	MB446		To instructional at Yeovilton 6.3.49, coded '205' (ex 700 Sqdn Yeovilton).
	MB495		At HMS Ariel, Culcheth by 4.47 to at least 4.48.
	MB504		To Class II 26.9.50 (ex Abbotsinch). At Bramcote 10.50-6.53. On Gosport dump 7.55.
	MB555		To Class II 26.9.50 (ex Abbotsinch).
	MB558		To Class II at Bramcote 26.9.50 (ex Abbotsinch). At Bramcote 10.50.
	MB560		At Bramcote 7.53, coded 'MV/-' (ex 767 Sqdn Milltown).
	MB561		To instructional at Bramcote 31.3.49 (ex Abbotsinch), coded 'AC/280' (ex 1830 Sqdn Abbotsinch). At Bramcote 6.49.
	MB581		At Bramcote 10.50, coded 'MV/205' (ex 767 Sqdn Milltown). Probably instructional.
	MB584?		At Bramcote 10.50, coded 'VL/201' (ex 767 Sqdn Yeovilton). Probably instructional. [This serial is in doubt as MB584 was converted to a T.2 between 11.49 and 9.50].
	MB641		To instructional 15.9.55 (ex Culdrose).
	MB642		At Yeovilton 7.50. Wreck destroyed in fire-fighting demonstration at Lee-on-Solent 26.8.50.
	MB742		At Bramcote 6.53. Probably instructional.
	MB743		At Yeovilton 7.50, coded '216' (ex 767 Sqdn Milltown).
	PP611	A22__?	To Class II at Culham 8.9.50.
	PP620		Believed to GI 18.1.50.
Firefly FR.4	TW688		To Class II 10.7.51 (ex 727 Sqdn Gosport).
	TW689		To Class II at Arbroath 25.1.51 (ex Abbotsinch). Previously at A&AEE Boscombe Down.
	TW690		To Class II at Arbroath 25.1.51 (ex Abbotsinch).
	TW691		To Class II at Arbroath 25.1.51 (ex Abbotsinch).
	TW693		To Class II 10.7.51 (ex Yeovilton).
	TW696		To Class II at Yeovilton 14.6.51 (ex Yeovilton).
	TW697		To Class II at Yeovilton 14.6.51 (ex Yeovilton) to at least 7.51.
	TW698		To Class II at Yeovilton 14.6.51 (ex Yeovilton).
	TW699		To Class II at Yeovilton 14.6.51 (ex Yeovilton).
	TW715		To Class II at Yeovilton 14.6.51 (ex Yeovilton).
	TW716		To Class II at Yeovilton 14.6.51 (ex Yeovilton).
	TW717		To Class II at Yeovilton 14.6.51 (ex Yeovilton).
	TW720		To Class II at Abbotsinch 30.1.51. At Yeovilton 7.51.
	TW721		To instructional 11.6.48.
	VG972		SOC 12.10.48. At Lee-on-Solent 8.50-9.51. Probably instructional. On Gosport dump 7.55.
Firefly 5	VT362		To Class II at Abbotsinch 26.9.50. At Yeovilton 7.51.
	VT369		To Class II at Abbotsinch 26.9.50, coded 'O/211' (ex 810 Sqdn). At RNEC Manadon by 8.54, coded 'O/211', but coded 'O/-' by 6.57.
	VT378		To Class II at Abbotsinch 26.9.50.
	VT381		To Class II at Abbotsinch 26.9.50.
	VT407	A224_?	To Class II at Abbotsinch 26.9.50. Engine No. E3243. At Bramcote 6.53-7.54, coded 'O/280' (ex 812 Sqdn HMS Ocean). Probably in range A240-2249.
	WB262		At Yeovilton 7.50, coded 'Q/221' (ex 814 Sqdn).
	WB349		To SAH Gosport 6.8.55 (ex Sembawang, via HMS Vengeance). WOC for instructional purposes 16.11.55.
	WB379		To SAH Gosport 6.8.55 (ex Sembawang, via HMS Vengeance). WOC for instructional purposes 16.11.55.

AIRCRAFT TYPE	SERIAL	'A' No.	DETAILS
Firefly 5(PF)	VX424		To Class II at Abbotsinch 26.9.50. At Yeovilton 7.51.
	VX435		To Class II at Abbotsinch 22.9.50.
Firefly AS.6	WB254		To Class II at Yeovilton 22.4.55 (ex CAD Ford, 1840 Sqdn 4.4.55). Reduced to scrap on site 26.11.56.
Firefly AS.7	WJ215		To instructional at Arbroath 15.7.53.
Firefly T.7	WM763		To Class II at St Merryn 17.2.54 (ex *"Operation Solitaire"* at St Merryn). To Worthy Down 23.10.54 and still there 6.56.
Gannet prototype	VR557		To instructional components at Culdrose 16.5.56 (ex CS(A) charge at RAE Bedford, via RNEC Manadon).
	WE488		To instructional at Worthy Down 28.2.54 (ex CS(A) charge at Ferranti). At Arbroath 7.55.
Gannet T.2	XG881		To Class II at Arbroath 26.9.61 (ex Abbotsinch ADW), coded 'GN/545' (ex 719 Sqdn Eglinton). In abeyance 23.2.62 and cancelled 17.10.62. To Fairey Aircraft, White Waltham 7.1.65 for conversion to T.5 standard and returned to service. [Crashed in sea off Brawdy 23.2.65].
Gnat T.1	XM694		Allocated to instructional at Culdrose 2.4.74 (ex RAE Bedford). Remained at Bedford and to RAE Apprentices.
Harrier GR.1	XV279		To RNAS Culdrose 27.1.77 on temporary Class GRB loan for apprentice familiarisation training (ex RAF Abingdon still in 1 Sqdn marks). No 'A' number allocated. Departed 6.77 for RAE Farnborough.
Hurricane I	L2045		To Technical Training 15.5.43 (ex RN).
	P3042		To HMS Fledgeling 1943, coded 'Y1I' (ex 759 Sqdn Yeovilton).
	P3061		To 6 SoTT Hednesford 1.9.43 (ex Yeovilton).
	V7068		To 2 SoTT Cosford 28.1.44 (ex RN).
Kranich I glider	VS208		To Class II at Arbroath (no 'A' number allocated). Disposal signalled 8.3.63.
Martlet I	AX826		To 6 SoTT Hednesford 6.12.42.
Master II	W9018		At Bramcote 1948.
	AZ668		At Bramcote 1948.
Meteor F.3	EE337		To Bramcote (ex storage at A&AEE Boscombe Down), to at least 10.56.
Mosquito B.20	KB410		At Bramcote 3.48-1950. Probably instructional.
Mosquito B.25	KA948		Broken up at Bramcote 1950, coded 'AR8Q' (ex 772 Sqdn Ayr).
	KA951		Broken up at Bramcote 1950, coded 'AR8U' (ex 772 Sqdn Ayr).
	KA964		At Yeovilton 7.50.
	KB574		At Bramcote 3.48-1950. Probably instructional.
	KB584		At Bramcote 3.48-1950. Probably instructional.
	KB699		At Yeovilton 7.50.
Oxford I	DF482		To instructional at Yeovilton 1.6.48.
	HM747		To instructional at Yeovilton 9.12.48 (ex Donibristle).
	LB413		To Class II at Lossiemouth 26.9.50. Classification cancelled.
	NM759		To Class II 26.9.50 (ex Lossiemouth store).
	PG984		At HMS Ariel, Culcheth by 4.47 to at least 4.48, coded 'FD5Q' (ex 762 Sqdn Ford).
	PH300		To Class II 26.9.50 (ex Lossiemouth store).
VAS.544	WT854		[Scimitar prototype] To Class II at Arbroath 25.10.56. To SAH Culdrose, date unknown. To P&EE Foulness in 1967.

AIRCRAFT TYPE	SERIAL	'A' No.	DETAILS
Scimitar F.1	XD242		To Class II 12.7.60 after touchdown accident at Yeovilton 14.5.60. To Arbroath 7.60 to at least 9.64. At MARTSU Lee-on-Solent 1.65-5.65. To Aberporth by 9.67 for missile-blast effect ground test.
Seafire L.III	LR857		At Yeovilton 7.50, coded 'G' (possibly ex 883 Sqdn).
Seafire F.15	"KF552"		At Arbroath by 9.52 to at least 5.53 [serial of a Harvard then at Arbroath]. Correct serial unknown.
	PK243		To Bramcote 2.6.49. Probably instructional. On dump at Gosport. To Lee-on-Solent by road 5.52.
	PR340		To instructional at Bramcote 21.2.49 (ex Lossiemouth). At Bramcote 11.50, coded 'LM/127' (ex 766 Sqdn Lossiemouth).
	PR353		To instructional at Bramcote 21.2.49 (ex Lossiemouth), coded 'LM/132' (ex 766 Sqdn Lossiemouth), until at least 11.50.
	PR359		To instructional at Bramcote 12.2.49 (ex Lossiemouth), coded 'LM/126' (ex 766 Sqdn Lossiemouth), until at least 11.50.
	PR374		To instructional at Bramcote 12.2.49 (ex Lossiemouth), coded 'LM/130' (ex 766 Sqdn Lossiemouth), until at least 11.50.
	PR403		SOC 17.3.52. At Anthorn and destroyed in a fire-fighting demonstration 5.7.52. Probably instructional.
	PR456		To instructional at Bramcote 21.2.49 (ex Lossiemouth), coded 'LM/106' (ex 766 Sqdn Lossiemouth), until at least 11.50.
	SR458		To instructional at Yeovilton 23.11.48, to at least 7.51.
	SR461		To instructional 4.7.49. At Arbroath by 9.52 until at least 5.53.
	SR468		Believed to instructional 22.7.48.
	SR473		To instructional at Arbroath 22.4.48, to at least 5.53.
	SR480		To Class II at Bramcote 14.2.49 (ex 767 Sqdn Yeovilton), coded 'VL/100', to at least 11.50.
	SR588		To Class II at Bramcote 26.9.50 (ex 1833 Sqdn Bramcote), until at least 10.52.
	SR602		Burnt in fire fighting demonstration at Culdrose 4.55. Probably instructional. Remains on fire dump at Chatham dockyard 1959-60.
	SR630		At Anthorn 6.51. Probably instructional.
	SR639		At Anthorn. Probably instructional.
	SW791		At Bramcote 1948.
	SW807		At HMS Ariel, Culcheth by 4.47 to at least 4.48.
	SW814		To Class II at Bramcote 26.9.50, coded 'BR/161' (ex 1833 Sqdn Bramcote), until at least 10.52.
	SW846		At Stretton 1.52. SOC 17.3.52. On Bramcote dump 6.52, coded 'CH/130' (ex 1832 Sqdn Culham). Probably instructional.
	SW919		To instructional 14.9.50 (ex 1832 Sqdn Culham), coded 'CH/115'.
Seafire F.17	SX296		To instructional at Bramcote 24.11.49 (ex Vickers-Armstrong), until at least 6.51. On Gosport dump 6.53.
	SX312		To instructional at Arbroath 28.4.49 (ex Vickers-Armstrong).
	SX361		To instructional at Bramcote 11.4.47, by road (ex 'C' Sqdn A&AEE Boscombe Down for RP trails).
Seafire F.47	PS944		To instructional at Yeovilton 10.6.49 (ex ETPS Farnborough).
	PS947		At Yeovilton by 7.51.
	PS951		To instructional at Bramcote 24.6.54, coded 'CW/168' (ex 759 Sqdn Culdrose).
	PS956		To instructional at Yeovilton 14.4.50 (ex Anthorn), to at least 7.50.
	VP441		To RNEC Manadon 20.1.54, probably as instructional, to at least 7.54. With Plymouth ATC at Biggin Hill 1963. To Culdrose 1964 (ex Plymouth or Biggin Hill), incomplete. Left Culdrose 7.69 for Lavenham(?) with HAPS, later to Hullavington. Being rebuilt by Confederate Air Force by 1980.

AIRCRAFT TYPE	SERIAL	'A' No.	DETAILS
Seafox	K8584		At Maharagama 1944-45.
Sea Fury prototype	VB857		To instructional at Arbroath 15.3.48 (ex CS(A) charge at RAE Farnborough).
Sea Fury F.10	TF895		To instructional at Arbroath 20.1.55 (ex CS(A) charge at Hawker Aircraft). Still at Arbroath 1955.
	TF903		To Class II at Donibristle 23.2.55 (ex 767 Sqdn Stretton).
	TF905		To Class II 26.9.50, possibly at Anthorn. At Yeovilton 7.51.
	TF910		To Class I at Yeovilton 1948 (ex Yeovilton). To St Merryn 26.11.53. To Class II at Bramcote 2.6.55 (ex St Merryn). Engine No. E3275.
	TF914	A23__	[Class II serial unidentified but presumed to be in range A2329 - A2331]. To Class II at Yeovilton 12.9.53. [Centaurus 18 engine to Class I on 9.1.51, to Class II on 12.9.53 as E3105; removed 4.5.55, WOC 19.1.59]. To St Merryn 3.12.53 for *"Operation Solitaire"*.
	TF920		To Class II 26.9.50 (ex Anthorn).
	TF923		To Class II 26.9.50 (ex Anthorn). Sold to Hawker Aircraft.
	TF928		To Class II 17.8.49. At Yeovilton 7.50.
	TF940		Instructional at Worthy Down 6.56, coded '09?' (ex 703 Sqdn Ford).
Sea Fury FB.11	TF960		At Yeovilton 7.51.
	VR923		To instructional 26.11.49. At Yeovilton 7.50.
	VW567		To instructional 6.12.49 (ex Anthorn). At Yeovilton 7.50.
Sea Fury T.20	VX301	A23__ ?	To instructional at Arbroath 6.10.53 (ex CS(A) charge). Reported on Donibristle dump 5.57, coded 'LM/201' (ex 738 Sqdn Lossiemouth). Probably in range A2329-2331.
Sea Hawk F.1	WF145		To instructional 9.7.59 (ex Brawdy).
	WF169		To instructional at Arbroath 24.8.59 (ex Abbotsinch). Still at Abbotsinch 7.68, coded '691' (ex 764 Sqdn Lossiemouth).
	WF180		To instructional at Yeovilton 25.4.56 (ex CS(A) charge at RAE Bedford). Reduced to instructional components 26.9.56.
	WF188		To instructional at Yeovilton 25.4.56 (ex CS(A) charge at RAE Bedford). Reduced to instructional components 26.9.56.
Sea Hawk FB.3	WF280		To instructional 23.3.61 (ex Abbotsinch).
	WM925		To instructional 23.3.61 (ex Abbotsinch). On Abbotsinch dump 4.62. Remains on Church Crookham dump 1963.
	WM963		To instructional at Abbotsinch 23.3.61 (ex Abbotsinch). WOC 25.4.61. On Abbotsinch dump 4.62.
	WM975		To instructional 23.3.61 (ex Abbotsinch). On Abbotsinch dump 4.62.
	WM976		To instructional 23.3.61 (ex Abbotsinch). On Abbotsinch dump 4.62.
	WM982		To instructional 23.3.61 (ex Abbotsinch). On Abbotsinch dump 4.62. On Portland dump 5.62.
	WM996		To instructional 23.3.61 (ex Abbotsinch). On Abbotsinch dump 4.62.
	WM999		To instructional 23.3.61 (ex Abbotsinch). At Arbroath 1963. On Arbroath dump 3.67.
	WN105		To instructional 23.3.61 (ex Abbotsinch). On Abbotsinch dump 4.62. On Culdrose dump 7.63, coded 'LM/-' (ex 736 Sqdn Lossiemouth).
	WN107		To instructional 23.3.61 (ex Abbotsinch). On Abbotsinch dump 4.62. On Culdrose dump 7.63.
Sea Hawk FB.5	WN108		To Short Bros & Harland Training School, Belfast 26.9.63 (ex RNAY Belfast). Still there 1975, coded '033' (ex Airwork FRU Hurn).

AIRCRAFT TYPE	SERIAL	'A' No.	DETAILS
Sea Hawk FGA.6	XE490		Crashed on delivery to Abbotsinch 10.1.56. Reduced to instructional components. Still present 7.60.
Sea Hornet F.20	PX219		To instructional at Arbroath 9.3.49 (ex CS(A) charge at Heston), until at least 5.53.
	TT188		To Class II at Gosport 13.12.50 (ex Fleetlands).
	TT195		To Class II at Yeovilton 3.2.49 (ex CS(A) charge at A&AEE Boscombe Down). No engines.
	VR844		To instructional 9.12.49. At Yeovilton 7.50, coded 'LP/006' (ex 703 Sqdn Lee-on-Solent).
Sea Hornet PR.22	TT187		To instructional at RNEC Manadon 4.9.52 (ex CS(A) charge). Used by fire section at Roborough Air Day 26.6.54. In scrapyard at Plymouth 5.59.
Sea Mosquito TR.33	TW289		To Class II at Stretton 26.9.50 (ex Stretton store). To Yeovilton by 7.51 and on dump there by 12.53.
Sea Otter ASR.2	RD877		At HMS Ariel, Culcheth by 4.47 to at least 4.48.
Sea Venom FAW.20	WM517		Held for instructional and display purposes 18.7.59. To Class II 21.7.59 (ex Abbotsinch), but no 'A' number allotted. Inscribed *"HMS Sanderling"* on fuselage side beneath cockpit. Reduced to spares and produce at Abbotsinch 10.9.62.
	WM518		At Abbotsinch, allocated to fire practice and escape drill. To Yeovilton and withdrawn 13.2.59. On Yeovilton dump 7.59.
Sea Venom FAW.22	WM573		To instructional 27.3.68.
	XG694		To instructional 4.9.64 at NARIU Lee-on-Solent (ex Belfast). No 'A' number known. Returned to service 8.12.65 with 831 Sqdn.
	XG694		To Lee-on-Solent 25.6.70 (received 31.7.70, ex Belfast), and declared Class II 27.7.70 but no 'A' number allotted. On the gate at Fleetlands by 8.70. To Fareham Technical College by 1974.
Sea Vixen FAW.1	XJ513		To FAA Museum, Yeovilton 30.1.70, coded 'VL/710' (ex 766 Sqdn Yeovilton), to at least 6.71. On Yeovilton dump by 4.74.
Spearfish	RA356		To instructional at Henstridge 30.4.52 (ex CS(A) charge). Reduced to spares and produce at Yeovilton 13.5.52.
Spitfire Vb	AD114		To RN Aircraft Training Establishment, Newcastle-under-Lyme 30.6.42.
Sturgeon S.1	RK791		To instructional at Yeovilton 23.6.50 (ex CS(A) charge at RAE Farnborough). On Yeovilton dump by 12.53.
Swordfish I	P4086		At Bramcote 3/4.48. Probably instructional.
Tiger Moth T.2	N6795		Serviceable instructional aircraft, re-categorised and repaired. Then TOC Yeovilton 30.4.48. At Stretton by 1.49. Sold 21.3.51 to become G-AKXE. [Class III?]
	T5900		Serviceable instructional aircraft, later re-categorised and repaired. Then TOC Yeovilton 30.4.48, coded 'VL/240'. At Stretton by 1.49. Sold 21.3.51 to become G-ANAY. [Class III?]
	T6183		Serviceable instructional aircraft, re-categorised and repaired. Then TOC Yeovilton 30.4.48. At Gosport by 1.49 and with 727 Sqdn Gosport 1.50. At Gosport by 7.50 until sold 5.2.51 to become G-AMUO. [Class III?]
	BB813		At Bramcote 9.52.
	BB814		[ex G-AFWI] To instructional at Arbroath 1951 (ex Stretton). Later returned to service [and served with several units until 1970. Returned to G-AFWI by 8.72].
	BB852		To instructional at Arbroath 1951 (ex Stretton). Later returned to service [and served with several units until 1970].

AIRCRAFT TYPE	SERIAL	'A' No.	DETAILS
Tiger Moth (contd)	NL979	Serviceable	instructional aircraft, re-categorised and repaired. Then TOC Yeovilton 30.4.48. At Stretton by 1.49. Sold 21.3.51 to become G-AMRH. [Class III?]
		?	A208_? At Bramcote 10.56. Engine No. E3091. [Presumably in A2080 series].
Vampire F.1	TG328		To instructional at Yeovilton 1.10.49 (ex 703 Sqdn Lee-on-Solent).
	TG421	A232_?	To instructional at Yeovilton 25.6.53 (ex CS(A) charge at RAE Farnborough). [Probably in A2321-A2325 range].
	VF268		To Class II at Stretton 27.10.54. Derelict at Yeovilton 8.60-6.62.
Wessex HU.5	XS490		To Air Medical School, Seafield Park 17.1.74 (ex MARTSU Lee-on-Solent), for crash recovery training. At Lee-on-Solent by 6.74, coded 'A/G' (ex 845 Sqdn). Dumped at Lee-on-Solent by 12.77.
	XT457		To Class II Arbroath 17.10.67 (ex RNAY Fleetlands). No 'A' number allocated. Later downgraded to Class III. Still at Arbroath 7.68. At Lee-on-Solent 7.71, coded 'B/C'. To Class DRB [see Introduction - Airframe Classifications] at Lee-on-Solent circa 1972/73. Rear fuselage to Fleetlands circa 1975, gone by 1977.
Whirlwind HAS.7	XM663		Crashed 14.4.59. To instructional at Arbroath 14.8.59 (ex RNAY Fleetlands). WOC at Arbroath 19.9.59. Remains still present 7.60-4.67. Parts in scrapyard of J.S.Shackleton, Siddal, Halifax noted 4.77-10.86. Perished/buried in the yard circa 1989.
Wyvern TF.1	VR132		Fuselage to RNEC Manadon 16.3.54 as instructional (ex 5 MU Kemble store on behalf of CS(A)), until at least 8.56. No engine. The mainplanes (complete with fuel tanks) went to P&EE Shoeburyness.
	VR136	A222_?	To Gosport 5.5.50 (ex CS(A) charge) as instructional. Derelict at Gosport 1959, coded "916" (spurious local code). Sometime after 7.59 it was pushed into a chalk pit, along with other aircraft, on the boundary of Gosport (used as a fire pit) and a bulldozer then filled the pit in! [Probably either A2226 or A2228].
Wyvern S.4	VZ782		Cat.5 12.7.56 (ex 'FD/082' 703 Sqdn Ford). Instructional at Bramcote 11.58.

Firebrand TF.5 EK844, seen here at Farnborough 11.9.48, became a Class II airframe at Bramcote.

Mosquito B.25 KB410 in use as a Class II airframe at Bramcote around 1949/50.

PART 2 - CHRONOLOGICAL ORDER

The following table lists, in the known date order of becoming instructional or struck off charge as an operational aircraft, all those aircraft in the list of unidentified airframes which seem likely to have been given an 'A' serial. It is evident that most of the missing aircraft between A2160 and A2399 appear in this list, so a rough estimate of the likely 'A' serial can be made. The 1955 allocations probably account for A2387 to A2391 and A2393 but this is not certain.

DATE	AIRCRAFT TYPE	SERIAL	DATE	AIRCRAFT TYPE	SERIAL
11.4.47	Seafire F.17	SX361	26.9.50	Firefly 5(PF)	VX424
8.9.47	Firebrand TF.IV	EK605	26.9.50	Oxford I	LB413
			26.9.50	Oxford I	NM759
13.1.48	Firebrand TF.IV	EK630	26.9.50	Oxford I	PH300
15.3.48	Sea Fury prototype	VB857	26.9.50	Seafire F.15	SR588
22.4.48	Seafire F.15	SR473	26.9.50	Seafire F.15	SW814
1.6.48	Oxford I	DF482	26.9.50	Sea Fury F.10	TF905
11.6.48	Firefly FR.4	TW721	26.9.50	Sea Fury F.10	TF920
22.7.48	Seafire F.15	SR468	26.9.50	Sea Fury F.10	TF923
12.10.48	Firefly FR.4	VG972	26.9.50	Sea Mosquito TR.33	TW289
23.11.48	Seafire F.15	SR458	13.12.50	Sea Hornet F.20	TT188
9.12.48	Oxford I	HM747			
			1951	Tiger Moth T.2	T5900
3.2.49	Sea Hornet F.20	TT195	1951	Tiger Moth T.2	BB814
12.2.49	Seafire F.15	PR359	1951	Tiger Moth T.2	BB852
12.2.49	Seafire F.15	PR374	25.1.51	Firefly FR.4	TW689
14.2.49	Seafire F.15	SR480	25.1.51	Firefly FR.4	TW690
21.2.49	Seafire F.15	PR340	25.1.51	Firefly FR.4	TW691
21.2.49	Seafire F.15	PR353	30.1.51	Firefly FR.4	TW720
21.2.49	Seafire F.15	PR456	14.6.51	Firefly FR.4	TW696
6.3.49	Firefly FR.1	MB446	14.6.51	Firefly FR.4	TW697
9.3.49	Sea Hornet F.20	PX219	14.6.51	Firefly FR.4	TW698
9.3.49	Firefly F.1	Z1901	14.6.51	Firefly FR.4	TW699
10.3.49	Firefly F.1	DK510	14.6.51	Firefly FR.4	TW715
17.3.49	Firefly F.1	DV130	14.6.51	Firefly FR.4	TW716
31.3.49	Firefly FR.1	MB561	14.6.51	Firefly FR.4	TW717
28.4.49	Seafire F.17	SX312	10.7.51	Firefly FR.4	TW688
2.6.49	Seafire F.15	PK243	10.7.51	Firefly FR.4	TW693
10.6.49	Seafire F.47	PS944			
14.6.49	Firebrand TF.5	EK792	25.2.52	Attacker F.1	WA509
4.7.49	Seafire F.15	SR461	27.2.52	Sea Fury prototype	SR666
19.7.49	Firefly FR.1	MB401	17.3.52	Seafire F.15	PR403
17.8.49	Sea Fury F.10	TF928	17.3.52	Seafire F.15	SW846
1.10.49	Vampire F.1	TG328	30.4.52	Spearfish	RA356
11.10.49	Firefly F.1	Z1899	19.5.52	Attacker F.1	WA470
14.10.49	Firebrand TF.5	EK779	4.9.52	Sea Hornet PR.22	TT187
8.11.49	Firefly F.1	Z1907			
24.11.49	Seafire F.15	SX296	10.2.53	Attacker FB.1	WA483
26.11.49	Sea Fury FB.11	VR923	8.6.53	Firebrand TF.5	EK843
6.12.49	Sea Fury FB.11	VW567	8.6.53	Firebrand TF.5	EK844
9.12.49	Sea Hornet F.20	VR844	25.6.53	Vampire F.1	TG421
			15.7.53	Firefly AS.7	WJ215
18.1.50 ?	Firefly FR.1	PP620	29.8.53	Firebrand TF.5	EK795
31.1.50	Firefly F.1	DK496	7.9.53	Attacker F.1	WA472
21.3.50	Firefly F.1	Z2099	12.9.53	Sea Fury F.10	TF914
21.3.50	Firefly F.1	Z2103	6.10.53	Sea Fury T.20	VX301
21.3.50	Firefly F.1	DK420	20.1.54	Seafire F.47	VP441
22.3.50	Firebrand TF.5	EK783	17.2.54	Firefly T.7	WM763
6.4.50	Firebrand TF.5A	EK728	28.2.54	Gannet prototype	WE488
14.4.50	Seafire F.47	PS956	3.54	Avenger S.4	XB317
5.5.50	Wyvern TF.1	VR136	5.4.54	Balliol prototype	VL892
25.5.50	Avenger I	JZ129	21.5.54	Attacker prototype	TS416
23.6.50	Sturgeon S.1	RK791	24.6.54	Seafire F.47	PS951
8.9.50	Firefly FR.1	PP611	27.10.54	Attacker FB.1	WA529
14.9.50	Seafire F.15	SW919	27.10.54	Vampire F.1	VF268
26.9.50	Firefly F.1	DV119			
26.9.50	Firefly FR.1	MB504	20.1.55	Sea Fury F.10	TF895
26.9.50	Firefly FR.1	MB555	23.2.55	Sea Fury F.10	TF903
26.9.50	Firefly FR.1	MB558	22.4.55	Firefly AS.6	WB254
26.9.50	Firefly 5	VT362	2.6.55	Sea Fury F.10	TF910
26.9.50	Firefly 5	VT369	6.8.55	Firefly 5	WB349
26.9.50	Firefly 5	VT378	6.8.55	Firefly 5	WB379
26.9.50	Firefly 5	VT381	15.9.55	Firefly FR.1	MB641
26.9.50	Firefly 5	VT407			

PART 3 - RECENT ADDITIONS

More recently, a number of airframes appear to have escaped allocation of an 'A' number but it is not certain if indeed they are/were Class GRB. The list is not exhaustive as airframes allocated directly to fire-fighting training were not normally allocated an 'A' number, although it was noted earlier that, surprisingly, some of those in use for this purpose at Predannack received an 'A' number in the 1993 re-allocations. Note that the SAH was renamed the School of Flight Deck Operations (SFDO) in November 1995.

AIRCRAFT TYPE	SERIAL 'A' No.	DETAILS
Gazelle HT.2	ZB648	To SAH Culdrose late-1993 (ex AMG Culdrose), coded 'CU/(5)40' (ex 705 Sqdn Culdrose, damaged in crash-landing 18.3.93). By road to Predannack 1.94 and current 9.97. [The boom was noted at Fleetlands 7.97].
Harrier T.4A(N)	ZB601	To ETS Yeovilton by 16.12.91, coded '-/721' (ex 899 Sqdn). Gone by 12.1.93 and next noted at St Athan 11.93. To BAe Dunsfold by 1.95 and current.
Lynx AH.1	XZ213	To Fleetlands apprentices by road 11.6.92 (ex RNAY Wroughton), marked "TAD213" (AAC instructional serial). Current.
Lynx Mk.28	QP-31	To Fleetlands by 1.93 (ex RNAY Almondbank store and Qatar Police) and stored. In use with apprentices by 6.95 and current.
Scout AH.1	XT640	To AES Lee-on-Solent (ex SAE Middle Wallop) and noted in the BDR compound by 6.94 (green/black colour scheme with *"Army"* titles). Noted 5.95 inscribed *"Not to be touched"*. Current 10.95. To SEAE Arborfield for BDR training by 4.96.
Wasp HAS.1	XV638	At Portland 21.6.83, coded '-/430' 829 Sqdn HMS Achilles Flt (ditched circa 5.83). Spuriously marked *"A430"* (indicating instructional use) at Portland by 2.84. To Air Movements School, Brize Norton late-1984 allocated 8826M.
Wessex HAS.3	XM838	To AES Lee-on-Solent by 7.82 (ex Portland store), coded 'LN/405' (ex 737 Sqdn HMS London Flt). In use for BDR by 7.83. Outside BDR hangar 5.86 and dumped by 7.86. To Predannack as 'LN/405' by 28.11.86. Current 10.92 lying on its side, fairly burnt, and only very burnt remains noted 5.93.
	XS119	To AES Lee-on-Solent by 11.82 (ex Portland store ?), coded 'PO/655' (ex 737 Sqdn Portland). Marked '-/655' by 7.85 and derelict outside the old RNHU hangars by 10.85 (BDR training ?). Parked near dump by 5.86. To Predannack circa 15.5.86, coded '-/655' (no tail pylon). Lying on its side by 9.87. Current as '55' 7.91, fairly burnt, but expired by 10.92.
Wessex HU.5	XT756	To AES Lee-on-Solent by road 7.7.92 (ex Wroughton), coded 'VL/ZJ' (ex 707 Sqdn Yeovilton). On the dump for BDR training by 11.7.92 and current 11.92 as '-/ZJ' (minus rear end). Moved to BDR compound by 4.94. (possibly the example noted as 'Z' 5.95 but scrapped by 9.95).
	XT769	To AES Lee-on-Solent by road 7.7.92 (ex Wroughton), coded 'CU/823' (ex 771 Sqdn Culdrose). Near the dump 11.7.92 but 'derelict' inside AES by 23.11.92 as '-/(8)23' (minus tail cone). To FAA Museum Yeovilton 7.9.93 and current.

CLASS III AIRFRAMES

The majority of Class III instructional airframes have been downgraded from a higher category, and details of these will be found elsewhere in these lists. A few machines, usually in a poor condition, have been downgraded directly into this category, and these are listed below. This classification no longer exists, having been merged into Class GRB during the re-organisation which took place in June 1973.

AIRCRAFT TYPE	SERIAL	DETAILS
Firefly 5(PF)	WB405	To Class III at Arbroath 28.8.50, having bounced over the barrier of HMS Vengeance on 18.5.50 and damaged WB315 and WB398, all three machines being with 815 Sqdn (WB405 was uncoded at the time).
Sea Fury prototype	SR666	To instructional at Arbroath 21.2.52 (ex CS(A) charge at Hawker Aircraft, Dunsfold), until at least 9.53.
Sea Venom FAW.22	XG736	Authorised to be reduced to spares and produce at Belfast 20.1.70, but reduced to Class III 2.70. Upgraded to Class II 3.3.71, but no 'A' number allocated. AT RNAY Belfast 1974. At the Ulster College of Further Education by 16.8.85 [Ulster Aviation Society aircraft ?]. Under restoration at Newtownards by 1989.
Sea Vixen FAW.1	XJ493	To Class III at Arbroath 27.1.63 (ex AIU Lee-on-Solent). Previously coded 'VL/721' with 766 Sqdn Yeovilton and crashed into the River Yeo 23.8.62.
Vampire F.1	TG314	To Class III 9.5.51 (ex CS(A) charge). Previously at A&AEE Boscombe Down from 6.6.50 until experimental equipment removed 28.12.50. To Arbroath 7.6.51 as Cat.1(GI), until at least 5.53.
Wessex HAS.1	XP146	To Class III at RNEC Manadon 30.4.63 (ex AIU Lee-on-Solent). Previously coded 'PO/663' with 737 Sqdn Portland and ditched after a night sortie from Portland on 17.8.62, being later salvaged.
	XS124	To Class III at Arbroath 1969 (ex Fleetlands). Previously coded 'E/067' with 820 Sqdn HMS Eagle from 7.65 until 1968.
Wessex HU.5	XT774	To Class III at Arbroath 9.3.70 (ex MARTSU Lee-on-Solent and AIU investigation, crashed 17.5.69 as 'B/F' 845 Sqdn). Remains In J.Shackleton's scrapyard, Siddal, Halifax by 10.75 and perished/buried there circa 1989.
Whirlwind HAR.3	XG582	To Class III 24.1.58. Previously 'P/529' with 705 Sqdn Lee-on-Solent and crashed into the sea on 3.12.57. Salvaged and handed back to the FAA at Portsmouth 16.12.57. Authorised for scrap 16.3.58.
Whirlwind HAS.7	XL879	To Class III at RNEC Manadon 1961 (ex Culdrose). Previously 'C/335' with 824 Sqdn Culdrose and collided with XL884 'C/336' 705 Sqdn 10.3.61. Believed to be the cockpit section which remained at Manadon (noted 11.85/7.87) until being burnt at the 1990 Open Day.

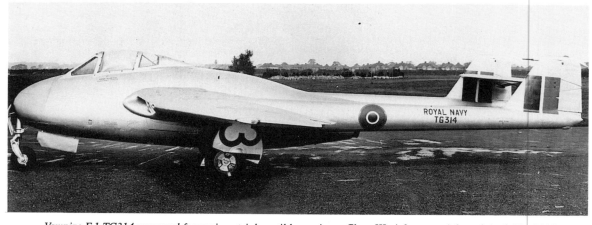

Vampire F.1 TG314 was used for various trials until becoming a Class III airframe at Arbroath in 6.51. (MAP).

SCHOOL OF AIRCRAFT HANDLING

From about 1966 aircraft of the School of Aircraft Handling at Culdrose have been allocated a unique series of side numbers in the range 'SAH-1' to 'SAH-24'. These numbers were carried on each side of the fuselage or fin, either in full or without the 'SAH-' prefix. They were intended to be comparable with normal side numbers or code markings for simulated deck operations. All known examples of these allocations and markings are listed, with such relevant dates and other details as are available including the local *Ace of Spades* badge. The 'SAH' series seems to have been discontinued in the late-1980's. The SAH was renamed the School of Flight Deck Operations in November 1995.

In addition to the machines in this list, the School has used a number of other aircraft, none of which has been reported as allocated or carrying 'SAH' numbers, and continues to receive 'new' airframes for training. To complete the record these other machines are given in a separate list.

ALLOCATED SAH NUMBERS

SAH No.	'A' No.	AIRCRAFT TYPE	SERIAL	REMARKS
SAH-1	A2420	Sea Hawk F.1	WF159	TOC by 25.7.59. Marked '1' by 15.7.60. To Predannack 1964.
	A2510	Sea Hawk FB.5	WM913	Marked 'SAH-1' by 7.66 (ex '7'). To Sealand by 9.71.
	A2554	Sea Hawk FGA.6	WV865	Marked 'SAH-1' by 7.71 (ex 'SAH-7'). To Luftwaffenmuseum 8.76.
	A2634	Sea Hawk FGA.6	WV794	TOC 17.12.74. Allocated by 7.76 but not carried. To Airwork, Perth 10.80.
	A2679	Gnat T.1	XP535	TOC 11.10.79. Marked '1' on fin by 11.79. WFU by 23.4.86 and sold 1987.
SAH-2	Class I	Sea Hawk FB.3	WF289	On charge 18.3.60 to 18.7.62. Marked '2' on nose by 15.7.60. SOC 13.2.63 and scrapped.
	A2532	Sea Hawk FGA.6	WV826	TOC 27.2.62. Marked '2' by 7.64 and 'SAH-2' by 7.66. To SWAPS, Rhoose 1.77.
	A2637	Sea Hawk FGA.6	WV797	TOC 6.2.75. Allocated by 7.76 but not carried. To Airwork, Perth 10.80.
	A2678	Gnat T.1	XR955	TOC 11.10.79. Marked '2' on fin by 11.79. WFU by 23.4.86 and sold 1987.
SAH-3	A2490	Sea Hawk FB.3	WM920	TOC 22.1.60. Allocated 'SAH-3'. Marked '3' by 15.7.60 and 'SAH-3' by 7.66. To Class III 26.10.66. To Predannack by 6.7.68.
	A2555	Sea Hawk FGA.6	XE330	TOC 13.3.67. 'SAH-3' by 7.67. To Predannack by 1.8.70.
	A2534	Sea Hawk FGA.6	XE368	TOC 10.7.68. Marked 'SAH-3' by 5.71. To Cornwall Aeronautical Park 1.76.
	A2632	Sea Hawk FGA.6	WV903	TOC 17.12.74. Marked '3' by 3.75. Marked '5' by 5.82. To Lee-on-Solent 9.5.85.
	A2676	Gnat T.1	XR572	TOC 11.10.79. Marked '3' on fin by 11.79. WFU by 23.4.86 and sold 1987.
SAH-4	A2489	Sea Hawk FB.3	WM918	On charge 29.2.60 to 29.10.65. Marked '4' on nose by 15.7.60. To RNAY Belfast 29.10.65.
	A2549	Sea Hawk FGA.6	WV909	TOC 7.7.65. Marked 'SAH-4' by 7.66. To Predannack by 4.71.
	A2557	Sea Hawk FGA.6	WV798	Marked 'SAH-4' by 5.71 (ex 'SAH-10'). To Thorpe Water Park 16.5.75.
	A2636	Sea Hawk FGA.6	XE390	On charge 6.2.75 to 1.3.83. Marked '4' by 1.76. To Lee-on-Solent 1.3.83.
	A2677	Gnat T.1	XR993	TOC 11.10.79. Marked '4' on fin by 11.79. WFU by 23.4.86 and sold 1987.

SAH No.	'A' No.	AIRCRAFT TYPE	SERIAL	REMARKS
SAH-5	Class I	Sea Hawk FB.3	WM908	On charge 18.2.60 to 15.2.62. Marked '5' by 15.7.60. Sold as scrap 19.12.62.
	A2530	Sea Hawk FB.5	WM969	TOC 14.5.64. Marked '5' by 7.64 and 'SAH-5' by 7.66. To Duxford 18.1.77.
	A2633	Sea Hawk FGA.6	XE369	On charge 17.12.74 to 22.2.83. Marked '5' by 3.75. To Lee-on-Solent 22.2.83.
	A2632	Sea Hawk FGA.6	WV903	Marked '5' by 5.82 (ex '3'). To '8' by 7.83.
	A2708	Gnat T.1	XR540	TOC 11.12.81. Marked '5' by 7.83. WFU by 23.4.86 and sold 1987.
SAH-6	Class I	Sea Hawk FB.3	WM988	On charge 18.2.60 to 8.12.61. Marked '6' by 15.7.60 (red Ace of Spades badge).
	A2517	Sea Hawk FB.5	WM961	TOC 13.10.61. Marked '6' by 7.64 and 'SAH-6' by 7.66. To Torbay Aircraft Museum by 6.71.
	A2511	Sea Hawk FB.5	WM983	Marked 'SAH-6' by 3.73 (ex 'SAH-9'). To Cornwall Aeronautical Park 29.5.75.
	A2635	Sea Hawk FGA.6	XE339	TOC 17.12.74. Marked '6' by 1.76. To '7' by 7.83.
	A2619	Kestrel FGA.1	XS695	TOC 12.5.78. Marked '6' by 5.82. To Lee-on-Solent 11.5.93.
	A2709	Gnat T.1	XR991	TOC 27.1.82. Marked '6' on fin by 7.83. WFU by 23.4.86 and sold 1987.
SAH-7	Class I	Sea Hawk FB.3	WN114	On charge 31.3.60 to 24.3.62. Marked '7' by 15.7.60 (red Ace of Spades badge).
	A2510	Sea Hawk FB.3	WM913	TOC 24.6.61. Marked '7' by 15.7.61. To 'SAH-1' by 7.66.
	A2522	Sea Hawk FB.3	WM993	TOC 23.2.62. Marked '7' by 7.66. To Class III 15.3.67. Fuselage to HMS Royal Arthur by 1972.
	A2554	Sea Hawk FGA.6	WV865	TOC 14.3.67. Marked 'SAH-7' by 3.68. To 'SAH-1' by 7.71.
	A2608	Gannet ECM.6	XA459	TOC 10.7.68. Allocated 'SAH-7' mid-1971 but not carried. To SWAPS, Rhoose 4.4.79.
	A2635	Sea Hawk FGA.6	XE339	Marked '7' on fin by 7.83 (ex '6'). To Lee-on-Solent 6.6.85.
SAH-8	A2509	Sea Hawk FB.5	WF299	TOC 1.9.61. Marked '8' by 7.64. Marked 'SAH-8' by 7.66. To Lee-on-Solent by 7.71.
	A2539	Gannet ECM.6	XG831	TOC 20.5.66. Allocated 'SAH-8' mid-1971 but not carried. To Cornwall Aero Park 11.5.80.
	A2632	Sea Hawk FGA.6	WV903	Marked '8' by 7.83 (ex '5'). To Lee-on-Solent 9.5.85.
SAH-9	A2511	Sea Hawk FB.5	WM983	TOC 22.7.61. Marked '9' by 7.64, 'SAH-9' by 7.66. To 'SAH-'6 by 3.73.
	A2540	Gannet ECM.6	WN464	TOC 20.5.66. Allocated by 3.73 but not carried. To Cornwall Aero Park 4.6.78.
SAH-10	A2557	Sea Hawk FGA.6	WV798	TOC 10.5.67. Marked 'SAH-10' by 3.68. To 'SAH-4' by 5.71.
	A2610	Sea Vixen FAW.2	XN647	Marked 'SAH-10' by 7.73. To Cornwall Aeronautical Park 4.6.78.
SAH-11	A2616	Sea Vixen FAW.2	XN651	Marked 'SAH-11' by 7.73. To fire pits 1978.
SAH-12	A2639	Sea Vixen FAW.2	XN650	Marked 'SAH-12' by 7.73. To SWAPS, Rhoose 25.4.79.
	A2628	Jet Provost T.4	XP558	TOC 22.5.74. Later allocated but not carried. To St Athan 19.3.79.
SAH-13	A2611	Sea Vixen FAW.2	XJ575	Marked 'SAH-13' by 7.73. WFU 12.80. To Cornwall Aeronautical Park 23.10.83.
SAH-14	A2622	Sea Vixen FAW.2	XJ602	TOC 28.9.73. Allocated but not carried. To Flight Refuelling 15.5.79.
SAH-15	A2623	Sea Vixen FAW.2	XN697	TOC 21.3.74. Allocated but not carried. To Flight Refuelling 18.12.78.

SAH No.	'A' No.	AIRCRAFT TYPE	SERIAL	REMARKS
SAH-16	A2621	Sea Vixen FAW.2	XJ584	Marked 'SAH-16' by 11.74. WFU 7.81. To Cornwall Aeronautical Park 23.10.83.
SAH-17	A2624	Sea Vixen FAW.2	XN692	Marked 'SAH-17' by 11.74. To Yeovilton 18.7.85.
SAH-18	A2573	Scimitar F.1	XD215	TOC 6.10.67. Allocated but not carried. To P&EE Foulness 1972.
SAH-19	A2574	Scimitar F.1	XD332	TOC 6.10.67. Allocated but not carried. To Cornwall Aeronautical Park 6.7.76.
SAH-20	A2627	Buccaneer S.1	XN967	TOC 2.5.74. Allocated but not carried. To Cornwall Aeronautical Park 4.6.78.
SAH-21	A2640	Wessex HAS.1	XP155	TOC 28.2.72. Allocated but not carried. To Lee-on-Solent 3.82.
SAH-22	A2641	Wessex HAS.1	XL729	TOC 3.71. Allocated but not carried. To fire pits by 19.9.78.
SAH-23	A2655	Buccaneer S.1	XN953	TOC 18.11.75. Allocated but not carried. To fire pits by 7.87.
SAH-24	A2650	Wessex HAS.1	XP160	TOC 20.8.75. Allocated but not carried. To Lee-on-Solent 13.9.88.

OTHER SAH AIRCRAFT

In the following list the first column shows the original 'A' number and the second column shows the 'A' number allocated in or after 1993, if appropriate.

A2600	-	Buccaneer S.1	XN934	TOC 7.7.76. WFU 3.10.79 for fire pits.
A2617	-	Buccaneer S.1	XN954	TOC 29.7.71. To HMS Royal Arthur 4.74.
A2500	-	DH.110 Mk.20X	XF828	TOC 28.11.60. To fire pits by 7.70.
A2531	-	Dragonfly HR.5	WG718	TOC 18.2.65 until at least 1.68.
A2493	-	Gannet AS.1	WN346	TOC by 10.68 until at least 10.71.
A2528	-	Gannet AS.1	XA363	TOC 13.9.63 until at least 10.71.
A2533	-	Gannet AS.4	XA456	TOC 22.2.63 until at least 10.66.
A2701	-	Gannet AEW.3	XL500	TOC by 10.80 until 1983.
-	?	Gazelle HT.2	ZB648	TOC late-1993. To Predannack 1.94.
A2614 [2]	A2605 [2]	Harrier GR.3	XV760	TOC 30.5.91. To Yeovilton 29.9.92.
A2606 [2]	A2607 [3]	Harrier GR.3	XV806	TOC 17.4.91. Current.
A2607 [2]	A2608 [3]	Harrier GR.3	XV741	TOC 24.4.91. Current.
A2608 [2]	A2609 [3]	Harrier GR.3	XV783	TOC 1.5.91. To Lee-on-Solent 10.8.93. TOC 24.4.96. Current.
A2609 [2]	A2610 [3]	Harrier GR.3	XW919	TOC 8.5.91. To RMCS Shrivenham 3.6.97.
A2615 [2]	A2611 [3]	Harrier GR.3	XV786	TOC 5.6.91. To Predannack 10.2.94.
A2610 [2]	A2612 [3]	Harrier GR.3	XZ969	TOC 17.5.95. Current.
?	A2684 [2]	Harrier GR.3	ZD667	TOC 30.7.93. Current.
?	A2685 [2]	Harrier GR.3	XZ996	TOC circa 19.7.93. Current.
-	A2691 [2]	Harrier GR.3	XV753	TOC 12.7.94. Current.
-	A2687 [2]	Harrier GR.3	XV808	TOC 11.7.94. Current.
-	A2692 [2]	Harrier T.4	XW271	TOC 3.11.94. Current.
-	A2610 [4]	Harrier T.4	XZ145	TOC 29.5.97. Current.
A2736	-	Hunter GA.11	XE682	TOC 22.11.85. To fire pits by 28.11.86.
A2731	A2645 [2]	Hunter GA.11	WT711	TOC 23.9.85. To Coventry 23.11.95.
A2732	A2646 [2]	Hunter GA.11	WT804	TOC 22.10.85. To Moreton-in-the Marsh 11.5.94.
A2733	A2647 [2]	Hunter GA.11	XE668	TOC 8.2.85. To Predannack 11.8.93.
A2737	A2650 [2]	Hunter GA.11	WV267	TOC 21.1.86. Left 13.1.94 en route USA.
A2754	A2664 [2]	Hunter GA.11	WW654	TOC 11.2.87. To Portsmouth 15.12.93.
?	A2616 [3]	Hunter PR.11	WT723	TOC 19.3.93. To Exeter 12.9.97.
?	A2617 [3]	Hunter T.7	XL601	TOC 25.3.93. To Exeter 23.5.97.
?	A2618 [3]	Hunter T.7	XF310	TOC 25.3.93. To Tasmania 19.5.97.

?	A2619 [2]	Hunter T.7	WV372	TOC 19.3.93. To North Weald 23.5.97.
A2738	A2651 [2]	Hunter T.7	XX466	TOC 14.5.86. To Predannack 10.8.93.
-	-	Scimitar proto	WT854	[VAS 544] TOC date unknown, until 1967.
A2499	-	Scimitar proto	WT859	TOC 29.10.60 until at least 7.72.
A2424	-	Sea Hawk F.1	WF182	TOC 9.1.57 until at least 12.59.
A2426	-	Sea Hawk F.1	WF183	TOC by 12.59.
A2428	-	Sea Hawk F.1	WF163	TOC by 12.59.
A2431	-	Sea Hawk F.1	WM901	TOC 31.1.57 until at least 12.59.
A2523	-	Sea Hawk FB.3	WM915	TOC by 11.67 until circa 3.73.
A2524	-	Sea Hawk FB.3	WM998	TOC 14.2.62 until at least 5.64.
A2425	-	Sea Hawk F.5	WF243	TOC by 12.59 for fire pits.
A2660	-	Sea Hawk FGA.6	WV908	TOC 28.10.76. Rebuilt to flying condition, first flight 23.5.78.
A2673	-	Sea Prince T.1	WF122	TOC 1.79 until 30.10.82.
A2674	-	Sea Prince T.1	WF125	TOC 1.79. To Predannack 20.2.79.
A2491	-	Sea Venom FAW.21	WW275	TOC 4.4.67. *Nothing further known.*
A2492	-	Sea Venom FAW.21	XG616	TOC 30.8.67 until at least 3.70.
A2529	-	VAS 508	VX133	TOC 7.1.64 until at least 11.68.
A2671	-	Wessex HAS.1	XS867	TOC 26.2.80. To Lee-on-Solent 4.82.
A2681	-	Wessex HAS.1	XP117	TOC 29.1.80. To fire pits by 11.10.85.
A2687	-	Wessex HAS.1	XS877	TOC by 10.80. To ETS by 9.6.88.
A2688	-	Wessex HAS.1	XP158	TOC by 6.80. To Lee-on-Solent 13.9.88.
A2690	-	Wessex HAS.1	XS887	TOC 3.80. To Cornwall Aero Park 1.8.87.
A2695	A2626 [3]	Wessex HAS.1	XS876	TOC 12.7.88. To fire pits by 6.95, then to HMS Sultan 14.5.96. TOC 12.8.97. Current.
A2705	A2627 [2]	Wessex HAS.1	XS866	TOC 22.6.88. To AES HMS Sultan 19.9.96. TOC 10.4.97. Current.
A2689	A2629 [2]	Wessex HAS.1	XM874	TOC by 6.80. To Lee-on-Solent 12.7.88.
A2668	A2631 [2]	Wessex HAS.1	XS885	TOC by 6.11.78. Current.
A2727	A2644 [2]	Wessex HAS.3	XM328	TOC 22.4.85. Current.
A2713 [2]	-	Wessex HAS.3	XM836	TOC 16.4.91 (fire pits). Scrapped 12.91.
A2710 [2]	A2633 [2]	Wessex HAS.3	XP137	TOC 13.9.88. Current.
A2712 [2]	A2634 [2]	Wessex HAS.3	XM870	TOC 13.9.88. Departed 27.7.93 to ?
A2751	A2661 [2]	Wessex HU.5	XT762	TOC 28.7.87. Current.
A2541	-	Whirlwind HAR.1	XA869	TOC by 7.66 until at least 1.68.
A2663	-	Whirlwind HAR.9	XN309	TOC 26.10.77 until circa 1979.
A2576	-	Whirlwind HAR.21	WV198	On loan 29.1.62-10.10.62.

Sea Hawk FB.5 A2517/WM961 marked SAH, at Torbay Aircraft Museum by 1971. (S.Brett)

OTHER LOCAL MARKINGS

In addition to the SAH numbers in use at Culdrose, spurious local markings have occasionally been employed by other stations on their instructional aircraft. In the cases of Arbroath, Gosport and Worthy Down these were in the form of a definite system of markings, of which the following examples are known.

LOCAL No.	'A' No.	AIRCRAFT TYPE	SERIAL	REMARKS
ARBROATH				
101	A2503	Sea Hawk FB.5	WM994	
102	A2505	Sea Hawk FB.5	WM943	
103	A2406	Sea Hawk F.1	WF201	
104	A2495	Sea Hawk FB.5	WM965	
105	A2443	Sea Hawk FB.3	WF294	
106	A2450	Gannet AS.1	WN343	
106	A2467	Gannet AS.1	WN454	
107	A2477	Sea Venom FAW.20	WM513	
108				
109				
110				
111	A2436	Gannet AS.1	WN453	
112	A2536	Sea Hawk FGA.6	WV914	
113	A2502	Sea Hawk FB.5	WM936	
114	A2494	Sea Hawk FB.5	WM937	
115	A2564	Hunter F.4	WV411	
116				
117				
118				
119		Attacker FB.2	WK329	
120				
121				
122	A2456	Sea Venom FAW.21	WW261	
123	A2506	Sea Venom FAW.21	XG655	
GOSPORT				
908	A2235	Firefly F.1	Z1889	
911	A2269	Firefly 5	VT373	
912	A2217	Firefly		
916	A222_ ?	Wyvern TF.1	VR136	
916		Firefly F.1	Z2103	
WORTHY DOWN				
101	A2320	Vampire F.1	VF317	
109	A2256	Seafire F.17	SW800	(as *"VM/109"*)
200	A2213	Firefly AS.5		(as *"VM/200"*)
202	A2258	Firefly FR.5	VT417	(as *"VM/202"*)
203	A2310	Wyvern TF.2	VW879	
300	A2318	Firefly AS.7	WJ216	

ARMY AIR CORPS INSTRUCTIONAL AIRFRAMES

Like the Royal Navy, the Army initially used 'M' serials for their instructional airframes but it was not until the 1960's that the Army began their own numbering system. This differed from the other two services in that the service serial numbers are retained but the letters 'TAD' are added in front. However, there have been a number of exceptions to this and it is not known whether the system has been applied to the following airframes. It was not until the last decade that these former FAA aircraft have found new homes at various AAC bases for instructional duties.

AIRCRAFT TYPE	SERIAL	REMARKS
Gazelle HT.2	XW860	To SAE Middle Wallop by road 22.5.92 (ex Wroughton) via Fleetlands, uncoded (ex 'CU/(5)44' 705 Sqdn Culdrose). Noted in the dope shop at Fleetlands 6.6.92 (resprayed in AAC scheme ?). Current at Middle Wallop 5.94. Transferred with SAE to Arborfield (early 1995 ?) and current with SEAE 4.96.
	XW863	To SAE Middle Wallop by road 10.1.92 (ex Wroughton), uncoded (ex 'CU/(5)42' 705 Sqdn Culdrose). Current 5.94 (presumably in AAC scheme ?). Transferred with SAE to Arborfield (early 1995 ?) and current with SEAE 4.96.
Wasp HAS.1	XS571	To 71 A/c Workshops, Detmold (ex Wroughton by road 21.6.84), coded '-/614' (ex 829 Sqdn Portland). Boom of XT436 fitted later. Last noted 5.89.
	XT436	To 71 A/c Workshops, Detmold (ex Wroughton by road 21.6.84), uncoded. Boom to XS571. To BDR at AAC Soest date ? (minus boom), but reported back at Detmold by 6.87 and believed to have perished.
	XT438	See A2704.
	XV627	To 71 A/c Workshops, Detmold (ex Wroughton by road 21.6.84), coded '-/321' (ex 829 Sqdn HMS Antelope Flt). Last noted 5.89.
	XV629	To AETW Middle Wallop by road 6.3.84 (ex Wroughton), uncoded. To BDRF by 6.84 and last noted 7.90.
Wessex HU.5	XS481	To 9 Rgt AAC Dishforth by road 21.7.92 (ex Wroughton), uncoded in SAR colour scheme and current 1.94. Dumped by 6.94 and current 11.95.
	XS488	[Previously 9056M] To 3/4 Rgt AAC Wattisham Air Mobile Training Centre by 4.96 (ex 1 SoTT Halton), coded '-/XK' (ex 847 Sqdn Yeovilton). Current.
	XS521	To REME Hospital, Birmingham by road 19.3.87 (ex Wroughton), coded '(Y)B' (ex 845 Sqdn Yeovilton). At Saighton Army Camp, Cheshire by 1.90 and burnt 4.90. Current 1.96 in a poor state.
	XT470	To 7 Rgt Netheravon by road 10.7.84 (ex Wroughton), coded '(Y)A' (ex 845 Sqdn Yeovilton). Last noted on the dump 10.88 and parts with IHM Weston-super-Mare 12.90.
	XT471	To 9 Rgt AAC Dishforth by road 21.7.92 (ex Wroughton), uncoded in SAR colour scheme. Dumped by 6.94 and current 11.95.
	XT474	To 4 Rgt Detmold (ex Wroughton by road 2.10.91), coded 'CU/820' (ex 771 Sqdn Culdrose). Arrived Harwich docks 8.10.91 and left that day on MV Hamburg. No subsequent sightings recorded.
	XT764	*[Allocated to RM Museum but this was cancelled 11.12.90].* To 4 Rgt Detmold (ex Wroughton by road 4.10.91), coded '(Y)G' (ex 845 Sqdn Yeovilton). Arrived Harwich docks 8.10.91 and left that day on MV Hamburg. No subsequent sightings recorded.

CHECK LIST

This publication is likely to prove of value to persons researching individual types of aircraft, and to those pursuing other specialised lines of research into British military aviation history. In view of the complexity of the various lists, it is appreciated that such researchers, and others with more general interests, may have difficulty in finding the information they require. This check list will be of assistance to them. In it will be found every aircraft mentioned within these pages, listed by both their original serial and their later 'A' or 'M' serial where this is known.

The symbols 'I', 'II', 'III' (the instructional categories), 'M' (for Naval 'M' serials) and 'AAC' (airframes transferred to the Army Air Corps) indicate the heading under which the entry may be found, although in some cases they may have served in some other category. For simplicity, the later categories 'GRA', 'GRB' and 'GR(2)' have not been used for this purpose. Where the airframes were re-allocated 'new' 'A' numbers in (or post) 1988 and/or 1993 the relevant section is indicated in the fourth column by reference to the year. Entries are listed in vertical columns, in alphabetical order of type, the name of the manufacturer being used where no type name was allocated.

ALBACORE

L7074	A78	II
X9112		II
A78	L7074	II

ATTACKER

TS409	A2313	II
TS416		II
WA469	A2396	II
WA470		II
WA472		II
WA481	A2362	II
WA482	A2407	II
WA483	A2312 ?	II
WA491	A2423	II
WA496	A2373	II
WA505	A2364	II
WA506	A2408	II
WA509		II
WA512	A2360	II
WA516		II
WA518		II
WA520	A2402	II
WA528	A2365	II
WA529		II
WA530	A2363	II
WA532	A2366	II
WA533	A2361	II
WK320	A2418	II
WK329		II
WP286	A2446	II
WZ279	A2400	II
WZ289	A2401	II
WZ299	A2445	II
A2312	WA483 ?	II
A2313	TS409	II
A2360	WA512	II
A2361	WA533	II
A2362	WA481	II
A2363	WA530	II
A2364	WA505	II
A2365	WA528	II
A2366	WA532	II
A2373	WA496	II
A2396	WA469	II
A2400	WZ279	II
A2401	WZ289	II
A2402	WA520	II
A2407	WA482	II
A2408	WA506	II
A2418	WK320	II
A2423	WA491	II
A2445	WZ299	II
A2446	WP286	II

AVENGER

FN758		II
FN827		II
JZ129		II
KE437		II
KE442	A2326	II
XB317		II
A367		II
A2326	KE442	II

AVRO 504N

K1813	1247M	M
K1974	1248M	M
K2349	1249M	M
K2386	1250M	M
K2402	1251M	M
1247M	K1813	M
1248M	K1974	M
1249M	K2349	M
1250M	K2386	M
1251M	K2402	M

BALLIOL

VL892	II

BARRACUDA

P9857		II
BV722		II
DR139		II
LS676		II
LS870		II
LS955	A455	II
MD612	A337	II
ME123		II
MX888		II
MX903		II
PM779		II
RJ963		II
RJ964		II
A325		II
A337	MD612	II
A417		II
A445	LS955	II
A463		II
A464		II
A466		II
A467		II
A471		II
A472		II
A551		II

BEAUFORT

A388	II

BLACKBURN YB.1

WB797	A2403	II
A2403	WB797	II

BUCCANEER

XK527	8818M	M	
XK531	8403M	M	
XK532	A2581/	II	
	8867M	M	
XK534	A2582	II	
XN924	A2553	II	
XN925	A2602/	II	
	8087M	M	
XN928	8179M	M	
XN929	8051M	M	
XN930	8180M	M	
XN932	A2552	II	
XN934	A2600	II	
XN953	8182M/	M	
	A2655/	II	
	A2600 [3]	II 1993	
XN954	A2617	II	
XN956	8059M	M	
XN962	8183M	M	
XN967	A2627	II	
XN972	8181M	M	
XT274	8856M	M	
XT277	8853M	M	
XT281	8705M	M	
XT284	8855M	M	
XT288	9134M	M	
XV152	8776M	M	
XV154	8854M	M	
XV155	8716M	M	
XV156	8773M	M	
XV161	9117M	M	
XV332	9232M	M	
XV337	8852M	M	
XV338	8774M	M	
XV340	8659M	M	
XV353	9144M	M	
XV354	8775M	M	
XV358	8658M	M]	
XV359	A2693 [2]	II 1993	
XV863	9115M/	M	
	9139M/	M	
	9145M	M	
XV864	9234M	M	
XV865	9226M	M	
8051M	XN929	M	
8059M	XN956	M	
8087M	XN925/	M	
	A2602	II	
8179M	XN928	M	
8180M	XN930	M	
8181M	XN972	M	

8182M	XN953/	M
	A2655/	II
	A2600 [3]	II 1993
8183M	XN962	M
8403M	XK531	M
8658M	XV358	M
8659M	XV340	M
8705M	XT281	M
8716M	XV155	M
8773M	XV156	M
8774M	XV338	M
8775M	XV354	M
8776M	XV152	M
8818M	XK527	M
8852M	XV337	M
8853M	XT277	M
8854M	XV154	M
8855M	XT284	M
8856M	XT274	M
8867M	XK532/	M
	A2581	II
9115M	XV863	M
9117M	XV161	M
9134M	XT288	M
9139M	XV863	M
9144M	XV353	M
9145M	XV863	M
9226M	XV865	M
9232M	XV332	M
9234M	XV864	M
A2552	XN932	II
A2553	XN924	II
A2581	XK532/	II
	8867M	M
A2582	XK534	II
A2600	XN934	II
A2600 [3]	XN953/	II 1993
	8182M/	M
	A2655	II
A2602	XN925/	II
	8087M	M
A2617	XN954	II
A2627	XN967	II
A2655	XN953/	II
	8182M/	M
	A2600 [3]	II 1993
A2693 [2]	XV349	II 1993

BUFFALO

AS417	A37	II
AS426	A39	II
AS427	A38	II
A37	AS417	II
A38	AS427	II
A39	AS426	II

CANBERRA

WH856	8742M	M	
WJ629	8747M	M	
WJ717	9052M	M	
WT308	A2601 [3]	II	1993
8742M	WH856	M	
8747M	WJ629	M	
9052M	WJ717	M	
A2601 [3]	WT308	II	1993

CORSAIR

JT207		II
JT221		II
JT601		II
JT681		II

DRAGONFLY/SIKORSKY S.51

VW209	A2339	II
VX596	A2465	II
VZ962		II
WG718	A2531	II
WG725	7703M	M
WH990	A2463	II
WN495	A2384	II
7703M	WG725	M
A2339	VW209	II
A2384	WN495	II
A2463	WH990	II
A2465	VX596	II
A2531	WG718	II

FAIREY IIIF

S1317	1028M	M
S1800	1929M	M
S1826	1827M	M
S1835	739M	M
S1851	1507M	M
S1859	1826M	M
739M	S1835	M
1028M	S1317	M
1507M	S1851	M
1826M	S1859	M
1827M	S1826	M
1929M	S1800	M

FIREBRAND

DK376		II
DK404		II
EK605		II
EK608	A2097	II
EK630		II
EK720		II
EK728		II
EK733	A2231	II
EK735	A2232	II
EK779		II
EK783		II
EK788	A2210	II
EK792		II
EK795		II
EK827	A2211	II
EK840	A2218	II
EK843		II
EK844		II
A494		II
A559		II
A703		II
A717		II
A2097	EK608	II
A2210	EK788	II
A2211	EK827	II
A2218	EK840	II
A2231	EK733	II
A2232	EK735	II

FIREFLY

Z1865		II
Z1868		II
Z1889	A2235	II
Z1899		II
Z1901		II
Z1907		II
Z1942		II
Z1972		II
Z1986		II
Z2013	A2014	II
Z2048	A2064	II
Z2097		II
Z2099		II
Z2103		II
Z2117	A2012	II
DK416		II
DK420		II
DK496		II
DK504	A2169	II
DK510		II
DK512	A2024	II
DK531	A2415	II
DK538	A2182	II
DT932	A714	II
DV119		II
DV130		II
MB388	A2010	II
MB401		II
MB408	A2395	II
MB413		II
MB415	A2173	II
MB446		II
MB495		II
MB504		II
MB553	A2071	II
MB555		II
MB558		II
MB560		II
MB561		II
MB572	A2023	II
MB581		II
MB584		II
MB592	A2241	II
MB618	A2240	II
MB641		II
MB642		II
MB742		II
MB743		II
PP596	A2257	II
PP611		II
PP620		II
PP642	A2255	II
TW687	A2299	II
TW688		II
TW689		II
TW690		II
TW691		II
TW693		II
TW694	A2007	II
TW696		II
TW697		II
TW698		II
TW699		II
TW715		II
TW716		II
TW717		II
TW719	A2301	II
TW720		II
TW721		II
VG972		II
VT362		II
VT369		II
VT373	A2269	II
VT378		II
VT381		II
VT407		II
VT417	A2258	II
VT421	A2291	II
VT429	A2382	II
VT434	A2245	II
VT476	A2375	II
VX394	A2328	II
VX420	A2394	II
VX424		II
VX435		II
WB250	A2374	II
WB254		II
WB262		II
WB313	A2392	II
WB349		II
WB379		II
WB405		III
WD848	A2378	II
WD850	A2383	II
WD909	A2386	II
WD910	A2413	II
WH630	A2385	II
WJ215		II
WJ216	A2318	II
WM763		II
A305		II
A480		II
A495		II
A543		II
A714	DT932	II
A2007	TW694	II
A2010	MB388	II
A2012	Z2117	II
A2014	Z2013	II
A2015		II
A2023	MB572	II
A2024	DK512	II
A2030		II
A2064	Z2048	II
A2071	MB553	II
A2099		II
A2104		II
A2106		II
A2169	DK504	II
A2173	MB415	II
A2182	DK538	II
A2213		II
A2217		II
A2235	Z1889	II
A2240	MB618	II
A2241	MB592	II
A2245	VT434	II
A2246		II
A2255	PP642	II
A2257	PP596	II
A2258	VT417	II
A2259		II
A2269	VT373	II
A2291	VT421	II
A2299	TW687	II
A2301	TW719	II
A2318	WJ216	II
A2328	VX394	II
A2374	WB250	II
A2375	VT476	II
A2378	WD848	II
A2382	VT429	II
A2383	WD850	II
A2385	WH630	II
A2386	WD909	II
A2392	WB313	II
A2394	VX420	II
A2395	MB408	II
A2413	WD910	II
A2415	DK531	II

FR POD Mk.20E

E.110	A2593	II
A2593	E.110	II

GANNET

VR557		II
WE488		II
WN341	A2414	II
WN343	A2450	II
WN344	A2437	II
WN346	A2493	II
WN354	A2412	II
WN364	A2466	II
WN373	A2422	II
WN376	A2435	II
WN391	A2470	II
WN393	A2421	II
WN421	A2419	II
WN453	A2436	II
WN454	A2467	II
WN462	A2416	II
WN464	A2540	II
XA342	A2471	II
XA363	A2528	II
XA456	A2533	II
XA459	A2608	II
XA460		I
XA508	A2472	II
XA510		I
XA518		I
XA523	A2459	II
XG797		I
XG831	A2539	II
XG871	A2474	II
XG881		II
XG882	8754M	M
XL500	A2701	II
8754M	XG882	M
A2412	WN354	II
A2414	WN341	II
A2416	WN462	II
A2419	WN421	II
A2421	WN393	II
A2422	WN373	II
A2435	WN376	II
A2436	WN453	II
A2437	WN344	II
A2450	WN343	II
A2459	XA523	II
A2466	WN364	II
A2467	WN454	II
A2470	WN391	II
A2471	XA342	II
A2472	XA508	II
A2474	XG871	II
A2493	WN346	II
A2528	XA363	II
A2533	XA456	II
A2539	XG831	II
A2540	WN464	II
A2608	XA459	II

GAZELLE

XW860		AAC
XW863		AAC
ZB648		II

GNAT

XM694		II
XP535	A2679	II
XR540	8636M/	M
	A2708	II
XR572	A2676	II
XR955	A2678	II
XR991	8637M/	M
	A2709	II
XR993	A2677/	II
	8878M	M
8636M	XR540/	M
	A2708	II

8637M	XR991/	M
	A2709	II
8878M	XR993/	M
	A2677	II
A2676	XR572	II
A2677	XR993/	II
	8878M	M
A2678	XR955	II
A2679	XP535	II
A2708	XR540	II
A2709	XR991	II

HARRIER

XV277	A2600 [2]/	II 1988
	A2602 [3]	II 1993
XV280	A2700 [2]/	II 1988
	A2608 [3]	II 1993
XV741	A2607 [2]/	II 1988
	A2608 [3]	II 1993
XV751	A2760 [2]/	II 1988
	A2672 [2]	II 1993
XV753	A2691 [2]	II 1993
XV755	A2604 [2]/	II 1988
	A2606 [3]	II 1993
XV760	A2614 [2]/	II 1988
	A2605 [2]	II 1993
XV783	A2608 [2]/	II 1988
	A2609 [3]	II 1993
XV786	A2615 [2]/	II 1988
	A2611 [3]	II 1993
XV806	A2606 [2]/	II 1988
	A2607 [3]	II 1993
XV808	A2687 [2]	II 1993
XW271	A2692 [2]	II 1993
XW630	A2759 [2]/	II 1988
	A2671 [2]	II 1993
XW919	A2609 [2]/	II 1988
	A2610 [3]	II 1993
XZ129	A2602 [2]/	II 1988
	A2604 [3]	II 1993
XZ145	A2610 [4]	II 1993
XZ969	A2610 [2]/	II 1988
	A2612 [3]	II 1993
XZ996	A2685 [2]	II 1993
ZB601		II
ZD667	A2684 [2]	II 1993
A2600 [2]	XV277/	II 1988
	A2602 [3]	II 1993
A2602 [2]	XZ129/	II 1988
	A2604 [3]	II 1993
A2602 [3]	XV277/	II 1993
	A2600 [2]	II 1988
A2604 [2]	XV755/	II 1988
	A2606 [3]	II 1993
A2604 [3]	XZ129/	II 1993
	A2602 [2]	II 1988
A2605 [2]	XV760/	II 1993
	A2614 [2]	II 1988
A2606 [2]	XV806/	II 1988
	A2607 [3]	II 1993
A2606 [3]	XV755/	II 1993
	A2604 [2]	II 1988
A2607 [2]	XV741/	II 1988
	A2608 [3]	II 1993
A2607 [3]	XV806/	II 1993
	A2606 [2]	II 1988
A2608 [2]	XV783/	II 1988
	A2609 [3]	II 1993
A2608 [3]	XV741/	II 1993
	A2607 [2]	II 1988
A2609 [2]	XW919/	II 1988
	A2610 [3]	II 1993
A2609 [3]	XV783/	II 1993
	A2608 [2]	II 1988
A2610 [2]	XZ969/	II 1988
	A2612 [3]	II 1993
A2610 [3]	XW919/	II 1993
	A2609 [2]	II 1988
A2610 [4]	XZ145	II 1993

A2611 [3]	XV786/	II 1993
	A2615 [2]	II 1988
A2612 [3]	XZ969/	II 1993
	A2610 [2]	II 1988
A2614 [2]	XV760/	II 1988
	A2605 [2]	II 1993
A2615 [2]	XV786/	II 1988
	A2611 [3]	II 1993
A2671 [2]	XW630/	II 1993
	A2759 [2]	II 1988
A2672 [2]	XV751/	II 1993
	A2760 [2]	II 1988
A2684 [2]	ZD667	II 1993
A2685 [2]	XZ996	II 1993
A2687 [2]	XV808	II 1993
A2691 [2]	XV753	II 1993
A2692 [2]	XW271	II 1993
A2700 [2]	XV280	II 1993
A2759 [2]	XW630/	II 1988
	A2671 [2]	II 1993
A2760 [2]	XV751/	II 1988
	A2672 [2]	II 1993

HART

K2464	695M	M
695M	K2464	M

HAWKER P.1052

VX272	7174M	M
7174M	VX272	M

HAWKER P.1127

XP980	A2700	II
XP984	A2658	II
A2658	XP984	II
A2700	XP980	II

HELLCAT

A372		II
A373		II

HILLER

XB480	A2577	II
A2577	XB480	II

HUNTER

WT711	A2731/	II
	A2645 [2]	II 1993
WT723	A2616 [3]	II 1993
WT745	8893M	M
WT804	A2732/	II
	A2646 [2]	II 1993
WV267	A2737/	II
	A2650 [2]	II 1993
WV322	9096M	M
WV372	A2619 [2]	II 1993
WV382	A2730/	II
	A2724 [2]	II 1988
WV404		I
WV405	A2563	II
WV411	A2564	II
WW654	A2754/	II
	A2664 [2]	II 1993
XE668	A2733/	II
	A2647 [2]	II 1993
XE673	8846M	M
XE682	A2736	II
XE707		I
XE712	A2730 [2]/	II 1988
	A2620 [2]	II 1993
XF303	A2565	II
XF310	A2618 [3]	II 1993
XF311	A2566	II
XF318	A2567	II
XF321	A2734/	II
	A2648 [2]	II 1993

XF363	A2560	II
XF365	A2561	II
XF370		I
XF947	A2568	II
XF967	9182M/	M
	9186M	M
XF976	A2569	II
XF984	A2570	II
XF995	9237M	M
XL600	A2729	II
XL601	A2617 [3]	II 1993
XX466	A2738/	II
	A2651 [2]	II 1993
8846M	XE673	M
8893M	WT745	M
9096M	WV322	M
9182M	XF967/	M
	9186M	M
9186M	XF967/	M
	9182M	M
9237M	XF995	M
A2560	XF363	II
A2561	XF365	II
A2563	WV405	II
A2564	WV411	II
A2565	XF303	II
A2566	XF311	II
A2567	XF318	II
A2568	XF947	II
A2569	XF976	II
A2570	XF984	II
A2616 [3]	WT723	II 1993
A2617 [3]	XL601	II 1993
A2618 [3]	XF310	II 1993
A2619 [2]	WV372	II 1993
A2620 [2]	XE712/	II 1993
	A2730 [2]	II 1988
A2645 [2]	WT711/	II 1993
	A2731	II
A2646 [2]	WT804/	II 1993
	A2732	II
A2647 [2]	XE668/	II 1993
	A2733	II
A2648 [2]	XF321/	II 1993
	A2734	II
A2650 [2]	WV267/	II 1993
	A2737	II
A2651 [2]	XX466/	II 1993
	A2738	II
A2664 [2]	WW654/	II 1993
	A2754	II
A2724 [2]	WV382/	II 1988
	A2730	II
A2729	XL600	II
A2730	WV382/	II
	A2724 [2]	II 1988
A2730 [2]	XE712/	II 1988
	A2620 [2]	II 1993
A2731	WT711/	II
	A2645 [2]	II 1993
A2732	WT804/	II
	A2646 [2]	II 1993
A2733	XE668/	II
	A2647 [2]	II 1993
A2734	XF321/	II
	A2648 [2]	II 1993
A2736	XE682	II
A2737	WV267/	II
	A2650 [2]	II 1993
A2738	XX466/	II
	A2651 [2]	II 1993
A2754	WW654/	II
	A2664 [2]	II 1993

HURRICANE

L1568	4534M	M
L2045		II

N2669	2876M	M
P3042		II
P3061		II
P3119	3585M	M
V6850	4574M	M
V7055	4663M	M
V7068		II
V7111	2757M	M
V7166	5034M	M
V7377	4562M	M
W9127	4533M	M
Z4790	4695M	M
LF656	5368M	M
LF690	5372M	M
LF709	5369M	M
LF718	5370M	M
LF719	5371M	M
LF765	5367M	M
2757M	V7111	M
2876M	N2669	M
3585M	P3119	M
4533M	W9127	M
4534M	L1568	M
4562M	V7377	M
4574M	V6850	M
4663M	V7055	M
4695M	Z4790	M
5034M	V7166	M
5367M	LF765	M
5368M	LF656	M
5369M	LF709	M
5370M	LF718	M
5371M	LF719	M
5372M	LF690	M
A105		II
A167		II
A201		II
A202		II
A203		II

JET PROVOST

XP558	A2628/	II
	8627M	M
8627M	XP558/	M
	A2628	II
A2628	XP558/	II
	8627M	M

JETSTREAM

XX479	A2611 [4]	II 1993
A2611 [4]	XX479	II 1993

KESTREL

XS695	A2619	II
A2619	XS695	II

KRANICH I GLIDER

VS208		II

LYNX

XW839	A2710/	II
	A2657 [2]/	II 1988
	A2624 [2]	II 1993
XX469	A2657	II
XX510	A2601 [2]/	II 1988
	A2772/	II 1988
	A2683 [2]	II 1993
XZ213	TAD213	II
XZ243	A2611 [2]/	II 1988
	A2613 [3]	II 1993
XZ249	A2721	II
QP-31		II

A2601 [2]	XX510/	II 1988	
	A2772	II 1988	
	A2683 [2]	II 1993	
A2611 [2]	XZ243/	II 1993	
	A2613 [3]	II 1993	
A2613 [3]	XZ243/	II 1993	
	A2611 [2]	II 1988	
A2624 [2]	XW839/	II 1993	
	A2710/	II	
	A2657 [2]	II 1988	
A2657	XX469	II	
A2657 [2]	XW839/	II 1988	
	A2710/	II	
	A2624 [2]	II 1993	
A2683 [2]	XX510/	II 1988	
	A2601 [2]/	II 1988	
	A2772	II 1988	
A2710	XW839/	II	
	A2657 [2]/	II 1988	
	A2624 [2]	II 1993	
A2721	XZ249	II	
A2772	XX510/	II 1988	
	A2601 [2]/	II 1988	
	A2683 [2]	II 1993	

MARTLET

AX826		II

MASTER

N9004	3831M	M
N9005	3819M	M
W9018		II
AZ668		II
3819M	N9005	M
3831M	N9004	M

METEOR

EE337		II
EE387	A2295	II
EE545	A2332	II
WF752	A2430	II
A2295	EE387	II
A2332	EE545	II
A2430	WF752	II

MOSQUITO

DD759	5912M	M
KA948		II
KA951		II
KA964		II
KB410		II
KB574		II
KB584		II
KB685	6006M	M
KB699		II
MM327	6154M	M
MM389	6143M	M
MT477	6116M	M
NS525	6155M	M
NS640	6156M	M
NS737	6153M	M
NS803	6120M	M
NT560	5915M/	M
	A2026	II
5912M	DD759	M
5915M	NT560	M
6006M	KB685	M
6116M	MT477	M
6120M	NS803	M
6143M	MM389	M
6154M	MM327	M
6153M	NS737	M
6155M	NS525	M
6156M	NS640	M
A2026	NT560/	II
	5915M	M

NIMROD

K2823	1146M	M
K2826	1046M	M
K2827	1190M	M
K2831	894M	M
K2833	622M	M
K2910	1183M	M
622M	K2833	M
894M	K2831	M
1046M	K2826	M
1146M	K2823	M
1183M	K2910	M
1190M	K2827	M

OSPREY

K2774	646M	M
K2777	1057M	M
K3631	1953M	M
K3635	1125M	M
K3640	922M	M
K3644	1000M	M
K3648	1228M	M
K3914	965M	M
K3915	873M	M
K3918	971M	M
K5755	1229M	M
K5760	1172M	M
646M	K2774	M
873M	K3915	M
922M	K3640	M
962M		M
965M	K3914	M
971M	K3918	M
1000M	K3644	M
1057M	K2777	M
1125M	K3635	M
1172M	K5760	M
1228M	K3648	M
1229M	K5755	M
1953M	K3631	M

OXFORD

DF482		II
HM747		II
LB413		II
NM661	A2315	II
NM759		II
PG984		II
PH300		II
A2315	NM661	II

PHANTOM II

XT595	8550M/	M
	8851M	M
XT857	8913M	M
XT859	8999M	M
XT864	8998M	M
XT867	9064M	M
XT874	9068M	M
XV569	9063M	M
XV570	9069M	M
XV577	9065M	M
XV581	9070M	M
XV582	9066M	M
XV586	9067M	M
XV587	9088M	M
8550M	XT595	M
8851M	XT595	M
8913M	XT857	M
8998M	XT864	M
8999M	XT859	M
9063M	XV569	M
9064M	XT867	M
9065M	XV577	M

9066M	XV582	M
9067M	XV586	M
9068M	XT874	M
9069M	XV570	M
9070M	XV581	M
9088M	XV587	M

SCIMITAR/VAS 544

WT854		II
WT859	A2499	II
XD215	A2573	II
XD226	A2562	II
XD242		II
XD243	A2588	II
XD271	A2589	II
XD272	A2585	II
XD274	A2584	II
XD275	A2587	II
XD276	A2591	II
XD278	A2586	II
XD280	A2583	II
XD324	A2590	II
XD332	A2574	II
A2499	WT859	II
A2562	XD226	II
A2573	XD215	II
A2574	XD332	II
A2583	XD280	II
A2584	XD274	II
A2585	XD272	II
A2586	XD278	II
A2587	XD275	II
A2588	XD243	II
A2589	XD271	II
A2590	XD324	II
A2591	XD276	II

SCOUT

XT640		II

SEAFIRE

"KF552"		II
LR857		II
MB364	A350	II
NF531	A509	II
NF630	A2106	II
NN336	A506	II
NN570	A505	II
NN585	A511	II
PK243		II
PR181	A2077	II
PR340		II
PR353		II
PR359		II
PR364	A2162	II
PR374		II
PR377	A2093	II
PR394	A2268	II
PR403		II
PR406	A2187	II
PR433	A2190	II
PR456		II
PR463	A2178	II
PS944		II
PS945	A2186	II
PS947		II
PS951		II
PS954		I
PS956		II
PX913	A438	II
RX217	A502	II
SR453	A2189	II
SR458		II
SR461		II
SR468		II
SR473		II
SR480		II
SR588		II

SR602		II
SR630		II
SR639		II
SW791		II
SW800	A2256	II
SW807		II
SW814		II
SW820	A2199	II
SW846		II
SW866	A2179	II
SW867	A2268	II
SW916	A2203	II
SW919		II
SX296		II
SX300	A646/	II
	A2054	II
SX300	A696	II
SX312		II
SX336	A517/	II
	A2055	II
SX341	A727	II
SX360?	A2080	II
SX361		II
VP441		II
A350	MB364	II
A438	PX913	II
A454		II
A456		II
A483		II
A486		II
A498		II
A502	RX217	II
A505	NN570	II
A506	NN336	II
A509	NF531	II
A511	NN585	II
A513		II
A518		II
A530		II
A564		II
A575		II
A577		II
A633		II
A634		II
A646	SX300/	
	A2054	II
A656		II
A661		II
A696	SX300	II
A707		II
A718		II
A791		II
A727	SX341	II
A2053		II
A2054	SX300/	
	A646	II
A2055	SX336	II
A2077	PR181	II
A2080	SX360 ?	II
A2090		II
A2093	PR377	II
A2106	NF630	II
A2113		II
A2115		II
A2162	PR364	II
A2178	PR463	II
A2179	SW866	II
A2186	PS945	II
A2187	PR406	II
A2189	SR453	II
A2190	PR433	II
A2199	SW820	II
A2203	SW916	II
A2256	SW800	II
A2268	PR394	II
A2268	SW867	II

SEAFOX

K4304	1463M	M

K8584		II
1463M	K4304	M

SEA FURY

SR666		II
TF895		II
TF899	A2036	II
TF900	A2270	II
TF903		II
TF904		I
TF905		II
TF908	A2349	II
TF910		II
TF912		I
TF914		II
TF918		I
TF920		II
TF922	A2351	II
TF923		II
TF928		II
TF940		I
TF943		I
TF946	A2350	II
TF947	A2348	II
TF950	A2358	II
TF955	A2352	II
TF960		II
TF963	A2355	II
TF973		I
VB857		II
VR923		II
VR927		I
VR930	8382M	M
VR937	A2381	II
VW567		II
VW651	A2209	II
VX301		II
VX664	A2379	II
VX665	A2343	II
WE722	A2359	II
WE733	A2356	II
WE734	A2380	II
WE801	A2377	II
WE825	A2372	II
WN487	A2357	II
8382M	VR930	M
A2036	TF899	II
A2209	VW651	II
A2270	TF900	II
A23..	TF914	II
A2343	VX665	II
A2348	TF947	II
A2349	TF908	II
A2350	TF946	II
A2351	TF922	II
A2352	TF955	II
A2355	TF963	II
A2356	WE733	II
A2357	WN487	II
A2358	TF950	II
A2359	WE722	II
A2372	WE825	II
A2377	WE801	II
A2379	VX664	II
A2380	WE734	II
A2381	VR937	II

SEA HAWK

WF143	A2368	II
WF144	A2452	II
WF145		II
WF146	A2410	II
WF147	A2367	
or	A2376	II
WF151	A2336	II
WF155	A2371	II
WF158	A2441	II
WF159	A2420	II
WF163	A2428	II
WF165	A2405	II
WF169		II
WF172	A2427	II
WF180		II
WF182	A2424	II
WF183	A2426	II
WF188		II
WF196	A2451	II
WF200	A2409	II
WF201	A2406	II
WF211	A2404	II
WF213	A2440	II
WF219	A2439	II
WF220	A2473	II
WF225	A2645/	II
	A2623 [2]	II 1993
WF243	A2425	II
WF257	A2462	II
WF259	A2483	II
WF277	A2454	II
WF280		II
WF284		I
WF289		I
WF294	A2443	II
WF299	A2509/	II
	A2662/	II
	8164M	M
WM901	A2431	II
WM903	A2347	II
WM907	A2484	II
WM908		I
WM913	A2510/	II
	8162M	M
WM915	A2523	II
WM918	A2489	II
WM920	A2490	II
WM924	A2433	II
WM925		II
WM936	A2502	II
WM937	A2494	II
WM939	A2482	II
WM943	A2505	II
WM961	A2517	II
WM963		II
WM965	A2495	II
WM969	A2530	II
WM975		II
WM976		II
WM981	A2460	II
WM982		II
WM983	A2511	II
WM988		I
WM993	A2522	II
WM994	A2503	II
WM996		II
WM998	A2524	II
WM999		II
WN105		II
WN107		II
WN108		II
WN114		I
WN115		I
WN116		I
WN118	A2432	II
WV792	A2559	II
WV794	8152M/	M
	A2634	II
WV795	8151M/	M
	A2661	II
WV797	8155M/	M
	A2637	II
WV798	A2557	II
WV825	A2593	II
WV826	A2532	II
WV828	A2592	II
WV831	A2558	II
WV836	A2545	II
WV841	A2521	II
WV860	A2547	II
WV861	A2548	II
WV865	A2554	II
WV870	A2546	II
WV903	8153M/	M
	A2632	II
WV904	A2497	II
WV908	8154M/	M
	A2660	II
WV909	A2549	II
WV911	A2526/	II
	A2626 [2]/	II 1988
	A2622 [2]	II 1993
WV914	A2536	II
XE327	A2556	II
XE330	A2555	II
XE339	8156M/	M
	A2635	II
XE366	A2515	II
XE368	A2534	II
XE369	A2580/	II
	8158M/	M
	A2633	II
XE390	8157M/	M
	A2636	II
XE490		II
8151M	WV795/	M
	A2661	II
8152M	WV794/	M
	A2634	II
8153M	WV903/	M
	A2632	II
8154M	WV908/	M
	A2660	II
8155M	WV797/	M
	A2637	II
8156M	XE339/	M
	A2535	II
8157M	XE390/	M
	A2636	II
8158M	XE369/	M
	A2580/	II
	A2633	II
8162M	WM913/	M
	A2510	II
A2336	WF151	II
A2347	WM903	II
A2367?	WF147	II
A2368	WF143	II
A2371	WF155	II
A2376?	WF147	II
A2404	WF211	II
A2405	WF165	II
A2406	WF201	II
A2409	WF200	II
A2410	WF146	II
A2420	WF159	II
A2424	WF182	II
A2425	WF243	II
A2426	WF183	II
A2427	WF172	II
A2428	WF163	II
A2431	WM901	II
A2432	WN118	II
A2433	WM924	II
A2439	WF219	II
A2440	WF213	II
A2441	WF158	II
A2443	WF294	II
A2451	WF196	II
A2452	WF144	II
A2454	WF277	II
A2460	WM981	II
A2462	WF257	II
A2473	WF220	II
A2482	WM939	II
A2483	WF259	II
A2484	WM907	II
A2489	WM918	II
A2490	WM920	II
A2494	WM937	II
A2495	WM965	II
A2497	WV904	II
A2502	WM936	II
A2503	WM994	II
A2505	WM943	II
A2509	WF299/	II
	A2662	II
A2510	WM913/	II
	8162M	M
A2511	WM983	II
A2515	XE366	II
A2517	WM961	II
A2521	WV841	II
A2522	WM993	II
A2523	WM915	II
A2524	WM998	II
A2526	WV911/	II
	A2626 [2]/	II 1988
	A2622 [2]	II 1993
A2530	WM969	II
A2532	WV826	II
A2534	XE368	II
A2536	WV914	II
A2545	WV836	II
A2546	WV870	II
A2547	WV860	II
A2548	WV861	II
A2549	WV909	II
A2554	WV865	II
A2555	XE330	II
A2556	XE327	II
A2557	WV798	II
A2558	WV831	II
A2559	WV792	II
A2580	XE369/	II
	8158M/	M
	A2633	II
A2592	WV828	II
A2593	WV825	II
A2622 [2]	WV911/	II 1993
	A2526/	
	A2626 [2]	II 1988
A2623 [2]	WF225/	II 1993
	A2645	II
A2626 [2]	WV911/	II 1988
	A2526/	
	A2622 [2]	II 1993
A2632	WV903/	II
	8153M	M
A2633	XE369/	II
	8158M/	M
	A2580	II
A2634	WV794/	II
	8152M	M
A2635	XE339/	II
	8156M	M
A2636	XE390/	II
	8157M	M
A2637	WV797/	II
	8155M	M
A2645	WF225/	II
	A2623 [2]	II 1993
A2660	WV908/	II
	8154M	M
A2661	WV795/	II
	8151M	M
A2662	WF299/	II
	A2509	II

SEA HORNET

PX219		II
PX239	A2051 or	
	A2059	II
TT187		II
TT188		II
TT192	A2294	II
TT195		II
VR844		II

A2051 or		
A2059	PX239	II
A2294	TT192	II

SEA HURRICANE

L1663	4501M	M
N2398	4759M	M
N2435	4577M	M
N2455	4693M	M
N2591	4725M	M
N2660	4560M	M
N2671	4664M	M
N2859	4685M	M
P2717	5054M	M
P3020	4505M	M
P3111	4503M	M
P3597	5044M	M
P3701	4576M	M
P3814	4559M	M
P3829	4561M	M
P5183	2807M	M
R4089	4504M	M
V6545	4747M	M
V6579	4578M	M
V6675	4687M	M
V6779	4662M	M
V6867	5033M	M
V6933	4536M	M
V6990	4350M	M
V7002	4506M	M
V7157	4499M	M
V7246	5035M	M
V7252	4686M	M
V7379	4756M	M
V7421	4726M	M
V7600	3584M	M
V7623	4757M	M
V7653	5036M	M
W9134	4749M	M
W9182	5207M	M
W9208	5039M	M
W9221	4502M	M
W9318	4748M	M
Z4851	4684M	M
Z4927	4535M	M
Z7078	4537M	M
Z7085	4660M	M
Z7091	4665M	M
Z7141	4746M	M
Z7145	5042M	M
Z7147	4507M	M
AF945	4758M	M
AF950	4694M	M
AF981	4696M	M
BW841	4659M	M
NF686	5373M	M
NF737	5374M	M
2807M	P5183	M
3584M	V7600	M
4350M	V6990	M
4499M	V7157	M
4501M	L1663	M
4502M	W9221	M
4503M	P3111	M
4504M	R4089	M
4505M	P3020	M
4506M	V7002	M
4507M	Z7147	M
4535M	Z4927	M
4536M	V6933	M
4537M	Z7078	M
4559M	P3814	M
4560M	N2660	M
4561M	P3829	M
4576M	P3701	M
4577M	N2435	M
4578M	V6579	M
4659M	BW841	M
4660M	Z7085	M
4662M	V6779	M
4664M	N2671	M
4665M	Z7091	M
4684M	Z4851	M
4685M	N2859	M
4686M	V7252	M
4687M	V6675	M
4693M	N2455	M
4694M	AF950	M
4696M	AF981	M
4725M	N2591	M
4726M	V7421	M
4746M	Z7144	M
4747M	V6545	M
4748M	W9318	M
4749M	W9134	M
4756M	V7379	M
4757M	V7623	M
4758M	AF945	M
4759M	N2398	M
5033M	V6867	M
5035M	V7246	M
5036M	V7653	M
5039M	W9208	M
5042M	Z7145	M
5044M	P3597	M
5054M	P2717	M
5207M	W9182	M
5373M	NF686	M
5374M	NF737	M

SEA KING

XV370	A2771/	II 1988
	A2682 [2]	II 1993
XV371	A2699 [2]	II
XV642	A2613 [2]/	II 1988
	A2614 [3]	II 1993
XV644	A2664/	II
	A2615 [3]	II 1993
XV654	A2698 [2]	II 1993
XV657	A2600 [4]	II
XV669	A2659	II
XV704		I
ZD631	A2621 [2]	II 1993
A2600 [4]	XV657	II 1993
A2613 [2]	XV642/	II 1988
	A2614 [3]	II 1993
A2614 [3]	XV642/	II 1993
	A2613 [2]	II 1988
A2615 [3]	XV644/	II 1993
	A2664	II
A2621 [2]	ZD631	II 1993
A2659	XV669	II
A2664	XV644/	II
	A2615 [3]	II 1993
A2682 [2]	XV370/	II 1993
	A2771	II 1988
A2698 [2]	XV654	II 1993
A2699 [4]	XV371	II 1993
A2771	XV370/	II 1988
	A2682 [2]	II 1993

SEAL

K3521	657M	M
K3577	1098M	M
K4202	1157M	M
K4203	1186M	M
K4204	1176M	M
K4214	1070M	M
K4218	1169M	M
K4224	1091M	M
K4786	1090M	M
K4792	1069M	M
K4793	1096M	M
K4794	1568M	M
657M	K3521	M
1069M	K4792	M
1070M	K4214	M
1090M	K4786	M
1091M	K4224	M
1096M	K4793	M
1098M	K3577	M
1169M	K4218	M
1175M	K4202	M
1176M	K4204	M
1186M	K4203	M
1568M	K4794	M

SEA MOSQUITO

LR387		I
TW289		II
VT726	6956M	M
6956M	VT726	M

SEA OTTER

RD877		II

SEA PRINCE

WF122	A2673	II
WF125	A2674	II
WF128	8611M	M
WP314	8634M	M
8611M	WF128	M
8634M	WP314	M
A2673	WF122	II
A2674	WF125	II

SEA VAMPIRE

VF315	A2193	II
VV137		I
XA165	8148M	M
8148M	XA165	M
A2193	VF315	II

SEA VENOM

WM503	A2447	II
WM505	A2398	II
WM509	A2479	II
WM512	A2478	II
WM513	A2477	II
WM514	A2455	II
WM517		II
WM518		II
WM520	A2476	II
WM543	A2486	II
WM553	A2480	II
WM557	A2475	II
WM564	A2411	II
WM569	A2417	II
WM570	A2458	II
WM573		II
WW146	A2461	II
WW148	A2448	II
WW189	A2518	II
WW194	A2488	II
WW218	A2508	II
WW219	A2449	II
WW223	A2453	II
WW261	A2456	II
WW267	A2513	II
WW269	A2457	II
WW270	A2520	II
WW275	A2491	II
WW285	A2464	II
XG616	A2492	II
XG621	A2498	II
XG622	A2504	II
XG637	A2512	II
XG655	A2506	II
XG694		II
XG736		III
A2398	WM505	II
A2411	WM564	II
A2417	WM569	II
A2447	WM503	II
A2448	WW148	II
A2449	WW219	II
A2453	WW223	II
A2455	WM514	II
A2456	WW261	II
A2457	WW269	II
A2458	WM570	II
A2461	WW146	II
A2464	WW285	II
A2475	WM557	II
A2476	WM520	II
A2477	WM513	II
A2478	WM512	II
A2479	WM509	II
A2480	WM553	II
A2486	WM543	II
A2488	WW194	II
A2491	WW275	II
A2492	XG616	II
A2498	XG621	II
A2504	XG622	II
A2506	XG655	II
A2508	WW218	II
A2512	XG637	II
A2513	WW267	II
A2518	WW189	II
A2520	WW270	II

SEA VIXEN/DH.110

WG240	A2481	II
XF828	A2500	II
XJ477	A2601	II
XJ482	A2598	II
XJ484	A2535	II
XJ486	A2599	II
XJ487	A2544	II
XJ493		III
XJ513		II
XJ521	A2612 [2]	II
XJ524	8804M	M
XJ526	8145M	M
XJ560	8142M	M
XJ571	8140M	M
XJ572	8803M	M
XJ575	A2611	II
XJ582	8139M	M
XJ583	A2507	II
XJ584	A2621	II
XJ602	A2622	II
XJ604	8222M	M
XJ607	8171M	M
XJ608	8802M	M
XJ609	8172M	M
XN647	A2610	II
XN650	A2612/	II
	A2620/	II
	A2639	II
XN651	A2616	II
XN652	8817M	M
XN658	8223M	M
XN685	8173M	M
XN688	8141M	M
XN691	8143M	M
XN692	A2624	II
XN694		I
XN697	A2623	II
XN699	8224M	M
XN700	8138M	M
XN704		I
XN705	8225M	M
XN706	A2613	II
XN707	8144M	M
XP919	8163M	M
XP921	8226M	M
XS583	8397M	M
XS587	8828M	M

8138M	XN700	M
8139M	XJ582	M
8140M	XJ571	M
8141M	XN688	M
8142M	XJ560	M
8143M	XN691	M
8144M	XN707	M
8145M	XJ526	M
8163M	XP919	M
8171M	XJ607	M
8172M	XJ609	M
8173M	XN685	M
8222M	XJ604	M
8223M	XN658	M
8224M	XN699	M
8225M	XN705	M
8226M	XP921	M
8397M	XS583	M
8802M	XJ608	M
8803M	XJ572	M
8804M	XJ524	M
8817M	XN652	M
8828M	XS587	M
A2481	WG240	II
A2500	XF828	II
A2507	XJ583	II
A2535	XJ484	II
A2544	XJ487	II
A2598	XJ482	II
A2599	XJ486	II
A2601	XJ477	II
A2610	XN647	II
A2611	XJ575	II
A2612 [2]	XJ521	II
A2612	XN650/	II
	A2620/	II
	A2639	II
A2613	XN706	II
A2616	XN651	II
A2620	XN650/	II
	A2612/	II
	A2639	II
A2621	XJ584	II
A2622	XJ602	II
A2623	XN697	II
A2624	XN692	II
A2639	XN650/	II
	A2612/	II
	A2620	II

SHARK

K4295	931M	M
K4357	990M	M
K5607	1482M	M
K5617	903M	M
K5633	1461M	M
K5641	1460M	M
K8450	1457M	M
K8451	1458M	M
K8452	1459M	M
K8475	1127M	M
K8479	1456M	M
K8500	1462M	M
K8895	1451M	M
K8906	1867M	M
K8929	3490M	M
L2374	1752M	M
903M	K5617	M
931M	K4295	M
990M	K4357	M
1127M	K8475	M
1451M	K8895	M
1456M	K8479	M
1457M	K8450	M
1458M	K8451	M
1459M	K8452	M
1460M	K5641	M
1461M	K5633	M
1462M	K8500	M
1482M	K5607	M
1752M	L2374	M
1867M	K8906	M
3490M	K8929	M

SIOUX

XV312	A2631/	II
	8430M	M
XV317	A2638	II
XW179	A2711	II
8430M	XV312/	M
	A2631	II
A2631	XV312/	II
	8430M	M
A2638	XV317	II
A2711	XW179	II

SKUA

L2869	1200M	M
L2870	1201M	M
L2871	1294M	M
1200M	L2869	M
1201M	L2870	M
"1291M"		M
1294M	L2871	M
"1296M"		M

SKYRAIDER

WT965		I

SPEARFISH

RA356		II

SPITFIRE

K9883	4727M	M
P7964	5262M	M
W3127	5537M	M
W3229	5572M	M
X4921	4750M	M
AR493	4697M	M
EP169	5369M	M
4697M	AR493	M
4727M	K9883	M
4750M	X4921	M
5262M	P7964	M
5396M	EP169	M
5537M	W3127	M
5572M	W3229	M

STURGEON

RK791		II

SWORDFISH

K5986	985M	M
L2761	1356M	M
L7698	1311M	M
P4086		II
HS618	A2001	II
985M	K5986	M
1311M	L7698	M
1356M	L2761	M
A2001	HS618	II

TIGER MOTH

K2587	5983M	M
N6795		II
N9211	5982M	M
R4752	6049M	M
T5900		II

T6183		II
T6296	8387M	M
T7682	5987M/	M
	A2034	II
T7695	A2086	II
W7951	A2195	II
BB731	A728/	II
	A2126	II
BB813		II
BB814		II
BB852		II
DE373	A680/	II
	A2127	II
DE627	A2087	II
DE661	A2033	II
NL750	A750/	II
	A2123	II
NL979		II
5982M	N2911	M
5983M	K2587	M
5987M	T7682/	M
	A2034	II
6049M	R4752	M
8387M	T6292	M
A680	DE373/	II
	A2127	II
A687		II
A728	BB731/	II
	A2126	II
A750	NL750/	II
	A2123	II
A752		II
A2033	DE661	II
A2034	T7682/	II
	5987M	M
A2086	T7695	II
A2087	DE627	II
A2088		II
A2123	NL750/	II
	A750	II
A2124		II
A2126	BB731/	II
	A728	II
A2127	DE373/	II
	A680	II
A2195	W7951	II

TUTOR

K1230	666M	M
666M	K1230	M

VAS 508/517

VV106	7175M	M
VX133	A2529	II
7175M	VV106	M
A2529	VX133	II

VAMPIRE

TG314		III
TG328		II
TG421		II
VF268		II
VF269	A2249	II
VF317	A2320	II
VV190	A2354	II
VV215	A2346	II
WW458	A2369	II
WW461	A2370	II
A2249	VF269	II
A2320	VF317	II
A2346	VV215	II
A2354	VV190	II
A2369	WW458	II
A2370	WW461	II

VENOM

VV613	A2327	II
WE279	A2399	II
WL806	A2429	II
A2327	VV613	II
A2399	WE279	II
A2429	WL806	II

WALRUS

K8563	1071M	M
L2186	1241M	M
L2192	1325M	M
L2203	1188M	M
L2215	1340M	M
L2270	1338M	M
L2272	1339M	M
X9580	6225M	M
1071M	K8563	M
1188M	L2203	M
1241M	L2186	M
1325M	L2192	M
1338M	L2270	M
1339M	L2272	M
1340M	L2215	M
6225M	X9580	M

WASP/P.531

XN332	A2579	II
XN333	A2519	II
XN334	A2525	II
XS463	A2647	II
XS476	A2656	II
XS529	A2743/	II
	A2692 [2]	II 1993
XS537	A2672	II
XS538	A2725	II
XS539	A2718 [2]/	I/II 1988
	A2640 [2]	II 1993
XS545	A2702	II
XS567	A2719 [2]	II 1988
XS568	A2715/	II
	A2637 [2]	II 1993
XS569	A2717/	II
	A2639 [2]	II 1993
XS570	A2699	II
XS571		AAC
XS572	8845M	M
XT429	A2720 [2]	I/II 1988
XT434	A2723 [2]/	II 1988
	A2643 [2]	II 1993
XT436		AAC
XT437	A2721 [2]/	II 1988
	A2641 [2]	II 1993
XT438	A2704	II/AAC
XT441	A2703	I/II
XT778	A2722 [2]	I/II 1988
	A2642 [2]	II 1993
XT779		I
XT780	A2716/	II
	A2638 [2]	II 1993
XT786	A2726	II
XT789		I
XT795	A2748	I/II
XV623	A2724	II
XV625	A2735/	I/II
	A2649 [2]	II 1993
XV626		I
XV627		AAC
XV629		AAC
XV638	("A430")/	II
	8826M	M
8826M	XV638/	M
	("A430")	II
8845M	XS572	M

Serial	Cross-ref	Mark
("*A430*")	XV638/	II
	8826M	II
A2519	XN333	II
A2525	XN334	II
A2579	XN332	II
A2637 [2]	XS568/	II 1993
	A2715	II
A2638 [2]	XT780/	II 1993
	A2716	II
A2639 [2]	XS569/	II 1993
	A2717	II
A2640 [2]	XS539/	I/II 1993
	A2718 [2]	II 1988
A2641 [2]	XT437/	II 1993
	A2721 [2]	II 1988
A2642 [2]	XT778/	I/II 1993
	A2722 [2]	II 1988
A2643 [2]	XT434/	II 1993
	A2723 [2]	II 1988
A2647	XS463	II
A2649 [2]	XV625/	I/II 1993
	A2735	II
A2656	XS476	II
A2672	XS537	II
A2692 [2]	XS529/	
	A2743	II 1993
A2699	XS570	II
A2702	XS545	II
A2703	XT441	I/II
A2704	XT438	II
A2715	XS568/	II
	A2638 [2]	II 1993
A2716	XT780/	
	A2637 [2]	II 1993
A2717	XS569/	II
	A2639 [2]	II 1993
A2718 [2]	XS539/	I/II 1988
	A2640 [2]	II 1993
A2719 [2]	XS567	II 1988
A2720 [2]	XT429	I/II 1988
A2721 [2]	XT437/	II 1988
	A2641 [2]	II 1993
A2722 [2]	XT778	I/II 1988
A2723 [2]	XT434/	II 1988
	A2643 [2]	II 1993
A2724	XV623	II
A2725	XS538	II
A2726	XT786	II
A2735	XV625/	I/II
	A2649 [2]	II 1993
A2743	XS529/	II
	A2696 [2]/II	1993
A2748	XT795	I/II

WELLINGTON

Serial	Cross-ref	Mark
MP519	5684M	M
5684M	MP519	M

WESSEX

Serial	Cross-ref	Mark
XL722	A2514	II
XL729	A2641	II
XM328	A2727/	II
	A2644 [2]	II 1993
XM329	A2609	II
XM832		I
XM835	A2516	II
XM836	A2713 [2]	II 1988
XM838		II
XM843	A2693/	I/II
	A2625 [2]	II 1993
XM845	A2682	II
XM868	A2706/	II
	A2630 [2]	II 1993
XM870	A2712 [2]/	II 1988
	A2634 [2]	II 1993
XM874	A2689/	II
	A2629 [2]	II 1993
XM916	A2718	II
XM917	A2692	II

Serial	Cross-ref	Mark
XM920	A2594	II
XM927	8814M	M
XP105	A2698	II
XP107	A2527	II
XP110	A2728/	II
	A2714 [2]/	II 1988
	A2636 [2]	II 1993
XP116	A2618	II
XP117	A2681	II
XP137	A2710 [2]/	II 1988
	A2633 [2]	II 1993
XP140	8806M	M
XP142	A2720	II
XP146		III
XP149	A2669	II
XP150	A2719/	II
	A2764	II 1988
XP151	A2684	II
XP155	A2640	II
XP157	A2680/	II
	A2780	II 1988
	A2689 [2]	II 1993
XP158	A2688	II
XP159	8877M	M
XP160	A2650/	II
	A2628 [2]	II 1993
XS119		II
XS120	8653M	M
XS122	A2707/	II
	A2632 [2]	II 1993
		III
XS124	A2648	II
XS125	A2670/	II
	A2690 [2]	II 1993
XS128	A2704 [2]	II 1988
XS153	9102M	M
XS241	8819M	M
XS479		AAC
XS481	A2746/	II
XS483	A2657 [3]	II 1993
	A2635 [3]	II 1993
XS485	9056M	M/AAC
XS488		II
XS490	A2763/	II
XS496	A2675 [2]	II 1993
	A2641 [3]	Ii 1993
XS498	A2762/	II
XS507	A2674 [2]	II 1993
	A2766/	II
	A2677 [2]	II 1993
XS508	A2597	II
XS509	A2765/	I/II
	A2676 [2]	II 1993
XS510	A2750/	II
	A2660 [2]	II 1993
XS511	A2770/	II
	A2681 [2]	II 1993
XS513	A2740/	II
	A2653 [2]	II 1993
XS514	A2747/	II
	A2658 [2]	II 1993
XS515	A2739/	II
	A2652 [2]	II 1993
XS516	A2625 [3]	II 1993
XS517	A2749/	I/II
	A2659 [2]	II 1993
XS520		AAC
XS521	A2753/	II
	A2663 [2]	II 1993
XS522	A2618 [2]/	II 1988
	A2670 [2]	II 1993
XS523	A2711 [2]	II 1988
XS862	A2694	II
XS865	A2705/	II
	A2627 [2]	II 1993
XS866	A2671	II
XS867	A2691/	II
XS868	A2686 [2]	II 1993
XS869	A2649	II
XS870	A2697	II
XS871	8457M	I/M

Serial	Cross-ref	Mark
XS872	A2666	I/II
XS873	A2686	II
XS876	A2695/	II
	A2626 [3]	II 1993
XS877	A2687	II
XS878	A2683	II
XS881	A2675/	II
	A2688 [2]	II 1993
XS882	A2696	II
XS885	A2668/	II
	A2631 [2]	II 1993
XS886	A2685	II
XS887	A2690	II
XS888	A2616 [2]	II 1988
XT255	8751M	M
XT256	A2615	II
XT257	8719M	M
XT448	A2596	II
XT449	A2752/	II
	A2662 [2]	II 1993
XT453	A2756/	II
	A2666 [2]	II 1993
XT455	A2741/	II
	A2654 [2]	II 1993
XT456	8941M	M
XT457		II
XT458	A2768/	II
XT460	A2679 [2]	II 1993
	A2744/	II
XT463	A2668 [2]	II 1993
	A2624 [3]	II 1993
XT466	8921M/	M
	A2617 [4]	II
XT467	8922M	M
XT468	A2757/	II 1988
	A2667 [2]	II 1993
XT469	8920M	M
XT470		AAC
XT471		AAC
XT474		AAC
XT475	9108M	M
XT480	A2617 [2]/	II 1988
	A2603 [2]	II 1993
XT482	A2745/	II
	A2656 [2]	II 1993
XT484	A2742/	II
	A2655 [2]	II 1993
XT485	A2769/	II
	A2680 [2]	II 1993
XT486	8919M	M
XT487	A2723	II
XT755	9053M	M
XT756		II
XT757	A2722	II
XT760	A2669 [2]	II 1993
XT761	A2767/	II
	A2678 [2]	II 1993
XT762	A2751/	II
	A2661 [2]	II 1993
XT764		AAC
XT765	A2755/	II
	A2665 [2]	II 1993
XT766	9054M	M
	A2620 [3]	II 1993
XT769		II
XT770	9055M	M
XT771	A2761/	II
	A2673 [2]	II 1993
XT772	8805M	M
XT773	9123M	M
XT774		III
8457M	XS871	M/I
8719M	XT257	M
8751M	XT255	M
8805M	XT772	M
8806M	XP140	M
8814M	XM927	M
8819M	XS479	M
8877M	XP159	M
8919M	XT486	M

Serial	Cross-ref	Mark
8920M	XT469	M
8921M	XT466/	M
	A2617 [4]	II 1993
8822M	XT467	M
8941M	XT456	M
9053M	XT755	M
9054M	XT766/	M
	A2620 [3]	II 1993
9055M	XT770	M
9056M	XS488	M
9102M	XS241	M
9108M	XT475	M
9123M	XT773	M
A2514	XL722	II
A2516	XM835	II
A2527	XP107	II
A2594	XM920	II
A2596	XT448	II
A2597	XS509	II
A2603 [2]	XT480/	II 1993
	A2617 [2]	II 1988
A2609	XM329	II
A2615	XT256	II
A2616 [2]	XS888	II 1988
A2617 [2]	XT480/	II 1988
	A2603 [2]	II 1993
A2617 [4]	XT466/II/1993	
	8921M	M
A2618	XP116	II
A2618 [2]	XS523/	II 1988
	A2670 [2]	II 1993
A2620 [3]	XT766/	II 1993
	9054M	M
A2624 [3]	XT463	II 1993
A2625 [2]	XM843/	I/II 1993
	A2693	II
A2625 [3]	XS517	II 1993
A2626 [3]	XS876/	II 1993
	A2695	II
A2627 [2]	XS866/	II 1993
	A2705	II
A2628 [2]	XP160/	II 1993
	A2650	II
A2629 [2]	XM874/	II 1993
	A2689	II
A2630 [2]	XM868/	II 1993
	A2706	II
A2631 [2]	XS885/	II 1993
	A2668	II
A2632 [2]	XS122/	II 1993
	A2707	II
A2633 [2]	XP137/	II 1993
	A2710 [2]	II 1988
A2634 [2]	XM870/	II 1993
	A2712 [2]	II 1988
A2635 [3]	XS485	II 1993
A2636 [2]	XP110/	II 1993
	A2728/	II
	A2714 [2]	II 1988
A2640	XP155	II
A2641	XL729	II
A2641 [3]	XS498	II 1993
A2644 [2]	XM328/	II 1993
	A2727	II
A2648	XS125	II
A2649	XS869	II
A2650	XP160/	II
	A2628 [2]	II 1993
A2652 [2]	XS516/	II 1993
	A2739	II
A2653 [2]	XS514/	II 1993
	A2740	II
A2654 [2]	XT455/	II 1993
	A2741	II
A2655 [2]	XT484/	II 1993
	A2742	II
A2656 [2]	XT482/	II 1993
	A2745	II
A2657 [3]	XS483/	II 1993
	A2746	II

A2658 [2]	XS515/	II 1993	A2698	XP105	II	
	A2747	II	A2704 [2]	XS153	II 1988	
A2659 [2]	XS520/	I/II 1993	A2705	XS866/	II	
	A2749	II		A2627 [2]	II 1993	
A2660 [2]	XS511/	I/II 1993	A2706	XM868/	II	
	A2750	II		A2630 [2]	II 1993	
A2661 [2]	XT762/	II 1993	A2707	XS122/	II	
	A2751	II		A2632 [2]	II 1993	
A2662 [2]	XT449/	II 1993	A2710 [2]	XP137/	II 1988	
	A2752	II		A2633 [2]	II 1993	
A2663 [2]	XS522/	II 1993	A2711 [2]	XS862	II 1988	
	A2753	II	A2712 [2]	XM870/	II 1988	
A2665 [2]	XT765/	II 1993		A2634 [2]	II 1993	
	A2755	II	A2713 [2]	XM836	II 1988	
A2666	XS872	II	A2714 [2]	XP110/	II 1988	
A2666 [2]	XT453/	II 1993		A2728/	II	
	A2756	II		A2636 [2]	II 1993	
A2667 [2]	XT468/	II 1993	A2718	XM916	II	
	A2757	II 1988	A2719	XP150/	II	
A2668	XS885/	II		A2764	II 1988	
	A2631 [2]	II 1993	A2720	XP142	II	
A2668 [2]	XT460/	II 1993	A2722	XT757	II	
	A2744	II	A2723	XT487	II	
A2669	XP149	II	A2727	XM328/	II	
A2669 [2]	XT760	II 1993		A2644 [2]	II 1993	
A2670	XS128/	II	A2728	XP110/	II	
	A2690 [2]	II II 1993		A2714 [2]/	II 1988	
A2670 [2]	XS523/	II 1993		A2636 [2]	II 1993	
	A2618 [2]	II 1988	A2739	XS516/	II	
A2671	XS867	II		A2652 [2]	II 1993	
A2673 [2]	XT771/	II 1993	A2740	XS514/	II	
	A2761	II		A2653 [2]	II 1993	
A2674 [2]	XS507/	II 1993	A2741	XT455/	II	
	A2762	II		A2654 [2]	II 1993	
A2675	XS881/	II	A2742	XT484/	II	
	A2688 [2]	II 1993		A2655 [2]	II 1993	
A2675 [2]	XS496/	II 1993	A2744	XT460/	II	
	A2763	II		A2668 [2]	II 1993	
A2676 [2]	XS510/	I/II 1993	A2745	XT482/	II	
	A2765	II		A2656 [2]	II 1993	
A2677 [2]	XS508/	II 1993	A2746	XS483/	II	
	A2766	II		A2657 [3]	II 1993	
A2678 [2]	XT761/	II 1993	A2747	XS515/	II	
	A2767	II		A2658 [2]	II 1993	
A2680	XP157/	II	A2749	XS520/	I/II	
	A2780/	II 1988		A2659 [2]	II 1993	
	A2689 [2]	II 1993	A2750	XS511/	II	
A2680 [2]	XT485/	II 1993		A2660 [2]	II 1993	
	A2769	II	A2751	XT762/	II	
A2681	XP117	II		A2661 [2]	II 1993	
A2681 [2]	XS513/	II 1993	A2752	XT449/	II	
	A2770	II		A2662 [2]	II 1993	
A2682	XM845	II	A2753	XS522/	II	
A2683	XS878	II		A2663 [2]	II 1993	
A2684	XP151	II	A2755	XT765/	II	
A2685	XS886	II		A2665 [2]	II 1993	
A2686	XS873	II	A2756	XT453/	II	
A2686 [2]	XS868/	II 1993		A2666 [2]	II 1993	
	A2691	II	A2757	XT468/	II 1988	
A2687	XS877	II		A2667 [2]	II 1993	
A2688	XP158	II	A2761	XT771/	II	
A2688 [2]	XS881/	II		A2673 [2]	II 1993	
	A2675		A2762	XS507/	II	
A2689	XM874/	II		A2674 [2]	II 1993	
	A2629 [2]	II 1993	A2763	XS496/	II	
A2689 [2]	XP157/	II 1993		A2675 [2]	II 1993	
	A2680/	II	A2764	XP150/	II 1988	
	A2780	II 1988		A2719	II	
A2690	XS887	II	A2765	XS510/	I/II	
A2690 [2]	XS128/	II 1993		A2676 [2]	II 1993	
	A2670	II	A2766	XS508/	II	
A2691	XS868/	II		A2677 [2]	II 1993	
	A2686 [2]	II 1993	A2767	XT761/	II	
A2692	XM917	II		A2678 [2]	II 1993	
A2693	XM843/	I/II	A2768	XT458/	II	
	A2625 [2]	II 1993		A2679 [2]	II 1993	
A2694	XS865	II	A2769	XT485/	II	
A2695	XS876/	II		A2680 [2]	II 1993	
	A2626 [3]	II 1993	A2770	XS513/	II	
A2696	XS882	II		A2681 [2]	II 1993	
A2697	XS870	II				

A2780	XP157/	II 1988
	A2680/	II
	A2689 [2]	II 1993

WHIRLWIND

WV190	A2537	II	A2538	XJ393	II	
WV193		I	A2541	XA869	II	
WV194		I	A2542	XA862	II	
WV195		I	A2543	XA870	II	
WV198	A2576	II	A2550	XA866	II	
XA862	A2542	II	A2551	XA868	II	
XA866	A2550	II	A2571	XG577	II	
XA868	A2551	II		9050M	M	
XA869	A2541	II	A2572	XJ402	II	
XA870	A2543	II	A2575	XG574	II	
XA871	A2468	II	A2576	WV198	II	
XG574	A2575	II	A2578	XJ399	II	
XG577	A2571/	II	A2595	XL868	II	
	9050M	M	A2603	XK911	II	
XG581	A2469	II	A2604	XN259	II	
XG582		III	A2605	XN308	II	
XG596	A2651	II	A2606	XN305	II	
XJ393	A2538	II	A2607	XK944	II	
XJ397	A2485	II	A2614	XN314	II	
XJ399	A2578	II	A2625	XL846	II	
XJ402	A2572	II	A2626	XL847	II	
XK908	A2442	II	A2629	XM667	II	
XK911	A2603	II	A2630	XL853	II	
XK933	A2496	II	A2642	XL836	II	
XK937	8432M	M	A2643	XN311/	II	
XK943	A2653/	II		A2760	II	
	8796M	M	A2644	XN358	II	
XK944	A2607	II	A2646	XK988	II	
XK988	A2646	II	A2651	XG596	II	
XL836	A2642	II	A2652	XN261	II	
XL839	A2665	II	A2653	XK943/	II	
XL846	A2625	II		8796M	M	
XL847	A2626	II	A2654	XN302/	I/II	
XL853	A2630	II		A2758/	II	
XL868	A2595	II		9037M	M	
XL879		III	A2663	XN309	II	
XL880	A2714	II	A2665	XL839	II	
XM663		II	A2712	XN359/	I/II	
XM667	A2629	II		A2759	II	
XN259	A2604	II	A2713	XN386	II	
XN261	A2652	II	A2714	XL880	II	
XN302	A2654/	I/II	A2758	XN302/	II	
	A2758/	II 1988		A2654/	I/II	
	9037M	M		9037M	M	
XN305	A2606	II	A2759	XN359/	I/II	
XN307	A2501	II		A2712	II	
XN308	A2605	II	A2760	XN311/	II	
XN309	A2663	II		A2643	II	
XN311	A2643/	II				
	A2760	II 1988	**WILDCAT**			
XN314	A2614	II				
XN358	A2644	II	FN174	A132	II	
XN359	A2712/	I/II				
	A2759	II 1988	A132	FN174	II	
XN386	A2713	II				
XN387	8564M	M	**WYVERN**			
			VR132		II	
8432M	XK937	M	VR135	A2227	II	
8564M	XN387	M	VR136		II	
8796M	XK943/	M	VW870	A2438	II	
	A2653	II	VW873	A2397	II	
9037M	XN302/	M	VW874	A2298	II	
	A2654/	I/II	VW877	A2308	II	
	A2758	II	VW878	A2309	II	
9054M	XG577/	M	VW879	A2310	II	
	A2571		VW880	A2311	II	
A2442	XK908	II	VZ777	A2444	II	
A2468	XA871	II	VZ782		II	
A2469	XG581	II	WL881	A2434	II	
A2485	XJ397	II				
A2487	XG584	II	A2227	VR135	II	
A2496	XK933	II	A2298	VW874	II	
A2501	XN307	II	A2308	VW877	II	
A2537	WV190	II	A2309	VW878	II	
			A2310	VW879	II	
			A2311	VW880	II	
			A2397	VW873	II	
			A2434	WL881	II	
			A2438	VW870	II	
			A2444	VZ777	II	

INSTRUCTIONAL ENGINES

All known numbers of installed engines are included in the details of their relevant airframes. As noted in the Introduction, there are also many engines which are used solely for some form of engine instruction and never fitted into airframes. No attempt was made to list these in the original monograph. For the sake of completeness, this section gives a few details which have come to light since then, but primarily concentrates on the re-allocation of 'E' numbers which occurred in 1988 and 1993.

ENGINE No.	ENGINE TYPE	DETAILS
E4307	Nene II	Ex Tudor 8 VX195, 1.9.48 to 27.6.51. To A.V.Roe 3.4.50, then RAE Farnborough. To Arbroath 16.6.55.
E4310	Nene Is	[Entry amended from E3410] To Arbroath 6.8.55, but unsuitable.
E4326	Double Mamba	[Not fitted to an aircraft] Ex Gannet VR546. To GI at Arbroath 5.7.56.
E4327	Ghost	[Not fitted to an aircraft] Ex Sea Venom XA539. To GI at Arbroath 5.7.56.
E4332	Wasp	[Not fitted to an aircraft] Ex Harvard III EZ277 or EZ377. To GI at Arbroath 16.10.56.
E4344	Gipsy Major	Ex Tiger Moth T6306. To Class II at Arbroath 13.2.57.
E4406	Leonides 50	[Not fitted to an aircraft] To GI at Arbroath 30.7.58. WOC 19.1.59.
E4411	Double Mamba 10101	[Not fitted to an aircraft] To GI at Arbroath 15.10.58.

September 1988

The following ECU's not fitted to an airframe were current in September 1988. Some of the 'E' numbers are original allocations but several are re-allocations as a result of the re-organisation of the system which took place that year. At the time of writing it has proved impossible to trace the original allocations and histories for the majority of these engines but the following details are known.

E4601	Conway 1011	[ex E4518] Manadon. Re-allocated E4618 in 1993.
E4602	Whittle W2/1700	[ex E4452] Manadon. Current 6.90.
E4606	Gnome 11201	Fleetlands 5.87. Current 1993.
E4607	Gnome 11201	Fleetlands 5.87. Current 1993.
E4608	Gnome 11301	Fleetlands 5.87. Current 1993.
E4609	Gnome 11301	Fleetlands 5.87. Current 1993.
E4610	Gnome 10301	To Manadon 11.6.80. Current 1993.
E4611	Junkers Juno	Manadon. Current 1993.
E4612	Gipsy Major Mk.1	Manadon. Current 1993. To Cranwell by 6.96.
E4613	Ghost 103	To Manadon 1966. Current 1993.
E4614	Gnome 11301	[ex E4810, from A2751/XT762] Lee-on-Solent. Current 1993.
E4615	Gnome 11301	[ex E4811, from A2751/XT762] Lee-on-Solent. Current 1993.
E4641	Viper 10201	Manadon. Current 6.90.
E4642	Viper 10201	To Manadon 6.73. Re-allocated E4620 in 1993.
E4644	Gem BS360	Manadon. Re-allocated E4621 in 1993.
E4657	Gnome 10101	Fleetlands. Current 6.89.
E4660	Double Mamba 1010	To Manadon 3.9.82. Current 6.92.
E4673	BS Gnome	To Manadon 1966 (presented by Rolls-Royce). Re-allocated E4622 1993.
E4674	Rolls-Royce RB 108	Manadon. Re-allocated E4623 in 1993.
E4677	Turbomecca Palouste	Manadon. Re-allocated E4624 in 1993.
E4678	Double Mamba	To Manadon 9.89 (ex Wroughton). Current 6.90.
E4679	Double Mamba	To Manadon 9.89 (ex Wroughton). Sectioned. Current 6.90.
E4680	Gem Mk.100	To Manadon 9.89 (ex Fleetlands). Re-allocated E4626 in 1993.
E4681	Gnome 12101	Fleetlands.
E4683	Marine Gnome 1054	Fleetlands.
E4684	Gnome 11301	To Yeovilton circa 1975. Re-allocated E4627 in 1993.
E4685	Gnome 11101	Fleetlands.
E4690	Nimbus 10301	Portland - on loan to Malaysia.
E4715	Pegasus Mk.5	To Manadon 10.8.76 Re-allocated E4629 in 1993.
E4723	Gnome 10101	To Fleetlands 6.81. Sectioned. Re-allocated E4630 in 1993.
E4724	Astazou 111N	To Manadon 4.10.77. Current 6.90.

E4726	Gem BS360	Lee-on-Solent.
E4738	Gnome 10301	Manadon.
E4770	Gem BS360	To Fleetlands 4.85. Re-allocated E4631 in 1993.
E4772	Gem BS360-07	To Manadon 1984. Re-allocated E4632 in 1993.
E4773	Gem BS360	Manadon. To Fleetlands 7.89. Re-allocated E4633 in 1993.
E4774	Nimbus 10301	To Fleetlands 7.1.92. Current 6.92.
E4777	Avon 12201	Yeovilton. Current 6.91.
E4780	G.E. T700	To Manadon 11.87. Re-allocated E4635 in 1993.
E4781	G.E. T700	To Manadon 11.87. Re-allocated E4636 in 1993.

November 1993

As with the 'A' numbers the system was re-organised once again in 1993 and the range E4600 to E4699 was used for ECU's not fitted to an airframe, although it can be seen that some 'E' numbers were listed as *"spare"*. Previous identities are included where known and the following were current in November 1993.

E4600	Viper 10201	Manadon.
E4601	Viper 10201	Manadon.
E4602	Gnome 11301	Yeovilton.
E4603	Gnome 11201	[ex E4812, from A2752/XT449] Manadon.
E4604	G.E. T700	Manadon.
E4605	Gnome 11301	Yeovilton.
E4606	Gnome 11201	Fleetlands.
E4607	Gnome 11201	Fleetlands.
E4608	Gnome 11301	Fleetlands.
E4609	Gnome 11301	Fleetlands.
E4610	Gnome 10301	Manadon.
E4611	Junkers Juno	Manadon.
E4612	Gipsy Major Mk.1	Manadon.
E4613	Ghost 103	Manadon.
E4614	Gnome 11301	[ex E4810, from A2751/XT762] Lee-on-Solent.
E4615	Gnome 11301	[ex E4811, from A2751/XT762] Lee-on-Solent.
E4616	Gnome 11301	[ex E4638, from A2628/XS523] Fleetlands.
E4617	Gnome 11301	[ex E4637, from A2628/XS523] Fleetlands.
E4618	Conway 1011	[ex E4601] Manadon.
E4619	*"Spare"*	
E4620	Viper 10201	[ex E4642] Manadon.
E4621	Gem BS360	[ex E4644] Manadon.
E4622	BS Gnome	[ex E4673] Manadon.
E4623	Rolls-Royce RB 108	[ex E4674] Manadon. To Cranwell by 6.96.
E4624	Turbomecca Palouste	[ex E4677] Manadon. To Cranwell by 6.96.
E4625	*"Spare"*	
E4626	Gem Mk.100	[ex E4680] Manadon.
E4627	Gnome 11301	[ex E4684] Yeovilton.
E4628	*"Spare"*	
E4629	Pegasus Mk.5	[ex E4715] Manadon.
E4630	Gnome 10101	[ex E4723] Sectioned. Fleetlands.
E4631	Gem BS360	[ex E4770] Fleetlands.
E4632	Gem BS360-07	[ex E4772] Manadon.
E4633	Gem BS360	[ex E4773] Fleetlands.
E4634	*"Spare"*	
E4635	G.E. T700	[ex E4780] Manadon. To MoD(PE) store Aston Down by 6.96.
E4636	G.E. T700	[ex E4781] Manadon. To NAWC Trenton, New Jersey by 6.96.
E4637	*"Spare"*	
E4638	Nimbus Mk.103	Manadon.
E4639	Nimbus Mk.103	Manadon.

GLOSSARY OF TERMS

AAC	Army Air Corps
AACU	Anti-Aircraft Co-operation Unit
A&AEE	Aeroplane and Armament Experimental Establishment
ADS	Aircraft Direction School
ADW	Awaiting disposal and write-off
AES	Air Electrical School *and* Air Engineering School
AESS	Air Engineering and Survival School
AETW	Air Engineering Training Wing *[later SAE]*
AHU	Aircraft Holding Unit
AIU	Accident Investigation Unit
AMG	Aircraft Maintenance Group *[formerly NASU]*
APS	Aircraft Preservation Society
ARWF	Advanced Rotory Wing Flight
ASF	Aircraft Servicing Flight
ASU	Aircraft Storage Unit
ATC	Air Training Corps
ATS	Armament Training Station
BDR	Battle Damage Repair
BRM	British Rotorcraft Museum (later IHM)
BRNC	Britannia Royal Naval College
C(A)	Controller (Air) - became Controller Services (Air)
CAD	Channel Air Division
CASEVAC	Casualty Evacuation
Cat.B	Beyond repair on site
Cat.1(GI)	Non-flying - Ground Instructional
Cat.3	Repairable on site but beyond unit capacity
Cat.5	Write-off
Cat.5(GI)	Damaged/surplus but suitable for Ground Instructional use
CAW	College of Air Warfare
CFS	Central Flying School
CoA	Certificate of Airworthiness
Comm	Communications
CS(A)	Controller Services (Air) - became MoD(PE)
CTE	Central Training Establishment [RAF Manston]
CTTS	Civilian Technical Training School
DLCO	Deck Landing Control Officer
DRA	Defence Research Agency
DRB	Disposal Reserve (B)
DTD	Director of Technical Development
ECU	Engine Change Unit
EFTS	Elementary Flying Training School
EP&TU	Exhibition, Production & Transportation Unit (formerly RAFEF)
EST	Engineering Simulation Training
ET	Engineering Training
ETPS	Empire Test Pilots School
ETS	Engineering Training School
FAA	Fleet Air Arm
FAAM	Fleet Air Arm Museum
FCR	Fire/Crash Rescue Training
FF&SS	Fire Fighting and Safety School
FIR	Frontline Immediate Replacement
FONA	Flag Officer Naval Aviation
FONAC	Flag Officer Naval Air Command *[became FONA 23.3.90]*
FORA	Flag Officer Reserve Aircraft
FR	Flight Refuelling
FRADU	Fleet Requirements and Development Unit
FRU	Fleet Requirements Unit
FTS	Flying Training School

G.E.	General Electric
GI	Ground Instruction
GRA	Ground (Training) Reserve (A)
GRB	Ground (Training) Reserve (B)
HAD	Home Aircraft Depot
HAS	Hardened Aircraft Shelter *and* Helicopter Ant-Submarine
HMAS	Her/His Majesty's Australian Ship
HMS	Her/His Majesty's Ship
HSA	Hawker Siddeley Aviation
HQ	Headquarters
IHM	International Helicopter Museum, Weston-super-Mare
IWM	Imperial War Museum
JATE	Joint Air Transport Establishment
LTS	Long Term Storage
LTS 1	Long Term Storage - 6 monthly modifications
LTS 2	Long Term Storage - Yearly modifications
LTS 2(U)	Long Term Storage - Yearly unworked
LTS 3	Long Term Storage - Plastic cocoon
MAEE	Marine Aircraft Experimental Establishment
MARTSU	Mobile Aircraft Repair, Transport and Salvage Unit *[see MASU]*
MASU	Mobile Aircraft Support Unit *[amalgamation of MARTSU and NATIU, April 1986]*
MLD	Marine Luchtvaart Dienst (Netherlands Navy)
MoD(PE)	Ministry of Defence Procurement Executive
MSFU	Merchant Ship Fighter Unit
MTPS	Maintenance Test Pilots School
MU	Maintenance Unit
MV	Merchant Vessel
NAS	Naval Air Station
NASU	Naval Air Support Unit *[re-titled Aircraft Maintenance Group circa 3.88]*
NATIU	Naval Air Trial Installation Unit *[see MASU]*
NATSU	Naval Aircraft Transport and Salvage Unit
NBC	Nuclear, Biological and Chemical
NEAM	North East Aircraft Museum (Sunderland)
NTPS	Naval Test Pilots School
OCU	Operational Conversion Unit
OTU	Operational Training Unit
PBM	Planned Base Maintenance
P&EE	Proof and Experimental Establishment
PF	Power folding wings
qv	which see
RAE	Royal Aircraft Establishment
RAF	Royal Air Force
RAFC	Royal Air Force College
RAFEF	Royal Air Force Exhibition Flight (EP&TU from 12.92)
RAN	Royal Australian Navy
RARA	Rear Admiral Reserve Aircraft
Rgt	Regiment
RIW	Repair In Works
RN	Royal Navy
RNARY	Royal Naval Aircraft Repair Yard - became RNAY
RNAS	Royal Naval Air Station
RNAY	Royal Naval Aircraft Yard
RNEC	Royal Naval Engineering College
RNethAF	Royal Netherlands Air Force
RNHF	Royal Naval Historic Flight
RNHU	Royal Naval Hovercraft Unit
RNVR	Royal Naval Volunteer Reserve
RRE	Royal Radar Establishment
RS	Radio School
SAD	Southern Air Division *and* Scottish Air Division
SAE	School of Aeronautical Engineering *[formerly AETW; later SEAE]*

SAH	School of Aircraft Handling [renamed School of Flight Deck Operations 11.95]
SAR	Search and Rescue
SARTU	Search and Rescue Training Unit
SAY	Scottish Aircraft Yard
SEAE	School of Electrical and Aeronautical Engineering *[formerly SAE]*
SFDO	School of Flight Deck Operations [formerly SAH]
Sic	Seemingly in error
SIF	Servicing Instruction Flight
SNATSU	Southern Naval Aircraft Transport and Salvage Unit
SoAC	School of Army Co-operation
SOC	Struck off Charge
SONC	School of Naval Co-operation
SoTT	School of Technical Training
Sqdn	Squadron
Stn Flt	Station Flight
STS	Short term storage
TOC	Taken On Charge
TTU	Torpedo Training Unit
USA	United States of America
USMC	United States Marine Corps
USN	United States Navy
VGS	Volunteer Gliding School
WFU	Withdrawn from use
WOC	Written Off Charge
WRNS	Womens Royal Naval Service

Sea Vixen FAW.2 XN707, seen here at Abbotsinch, went to No.1 School of Technical Training at RAF Halton as 8144M in 6.71.
(John Huggon)

BRITISH AVIATION RESEARCH GROUP

If you wish to know more about current military aviation then why not subscribe to

British Aviation Review

Published monthly, *British Aviation Review* builds annually into over 1200 pages of comprehensive information on military aviation, covering both modern and recent history, in the United Kingdom and overseas.

British Aviation Review covers news on the United Kingdom Army Air Corps, Fleet Air Arm and Royal Air Force, plus sections devoted to items such as manufacturers' news as well as European, United States and other air arms worldwide. In depth articles, covering topics such as specific aircraft types and orders of battle, are also regular features.

For more details, plus a free sample copy, send a SAE/IRC to:

The Honorary Membership Secretary - BARG,
"Aorangi",
Beech Road,
Tokers Green,
Reading,
RG4 9EH
United Kingdom

British Aviation Review is a publication of the British Aviation Research Group, formed 1958.

Tiger Moth T.2 BB814 became a Class II airframe at Arbroath.

Sea Fury F.10 TF903 Class II airframe at Donibristle in 1956.

Hunter T.7 XF321/A2734 at RNEC Manadon 10.94, in the red, white and black colour scheme of RAE Bedford. (Keith A.Saunders)

Buccaneer S.2B A2693 [2]/XV359, ex No.12 Sqdn RAF, at Predannack 18.5.94. (Geoff Wakeham)

AIR-BRITAIN - THE INTERNATIONAL ASSOCIATION OF AVIATION HISTORIANS - FOUNDED 1948

Since 1948, Air-Britain has recorded aviation events as they have happened, because today's events are tomorrow's history. In addition, considerable research into the past has been undertaken to provide historians with the background to aviation history. Over 16,000 members have contributed to our aims and efforts in that time and many have become accepted authorities in their own fields.

Every month, *AIR-BRITAIN NEWS* covers the current civil and military scene. Quarterly, each member receives *AIR-BRITAIN DIGEST* which is a fully-illustrated journal containing articles on various subjects, both past and present.

For those interested in military aviation history, there is the quarterly *AEROMILITARIA* which is designed to delve more deeply into the background of, mainly, British and Commonwealth military aviation than is possible in commercial publications and whose format permits it to be used as components of a filing system which suits the readers' requirements. This publication is responsible for the production of the present volume and other monographs on military subjects. Also published quarterly is *ARCHIVE*, produced in a similar format but covering civil aviation history in depth on a world-wide basis. Both magazines are well-illustrated by photographs and drawings.

In addition to these regular publications, there are monographs covering type histories, both military and civil, airline fleets, Royal Air Force registers, squadron histories and the civil registers of a large number of countries. Although our publications are available to non-members, prices are considerably lower for Air-Britain members, who have priority over non-members when availability limited. Normally, the accumulated price discounts for whi members qualify when buying monographs far exceed the annu subscription rates.

A large team of aviation experts is available to answer membe queries on most aspects of aviation. If you have made a study of a particular subject, you may be able to expand your knowledge joining those with similar interests. Also available to members libraries of colour slides and photographs which supply slides a prints at prices considerably lower than those charged commercial firms.

There are local branches of the Association in Blackpo Bournemouth, Central Scotland, Gwent, Heston, London, Lut Manchester, Merseyside, North-East England, Rugby, Southampto South-West Essex, Stansted, West Cornwall and West Midlanc Overseas in France and the Netherlands.

If you would like to receive samples of Air-Britain magazines, plea write to the following address enclosing 50p and stating yo particular interests. If you would like only a brochure, please send stamped self-addressed envelope to the same address (preferat 230mm by 160mm or over) - Air-Britain Membership Enquiri (Mil), 1 Rose Cottages, 179 Penn Road, Hazlemere, High Wycomt Bucks., HP15 7NE.

MILITARY AVIATION PUBLICATIONS
[* Currently out of print]

Royal Air Force Aircraft series: (prices are for members/non-members and are post-free)

J1-J9999	(£8.00/£12.00)	K1000-K9999	see The K-File below	L1000-N9999	(£12.00/£18.00)
P1000-R9999	(£11.00/£14.00)*	T1000-V9999	(£16.00/£19.50)	W1000-Z9999	in preparation
AA100-AZ999	(£6.00/£9.00)*	BA100-BZ999	(£6.00/£9.00)	DA100-DZ999	(£5.00/£7.50)
EA100-EZ999	(£5.00/£7.50)	FA100-FZ999	(£5.00/£7.50)	HA100-HZ999	(£6.00/£9.00)
JA100-JZ999	(£6.00/£9.00)	KA100-KZ999	(£6.00/£9.00)	LA100-LZ999	(£7.00/£10.50)
MA199-MZ999	(£8.00/£12.00)	NA100-NZ999	(£8.00/£12.00)	PA100-RZ999	(£10.00/£15.00)
	SA100-VZ999	(£6.00/£9.00)	WA100-WZ999	(£5.00/£7.50)*	

Type Histories

The Halifax File	(£6.00/£9.00)*	The Lancaster File	(£8.00/£12.00)*	The Washington File	(£2.00/£3.00)*
The Whitley File	(£4.50/£6.75)*	The Typhoon File	(£4.00/£6.00)*	The Stirling File	(£6.00/£9.00)*
The Anson File	(£15.00/£22.50)	The Harvard File	(£7.00/£10.50)	The Hampden File	(£11.00/£16.50)
The Hornet File	(£9.00/£13.50)	The Beaufort File	(£10.00/£15.00)	The Camel File	(£13.00/£19.50)
The Norman Thompson File (£13.50/£17.00)		The Defiant File	£12.50/£16.00	The S.E.5 File	(£16.00/£20.00)
		The Battle File	in preparation		

Hardbacks

The Squadrons of the Royal Air Force and Commonwealth (£15.00/£15.00)*
The Squadrons of the Fleet Air Arm (£24.00/£36.00)
Fleet Air Arm Aircraft 1939 - 1945 (£24.00/£30.000)
Royal Navy Shipboard Aircraft Developments 1912 - 1931 (£10.00/£10.00)
Royal Navy Aircraft Serials and Units 1911 - 1919 (£10.00/£10.00)
Central American and Caribbean Air Forces (£12.50/£15.50)
The British Aircraft Specifications File (£20.00/£25.00)
The K-File - The Royal Air Force of the 1930s (£23.00/£30.00)
Aviation in Cornwall (£14.00/£17.50)
Royal Air Force Flying Training and Support Units (£20.00/£25.00)

Individual Squadron Histories

Strike True - The History of No.80 Squadron, Royal Air Force (£4.00/£6.00)*
With Courage and Faith - The History of No.18 Squadron, Royal Air Force (£5.00/£7.50)*
Scorpions Sting - The Story of No.84 Squadron, Royal Air Force (£11.00/£16.50)
Rise from the East - The Story of No.247 Squadron, Royal Air Force (£13.00/£16.50)
United in Effort - The Story of No.53 Squadron, Royal Air Force (£15.00/£19.00)
* Currently out of print

Except where out of print, the above are available from:
Air-Britain Sales Department, 5 Bradley Road, Upper Norwood, London SE19 3NT

Access, Visa, Mastercard accepted with number and expiry date